Donald Horne is one of Australia's most original and influential writers. He is associate Professor of Political Studies at the University of New South Wales. From 1985, he will chair the Australia Council. His other books include *The Lucky Country*, which has sold more than 250,000 copies and *The Education of Young Donald*, the first volume of his autobiography.

D1099962

First published in 1984 by Pluto Press Limited,
The Works, 105a Torriano Avenue, London NW5 2RX
and Pluto Press Australia Limited, PO Box 199, Leichhardt,
New South Wales 2040, Australia

7 6 5 4 3 2

89 88 87 86 85

Cover designed by Ashted Dastor

Typeset by Photobooks (Bristol) Ltd.
and printed by Guernsey Press Company Limited, Guernsey, C.I.

British Library Cataloguing in Publication Data
Horne, Donald
  The great museum.
  1. Europe—History—1789–1900
  2. Europe—History—20th century
  I. Title
  940.2'8   D299

ISBN 0-86104-788-5 (pbk)

Donald Horne

The great museum

The Re-Presentation of History

Pluto Press
London and Sydney

Contents

Prologue: 'The dreamlands'

Devotees of the cult are often seen in the great churches of Europe. You know them by the long, thin books they carry, bound in green or maroon. Sometimes they walk the aisles, studying the printed pages. Sometimes they sit, lips moving as they pass on the words to fellow-devotees; or they read silently, in private contemplation. From time to time some look up towards a part of the church, although they seem regretful about looking away from the print. The books are *Michelin Guides*. The devotees are tourists. They are trying to imagine the past.

They are engaging in that area of the great public display of a modern industrial society, that has turned parts of Europe into a museum of authenticated remnants of past cultures, resurrected so richly and professionally that the people of those days would probably not even recognise their own artifacts.

Since 'reality' does not exist in itself, we create it – with the result that each society and each age has different versions of what 'reality' might be. This makes the tourist experience a voyage through many different 'dreamlands'. Most of the sights we see as we pass through Europe in our hundreds of thousands are relics of previous declarations of reality – discarded 'dreamlands' which, in their own terms, we can never altogether understand; they have, however, now been turned into 'dreamlands' of a modern kind. To these are then added contemporary tourist monuments, with their own dreams. And all of them, in the future, so long as the habit of tourism survives, will go on being turned into whatever dreams some new age requires.

Dominant versions of reality tend to suit dominant groups and to uphold a certain social order. As tourists moving among Europe's sights, we are moving among symbols that explain the world in ways that justify the authority of the few over the many.

But we find conflicting languages of legitimacy: from the past, there are the great legitimating languages of religion and hereditary right; in modern times, there are the legitimating languages of nationalism, of economic growth, of social class, and of revolution – all of which turn the past to new purposes. In this sense there is a rhetoric of monuments, which can change with changes in the social order. That is what this book is about: what was 'meant', in their own time, by what we now see as monuments to the past? What social interests did they serve? What social interests do they, along with modern monuments, serve now?

I did not write this book about the social meanings of sightseeing in Europe because of some overriding interest in either tourism or in Europe; I wrote it because tourism is now a significant part of the 'public culture' of modern industrial states – whether capitalist or Communist. Tourism takes its place among the many other marvels of our public culture: the 'news', both broadcast and printed, with its personality cults and acts of political theatre, its heroes and villains, fools and victims, refining existence into a few simple processes – or even single, isolated events – and suggesting to us that this is all that matters; the movies, paperbacks, magazines, pop music and television serials – products of what, in *Antimemoirs*, Malraux called 'the dream factories' – offering more narrative in a week than was available to past societies in a year or a lifetime; and the rituals in which the people themselves may participate, to show that they belong – the sporting ceremonies, the fairs and expositions, the ceremonies of nation or class and the voting rituals that now give magic to power. From soap opera to museum exhibit, these are reaffirmations of what life is supposed to be about, modern manifestations of what began as stampings and chantings around tribal fires and paintings on cave walls. They are an important part of what makes us human. In this sense, sightseeing helps people in modern industrial societies define who they are, and what matters in the world.

And these activities of the public culture are shared in a way unimaginable in earlier societies. Before the industrial societies there was no shared public culture. Ruling-class display (some of the relics of which are now in museums) dominated the towns, the courts of the magnates and the religious ceremonies; the culture of the peasants, who made up the mass of the people, was not something with which rulers had to concern themselves. The power of the rulers was justified and explained in various legitimising devices. Peasant wisdom, on the other hand, was generally passed down only among the peasants themselves, from generation to generation. The rulers exhibited their legitimacy; other than that, there was not much reason for them to care what the peasants did or thought. If there was an uprising, it would be put down. The most significant statement the rulers could make to the ruled was to display, on a pole, the head of an executed rebel.

Modern industrial states are also partly held together by fear – above all, fear of the police and/or fear of economic deprivation. They are, however, far too complex to function on fear alone. What is necessary now is a culture shared by rulers and ruled, ways of doing things and seeing the world so ingrained as to have become 'common sense'. Elements in this public culture are taught in classrooms (and sometimes untaught in the counter-culture of the playgrounds); they become the unexamined assumptions of the news services; they are expounded in bodies of knowledge; they are also dramatised in myths and rituals, in arts and entertainments. And, of course, they take their place in tourism.

The significance of tourism to public cultures is not limited by geographical boundaries. In the United States tourism can be as significant a political act as it is in the Soviet Union. Disneyland has a vinyl-covered, computerised, walking-and-talking 'Mr Lincoln'; Red Square has Lenin's mummified body. Tourists can 'do', in three days, the Taj Mahal at Agra, the erotic temple carvings at Khajuraho and the sacred River Ganges at Varanasi. One can 'do' China in two weeks. Mexico offers one of the world's best-value 'lost civilisations'. Tourists can live in authentically reconstructed grass-roofed *bures* in Fiji and enjoy a tribal feast every night. A drive through a game park in Africa can provide a unique sensation of being 'close to nature'. Kyoto offers nostalgia as convincingly as Avignon. As the Swiss found national identity in the Alps, Australians have found identity in the red granite of Ayers Rock. But in order to expose the social meanings of tourism, I chose Europe for convenience: it offered the most variety in a manageable area.

To supplement earlier experience, I made two expeditions,

visiting, as participant–observer, every capital city in Europe, apart from Tirana, and a number of provincial centres. But the book is not a comprehensive survey; it is merely an offering of specimens. To emphasise the universality of the tourist experience, I have deliberately given more emphasis than some western Europeans might expect to tourism in eastern and northern Europe.

It has been suggested that perhaps I chose Europe because I am an Australian and Australians, like other people who do not live in Europe, tend to give Europe a single identity. Perhaps so, although I didn't see it like that. What I did discover was that it was unavoidable that the book would end up being not only a book about tourism, but also a book about Europe. It became a book about European power and imagination and the re-presentation, through its monuments, of Europe's history.

I made another discovery. The objects on tourist schedules become symbols which can reinforce the dominant values of the public culture: I already knew that in European tourism there is one value that would always be reiterated – the continuing legitimation of male authority. However, it was not until I worked over my notes that I recognised that this was so consistent as to be almost universal. European tourism is so patriarchal that to go on repeating the point would be tedious. With exceptions such as the Virgin Mary or Joan of Arc, women are simply not *there*. They make their appearance as dummies of sturdy peasant women in folk-museum reconstructions of peasant kitchens, or in other useful supporting roles; they may be seen nude, or partly nude, created as an object for the male gaze. Even where women are used as personifications of a nation or idea ('Polonia', 'Finlandia', 'Liberty') the artists usually expose at least one breast. For several generations, one of the most important motives for visits to European art museums was to peer at displayed female flesh – a predilection that Europeans also indulged in those non-European cultures where nudity in women was portrayed in painting or sculpture not to gratify the male gaze, but to express female sexuality.

To handle the themes in this book has demanded enough boldness to pass over areas of expertise: it seemed essential to write something which would interest both specialists and non-specialists.

The balancing act between writing for the general interested reader and for the scholarly is always difficult; it is essential for our general intellectual culture, and for our belief in ourselves as humans, that we should keep on trying. There is a further difficulty: I have tried to keep down the abstract theorising and to tell the story as much as possible through images. I have tried both to present these images within the range of stereotyped tourist experience and also to indicate some of the ironies of that experience. This inevitably produces an effect that can seem to disparage both tourism and tourists. I should explain at once that I am myself an enthusiastic (if sceptical) tourist, and that if sightseers engage in follies it is because they have been taught to do so. This does raise the question of whether there is any intellectual validity at all in the sightseeing experience. That question I leave to the epilogue.

Part one

The way of the tourist

1. The tourist pilgrims

The new pilgrims

The social significance of tourism can be clarified if one imagines the modern sightseer as a 'pilgrim', and what is looked at as a 'relic'.

In its complex organising of voluntary journeys, the modern tourist business is matched only by medieval pilgrimages to the shrines of dead saints who cured the sick, punished enemies and raised essential revenues for the cathedrals where they were housed. Then, the great highways of Europe were the pilgrim routes to the tombs of St James in Compostela, of St Peter in Rome and of Jesus Christ in Jerusalem; these were later joined in fame by the three Russian pilgrim routes – to Kazan, Novgorod and Kiev. In the eleventh century, in a Rome where the soil had gone sour and there were only small huddles of people living among the ruins and the churches, the pilgrim business was the main industry, supporting the lodging-house keepers, the middle men and the clerics.

Simple pilgrimages in the medieval style survive. In that devout catholic country, Poland, for example, those who follow the cult of Mary still make pilgrimages on foot. Between 300 and 500 people set out in organised groups to reach a special place of pilgrimage on a significant date, staying overnight in bare quarters. Other pilgrim churches are visited on the way to some lustrous baroque Polish church, with a cream and black façade, perhaps on a hill overlooking woods and plains where, inside, among the gold, black and bronze decorations, are the holy objects – the goal of their journey. In the drab town of Wadowice, birthplace of Pope John Paul II, a new pilgrim cult is beginning. The yellow house where he was born, situated just across the road from the church, was bought by the church after his election to the papacy;

it is now a museum. An enlarged photograph of him, set on a carpet on the main portal, looks out on to a square dominated by a monument to the Soviet liberators.

But it is tourists who are the main modern pilgrims, carrying guide books as devotional texts. Moving from one architectural feature of the church to the next, or, in museums, passing from glass case to glass case or from painting to painting or, in the streets, from famous square to historic fountain, they may scarcely look at the exhibit or the monument: their essential function is to read the guide books, the explanatory cards or commemorative plaques, or to listen to hired cassettes. What matters is what they are told they are seeing. The fame of the object becomes its meaning; what finally matters may be a souvenir postcard, perhaps even the admission ticket, kept for years afterwards with other mementoes of passing visions of how life might have been.

Even when tourists have no interest in the countries they visit and are travelling merely for conviviality, solitude, sunshine, snow, fresh air, water, gluttony, shopping, sport, sex or gambling, and when whatever curiosity they have can be satisfied by the foreign names on the menu, they are nevertheless likely to go on a 'sights-of-the-city' coach tour and visit a souvenir shop. And just as coral polyps secrete the limestone that builds the reef, even tourists at a pleasure resort are, as it were, secreting all around them structures that themselves then become monuments, to be 'done' on a coach tour of the hotels and pleasure spots. At the Metropol in East Berlin, the German Democratic Republic's most expensive hotel, tourists who cannot afford to stay there come to the hotel on a tour to be shown its three salons (in romanesque, late gothic, rococo styles), and its disco, rotisserie, restaurant, boutiques, art objects, and bar, with their cultural affirmations.

The ceremonial agenda

In Italy one *must* see Rome. In Rome one *must* see the Vatican. In the Vatican one *must* see the Sistine Chapel: in the Vatican Museum, along each of the four different routes – the green, the yellow, the purple and the orange, each with its own sales kiosk – there is both ceremony and a controlled hysteria as the Sistine Chapel is approached; then, before the moment of entry, a taped voice exacerbates the tension by calling out for solemnity, in four languages, one after the other: 'You are about to enter Sistine Chapel. Please treat it with reverent silence.' Control breaks down. Inside, everyone is talking. They have arrived.

Sightseeing has established its own rituals. In what Erving Goffman calls the 'ceremonial agenda of obligatory rites', there are established for us the monuments and exhibits we must see, and sometimes the order in which we must see them. The ceremonial agenda can lead us along an obligatory route through a city, whether a riverside walk in Leningrad or an inspection of the 'Royal Mile' in Edinburgh, as if we were programmed robots. Seeing the sights in the prescribed priorities (and dismissing everything else) is one of the most disciplined of modern rituals. The ceremonial agenda can even direct us to view a scene from a special place. The tourist–pilgrim in Gent, Belgium, is directed to St Michielsbrug, the bridge which gives 'the most famous view in Europe'. With the help of a town plan, a skilled sightseer can reconstruct a prosperous medieval past by determining the differences between church, belfry, cloth hall and cathedral – but there is a disconcerting muddle of car parks and traffic. As tourists, we can be most faithful to the vision of the ceremonial agenda for Gent by standing on the bridge at night when the floodlights show us what to look at.

These ceremonies of seeing the sights in predetermined order recall the progress and rituals of the medieval pilgrims, but there is a confirmatory modern magic the pilgrims could not know. Each main sight has to be *photographed*. As Susan Sontag says in *On Photography*, 'Travel becomes a strategy for accumulating photographs.' It can mean 'putting oneself into a certain relation to the world that feels like knowledge – and, therefore, power'.

In St Paul's Cathedral, London, the tourists wait politely at the back of the nave while the small, outnumbered congregation finishes evensong. A few tourists may sit with them, but most have such an innate sense of respect that they would no more join the evening services at St Paul's than help change the guard at Buckingham Palace. Neither ceremony has any involvement for them. However, when the service is over the tourists participate. They make their distinctive act of worship at the altar. They photograph it.

Magic has to be worked with the sensitivity to light of silver salts so that, like artists, we can conquer the complexities of existence; by photographing a monument, we make it *real*. It also offers us joys of possession, akin to those of the aristocrats who used to collect famous paintings: by taking photographs of famous sights and then, at home, putting them into albums or showing them as slides, we gain some kind of possession of them. For some of us this can be one of the main reasons for our tourism. Between them, the camera and tourism are two of the uniquely modern ways of defining reality.

Taking photographs can connect tourists with what they see. Back home, their photographs or slides show the monuments and exhibits in their relation to the tourists themselves; either they are in the picture, or they took it. This explains one of the most poignant moments of confrontation between the two Europes in Berlin. Off-duty United States soldiers cross the line of concrete, barbed wire, watch towers and land mines that appears to divide humanity, make their obeisances at the checkpoints, then go to the Unter den Linden where the guards of the People's Army stand outside the doric portico of the Hohenzollerns' 'New Guard House', now named 'Monument to the Victims of Fascism and Militarism'. The American soldiers pose. They are photographed in front not of the Eiffel Tower or the Manneken-Pis, but of the men they are being trained to kill.

The ceremonial agenda can be part of the pattern of growing up. Children are taken to a museum for instruction in life's mysteries as once they might have been taken to a cathedral to see the stories in its stone carvings or stained glass or frescoes or mosaics. Now they learn human and cosmic significance from the 'exhibits'. The coaches drive up into the Kalegmedan Fortress, Belgrade, one of Europe's great surviving fortification systems. Built before the period of ferro-concrete, with walls within walls, it stands on a cliff and strategically overlooks the Danube and the Pannonian Plain; it is now a centre for tennis, basketball and mini-golf. Out of the coaches come school pupils for their day at the Military Museum, where they can learn nostalgia for the Golden Ages of struggle against the conquerors. In Brussels, coaches drive to Tervuren Park, stop near a statue of an elephant left over from the Brussels

International Exhibition, 1879, and school pupils go into a palace – renamed the 'Royal Museum of Central Africa' – where they can learn nostalgia for the Golden Age when Belgium was itself a conqueror.

The ceremonial agenda can also give a sense of completion. To those of European origin, the first sighting of the Acropolis buildings is likely to give a shiver of self-determination. Because it is part of being European, walking up the steps to the Propylaea gives almost everyone a sense of awe and pilgrimage. This is what we are prepared for: ascending ceremonial steps to a temple is one of the clichés of a late-night movie spectacular. As feet stumble on the cable wires of the arc-lights, as hands adjust f-stops or change to a telephoto lens and as eyes look out over a plain of modern houses and a blue sky with its delicate drifts of smog, the guides blow their whistles and their voices cry out in a dozen languages that here is the beginning of so many styles of architecture and art, and there, on the hill of Pnyx, is the beginning of the use of the word 'democracy', and down there, in the foundations of Pericles' Odeon, is the beginning of theatre, and over there, in the stadium, is the beginning of sport. Given words like 'portico' and 'statue', 'democracy', 'theatre' and 'sport', as tourists we can feel that we are with history.

In the Soviet Union, tourism has been described as the state religion. This is obvious enough from the immense queues that wait to enter the Lenin Mausoleum, with its understated solemnity of line in red granite and black labradorite, and the simple name 'Lenin' in red quartzite set in black; or in the crowds at night that stare at the red stars above the Kremlin and see them as marking the centre of the world; or in the queues outside the museums and monuments of revolution and patriotic war. But tourism as faith can also be seen in the long queues outside the art museums; sometimes they wait, long lines of patient pilgrims in the snow.

Modern 'relics'

The powers of saints' bones were as important to medieval Europe as the making of offerings to the gods was in pagan Rome; relics were the avenue for doing business with the supernatural and for paying respect to the culture heroes of the age. After making a pilgrimage to one of the cult centres of these demi-gods, a pilgrim might expect to be a changed person. Today, many catholics still treat relics as having supernatural powers – a phial of Christ's blood is believed to liquefy once a year in the cathedral at Naples. To most tourists, though, these splinters of wood, old teeth, rags, or old bone are now merely reminders of how enlightened we have become. What is more likely to interest the modern tourist is the reliquary, the decorated container in which a relic was kept. In the Munich collection of the Wittelsbachs, the royal family of Bavaria, there are 75 reliquaries. A piece of the holy manger, 8 separate pieces of the true cross, 3 pieces of the Virgin's gown, various leftovers of the Last Supper, pieces of the crown of thorns and the scourge, some of Christ's blood, relics of the massacred innocents and 80 scraps of the clothes or fragments of the bones of various saints – all are housed in miniature towers, caskets, crucifixes, crowns, pendants, monstrances, miniature altars, lockets, bas-reliefs, busts, cabinets and pyramids made from gold, silver, ebony, ivory, pearls, rock crystal, agate, lapis lazuli, amethyst, onyx, green jasper, rubies, emeralds, pearls and diamonds. To tour this collection is not a religious experience: it is a visit to the jeweller's.

The development of secular relics began when humanist Popes and others started collecting classical statues in Italy in the fifteenth century. The habit spread, and in the late eighteenth and early nineteenth centuries the present museums of classical antiquities began to form. In every major European city it became essential either to establish a museum of antiquities, or to devote special galleries in other museums to statues without heads or arms or legs, or with smashed noses, or battered ears, or chipped penises. These broken relics were designated 'originals' (which often meant pallid Roman copies in marble of Greek statues in bronze), or, failing 'originals', copies of them in plaster casts. With typical Bavarian grandiloquence, the kings of Bavaria put up three palace-museums in classical style around a new square, the Königsplatz, to confirm the pre-eminence of Munich in European culture; the attendants were clothed in sumptuous liveries to encourage respect for antiquity. The greatest archaeological museums (in Rome, Naples, Athens, Istanbul, Paris and East Berlin) have now themselves become museum pieces, each with its own style.

At about the same time, great princes began to collect paintings and started the sacralising of painted images into 'Old Masters'. Its modern form came when, in the nineteenth century, that secular temple, the public art museum, was created. It happened in Paris, when the Louvre became the Musée Napoléon and displayed the greatest collection of art treasures ever assembled, mostly looted from princely hoards in Europe; in Madrid, when the royal collections were moved into the Prado, the first modern building to house an art museum; but, most significantly, in Berlin when what became known as the Altes Museum was opened in 1830.

The Altes Museum was built as a pictures gallery to show all the characteristics of the new phenomenon: its buying policy was to bring together a representative collection to be displayed systematically (as had already been done in Vienna), and so educate the public in the history of art as it was defined by that prototype scholar of this new movement, the German art historian. It was to be controlled by its director, who would see his fellow-scholars as his most important public; and it was to honour the arts in a museum–palace that would reproduce the grandeur of the old royal palaces that housed the princely hoards. It became the prototype for the foundation of the other great museum–palaces of art in modern Europe: in Munich (1836), London (1838), Dresden (1855), Brussels (1885), Amsterdam (1885), Vienna (1891) and Moscow (1912). The collections in the Louvre, the Prado, the Hermitage and the large Italian museums were also extended and rearranged on the new educative principles.

These art museums were one aspect of the more general museum phenomenon that began in the eighteenth century at about the same time as the development of the first encyclopedias; they then became as characteristic a novelty of the nineteenth century as the stamp album. (The stamp album is itself a kind of do-it-yourself museum, involving classification, catalogues – the first stamp catalogue came out in Britain, in 1864 – auctions, dreams of unexpected finds and tests of authenticity.) As well as the art museums, the new European desire to order the universe evolved other great palaces of encyclopedic display – the natural history museums; the ethnology museums, stocked with either the loot of empire or the relics of Europe's suddenly vanquished peasant cultures; the science and industry museums, which attempted to make exhibits out of the 'modern'; the historical museums (at Düsseldorf and Dresden there were museums of sociology); and the museums of war.

Though a declared aim of them all was educational, one of the unintended functions of these museums was to put most people in their place. A much quoted survey carried out in France, in 1966, suggested that eight out of ten working-class people who visited an art museum associated it with a church; two-thirds could not remember the name of a single work. While most other museums are now more than glass cases of exhibits arranged for the benefit of the scholar, the art museums still maintain the holiness of paintings as authentic 'relics', and their own sanctity as cathedrals. In museums arranged on principles which Malraux calls 'as preposterous as would be a concert in which one listened to a programme of ill-assorted pieces following in unbroken succession', even the cultivated may feel too rushed to take from old paintings one of the great consolations that art offers life: assistance in constructing 'realities' that make a hypothetical sense of existence, which it does by giving meanings that can't be put into words.

An art museum is not the place to attempt to see the meanings of old paintings in terms of those who painted them and of those they were painted for. There is not usually any intellectual theme in a collection of paintings. The Groeningemuse, Brugge, where transparencies of Van Eyck paintings from other galleries are put together to make sense of the 'originals', is exceptional. Normally, paintings come together simply through the accidents of collecting. For these reasons, tourists with little or no knowledge of painting are expected to pay their respects solely to the fame, costliness and authenticity of these sacred objects, remote in their frames. As 'works of art' from which tourists must keep their distance, the value of paintings can depend not on their nature, but on their authenticated scarcity. The gap between 'art' and the tourist's own environment is thereby maintained.

'Authenticity' is the special magic of museums. In a technological museum, it is not that this is the *kind* of steam engine that Watt constructed that makes it interesting, but that it is the *very* steam engine Watt constructed. In an art museum, it is not that this painting is beautiful, but that it is an *authenticated* Rembrandt. In a history museum, it is not that this is the *kind* of hat that

Napoleon wore, but that this is the *very* hat Napoleon wore. Such an emphasis on authenticity provides a radiance of value and scarcity that hallows the object in itself, so that often a museum provides not an account of social processes but a collection of isolated objects, sacred in themselves.

In an industrial age, the importance of the authentic can be so great that techniques of restoration may be more interesting to tourists than what has been restored. Most of the big art museums now have displays of infra-red and X-ray photographs, descriptions of chemical analysis and pigment analysis, and other techniques of authentication and restoration: it is as if a famous surgeon were to display photographs of his or her most expensive operations in the waiting-room. At the Danish Viking Museum, Roskilde, tourists could watch several thousand pieces of wood dug out of Roskilde Fjord being reconstructed into the five ships that were sunk, full of stones, 1,000 years ago, to block a channel leading to a Viking trading-town. With workers showing their skills and with tools and diagrams on display, the museum looks like a shipbuilding yard. On show in Stockholm, the restored hull of a seventeenth-century Swedish warship, the *Wasa*, lies like a patient in an intensive-care ward. Put together from the 14,000 bits and pieces that were lifted out of the harbour where it sank in 1628, the *Wasa* is now propped up by steel pipes and sustained by rubber tubes, its temperature and humidity being tested several times during the day as if it were still near death. It may be more famous as the 'largest-ever organic matter preservation project' than as the only surviving baroque warship. Tourists see the film and follow the diagrams and learn about baths of rotting-preventatives and shrinkage-preventatives, and the subsequent six-month drying treatment. Looking at the old black wood itself can seem relatively uninteresting.

There is another sense in which modern tourism can be likened to a medieval pilgrimage. As well as the intrinsic holiness of venerated objects, it also offers cults of the dead – at the tombs, monuments and museums of secular saints.

Resting-places for the illustrious secular dead were developed first by accident, and later formalised. For instance, the Franciscan church of Santa Croce, Florence, began merely as a fashionable burial place. However, the Florentines buried there seemed so important that the church became a sacred place of European intellectual virtue. Inscriptions on its fifteenth-century tombs commemorated famous humanists as 'great sage' or 'glory of the age'; in the next century, Michelangelo's tomb went up; Galileo's body was moved there in the eighteenth century; a monument to Machiavelli was installed; a monument to Dante was erected in the piazza a century later.

In Westminster Abbey, London, there are so many tombs that parts of it look like a graveyard mason's catalogue; the Tikhvinskoye Cemetery, Leningrad, became a display area for the graves of famed writers, composers, painters and sculptors in late-nineteenth-century Russia; in the Var Frelsers Cemetery, Oslo, among the trees in a natural amphitheatre, the Norwegians, to show they were a nation, established a 'Grove of Honour' as the burial place of Ibsen and other Norwegian secular saints; in the Père Lachaise Cemetery, Paris, near the wall where the last of the Communard resisters were shot, there huddles the French Communist 'pantheon', with a few chosen leaders buried in single graves and the others arranged in the party's special vault. But it is the Paris Panthéon itself that symbolises most effectively the idea of a secular temple honouring great men of the Enlightenment by disposing of their bodies with a glory once reserved for saints – and by this means proclaiming civic and intellectual virtue.

With the wars of liberation in nineteenth-century Europe, symbolic cemeteries were created to commemorate the secular martyrs of the new nations; then, after the First World War, the cult of the fallen soldier became one of the deepest fountains of human meaning. Crops of crosses turned old fields into some of the most sacred places in the world. Traditionally, after a battle, soldiers' bodies had been shovelled into common holes; now they became focuses for national pilgrimage. The bodies of Unknown Soldiers were buried in the capital cities in nation-defining ceremonies; in national memorials there were urns of sacred earth, enriched by the blood of martyred innocents. Whole tourist programmes were developed to visit places sacred to fallen heroes.

The worship of secular saints has reached its climax in the canonisation of Lenin. Just as a saint's body was planted in a medieval cathedral to give it magic, Lenin's chemically preserved corpse (specially treated each year) is displayed under glass in the Lenin Mausoleum; its presence transforms Red Square into the world's most powerful cathedral. In the early years after Lenin died, some peasants believed that at night he walked about in the Kremlin, and in the factories and villages. With 10,000 people assembled on the marble steps to either side and the illustrious Soviet dead buried among the silver firs behind them, the Soviet hierarchy stands, twice a year, on the rock of Lenin's tomb and continues to build its church in the great reaffirmations of May Day and the Anniversary of the October Revolution.

Throughout the Communist world there are manifestations of the Lenin cult – thousands of statues and busts, hundreds of thousands of icons; cult centres in the Lenin Museums of the Soviet Union and some of the cities of eastern Europe. In East Berlin, a Lenin figure emerges sketchily from red Ukrainian granite, 18 metres high: it stands in front of a semicircle of shops, looking towards the TV tower and its revolving restaurant. At one end of Lenin Square, Sofia, Lenin stands, left hand on overcoat, as if explaining a new policy to the party headquarters at the other side of the square. In Budapest's main ceremonial area, Lenin, in long coat, seems about to cross the boulevard to the trade union buildings on the other side, where sculptured workers await him with their shirts off. The museums of eastern Europe house some of Lenin's relics: in Berlin, the very table at which he studied for several months in a library in the Unter den Linden; in Prague, the very postcard he once sent to the Czech socialists; in Sofia, the very note to his secretary asking for a Bulgarian–Russian dictionary. In Krakow, on the doorway of 16 Szewska St, next to a grocery shop, a plaque says: 'In this house, in April 1913, Vladimir Lenin delivered a lecture on contemporary Russia and the workers' movement.' And in the Soviet Union itself busts, paintings and photographs of Lenin are to be found as frequently as were crucifixes in the middle ages. They are associated with everything, and explain everything.

All of the characteristics of the modern tourist pilgrimage can be found at Salzburg.

Fifty years after Mozart died at the age of 35 and a pauper's hearse carried his body to a common grave in a place now unknown (thereby consoling generations of self-perceived neglected geniuses), a small organisation was founded in Salzburg, his birthplace. The Cathedral Musical Society and Mozarteum collected a few relics, and displayed them in one room. Now, a bronze statue of Mozart, pencil in hand, stands in Mozartplatz, near the American Express office, facing the Café Glockenspiel. At the Mozarteum building there are two concert halls and the Bibliotheca Mozartiana, with 30,000 volumes and a Mozart archive of hundreds of manuscripts and letters; next door, the Marionette Theatre specialises in Mozart performances. A museum of 100 dioramas and other exhibits visualises the history of theatre treatments of Mozart's operas. At the annual Mozart Festival, as many as 80 Mozart performances are put on in one month; sometimes half a dozen or so are playing at the same time.

All this activity fittingly commemorates a great man by the work that made him great. But, playing a less rational part, are the souvenirs of Mozart as celebrity and the relics of him as saint – the objects by which, as it were, we come to own him. As celebrity he is venerated in the shops – in Mozart souvenir busts, in Mozart toy grand pianos, in Mozart souvenir boxes of chocolates. This merchandise celebrates not the cult of Mozart, but the cult of commercialism which reduces everything to purchasable trivialities. As saint he is venerated in a collection of 'Mozartiana', some of it displayed in a replica of a house where he sometimes lived in Salzburg, more displayed in a summer house, transported from Vienna to Salzburg. Churches and aristocratic courtyards where Mozart's works had their first performances have plaques and guide-book annotations. Among the high, narrow houses of the Getrreidergasse, next to a shopping arcade and opposite a tax-free shop, there is Mozart's Birth House, opened as a museum in 1880 and a favourite shrine on the tourist pilgrim routes of central Europe. At the Birth House one climbs the stairs to the third storey of the steep, narrow building with its tiny courtyard, and then 'enters history' – the three rooms, low ceilinged with well-scrubbed floors, bought by Mozart's father after his success as an archbishop's violinist, are now used, in surrealist juxtapositions, to establish Mozart's reality by displaying material objects. At the spot where, reputedly, his mother gave birth to him, is stationed what was, reputedly, his favourite concert piano. On the spot where, reputedly, his cradle stood is placed the violin he played as a child. Under glass, there are smaller relics – buttons from his court coat, miniatures, revered odds and ends. And there are manuscripts – among the most sacred of secular relics, the actual pieces of paper on which the marks of genius were made, guaranteeing authenticity in a world of imitations.

Crisis in reality

Why should tourists be seeking the past? Why should the past have any particular resonance? Why has Europe become a great museum, reflecting certain views of the world? Throughout the age of industrialism there has been a nervousness in finding valid expressions of modernity. The tourist experience, with its seeking for an authentic (and well-researched) past, has been part of the same crisis in reality that has produced so much historical scholarship, so much sociology and so many experiments in art forms.

Tourism itself has a deep sense of history. One can stand in St Mark's Square, Venice, surrounded by pigeons and tourists, photographing the pigeons, and it can seem an epitome of modern tourism. So it is. But for 200 years it has also been one of the heartlands of tourism. The goods in the tourist shops are new, but tourists have been visiting its coffee houses since the eighteenth century. Rousseau, Goethe, Stendhal, Byron, Wagner, Longfellow, Rilke, Shelley, Proust, Mendelssohn, Henry James, Mann, Browning, Hemingway – all went to Venice to find the romantic and the poetic. There are paintings of Venice in almost every art museum. When John Ruskin wrote the three volumes of *The Stones of Venice*, he was casting up some of the grand images of modern tourism: from old buildings and artifacts he conjured spirits of meaning and beauty that were both an assault on the products of modern industrialism, and an escape from them. Venice is one symbol of modern tourism. It stands for poetry, romance, history, faith, frivolity, a return to the past. As sightseers tick off sights on their itineraries, whether they know it or not, they may be looking for escape from the dislocations of the industrial society – even if only on holiday. In nature, views, sights, ruins, or the strange customs of other lands, they are looking for new meanings – even if they go home confirmed in their old meanings.

Another symbol of the romantics' tourism is to be found in the Swiss Alps, which provided sustenance for the early nineteenth-century appetite for finding an invigorating melancholy in abysses, roaring torrents, avalanches and other catastrophes. They also satisfied the time's desire for a source of inner regeneration, obtained by intrusion into a natural order more enduring than that of humanity. Through their writings, Rousseau, Goethe and others helped 'invent' the Alps; there was soon a fashion for alpine journeys among the melancholy-seeking English. About the same time Scotland also opened out to the romantic travel imagination. With the development of steam trains, steamboats and Cook's Tours, both Switzerland and Scotland were recreated as 'tourist centres' for those seeking landscapes that would make them physically healthier and morally improved. Now the Alps and the Scottish Highlands have themselves become monuments.

Uneasiness with the present was so great that, for most of the nineteenth century, the past was nostalgically plundered to provide a modern sense of dignity and meaning. When, in the mid-nineteenth century, an Ottoman emperor wanted to build himself a new palace alongside the Bosphorous, he ordered it in the style of the Italian renaissance; nearby, there is a mosque with corinthian minarets. The Marquess of Bute, owner of Cardiff Castle, in his efforts to make a dream palace out of a medieval fortifications system, imposed on the simple stone decoration reminiscent of medieval romance: dragons, zodiac signs, coats of arms; portraits of the seasons and of the Saxon gods, the winds, the four elements and the great astronomers; representations of lovers' summer diversions and the exploits of Welsh heroes, as well as scenes from classical mythology, Chaucer's works and medieval romance. This elaborate fantasy was executed in carved wood, carved stone, stained glass, inlays, marble mosaic, gilding, handpainted tiles, murals, bronze doors, mirrors and chandeliers.

The rebuilding of the nineteenth-century cities was presided over by architects who had lost the power to present anything new. Architects were 'tourists' of the past: building with meticulous scholarship, they revived styles of bygone eras. An exhibition in Paris in 1979 – 'Le temps des gares' – showed how nineteenth-century architects were unable to accept the modernity of the railway station. Engineers who built the halls where the platforms were and where the trains came in used metal and glass to proclaim modern enterprise and ingenuity; the architects who designed the rest of the station could find no sense of progress and majesty in a steam engine, and so designed passenger buildings as Greek temples or Roman baths, romanesque basilicas, gothic cathedrals, renaissance chateaux, baroque abbeys. The Berlin U-Bahn station at Dahlem was, at Wilhelm II's suggestion, put up in 1913 as a rustic, half-timbered cottage with a thatched roof.

To romantic Germans, the gothic was above all an expression of the glories of medieval Germany. In Britain, the past could be a revival of the glories of gothic, and also of the Tudor, Elizabethan or Jacobean; in Budapest, it could be 'Brancovian', a style named after an eighteenth-century Romanian prince. The National Museum, Finland, was designed to look like palace, castle and church in order to accommodate all Finnish architectural styles. Equally, the Swiss National Museum, Zurich, was built by putting together a number of familiar Swiss styles – a spire here, a battlement there, a bit of everything that conformed to new notions of Old Switzerland.

All over Europe and the New World, carefully copied versions of classical temples glorified banks, museums, town halls, court houses, universities, parliament houses and other sustainers of dominant cultures. A tourist from Budapest, Edinburgh or Adelaide can go to the Königsplatz, Munich, look at the portico of the Glyptothek and compare it with the portico of the Hungarian Museum of Fine Arts, the National Gallery of Scotland or the Art Gallery of South Australia. Even in Athens, imitation classical buildings went up: in Venizelos Avenue, the National Library, the Academy and the University – all three designed by a Dane and paid for by an Austrian – were built with classical colonnades and pseudo-ancient statues. They gave dignity to a small town that had only one well-preserved classical building of its own.

The cults of simplicity are another form of consolation in the past. It is possible, for example, to walk around the 40 or so farmsteads of the open-air museum near Copenhagen and to reconstruct the entire farmhouse experience of non-Mediterranean Europe. The very sight of the thatched and the turfed roofs – brown with age and green with moss – or of the red, sun-dried brick, the white-washed walls, and the pinks and yellows of the half-timbered houses can arouse admiration for skill and for the sturdy husbanding of resources that confront modern wastefulness and factory methods. The timber beam is everywhere. For several generations of middle-class Europeans it has been a reassurance of traditions of rugged human sincerity and communal decision-making. On the village green, beside the village pond, a ring of stones is set under a lime tree: here, tourists are invited to imagine the farmers, sitting on their customary stones, formally debating their collective decisions. The farmhouse 'dwelling-rooms', with their built-in furniture, ostensibly feature all the elements of a simplicity-seeking modern urban commune, where people live together and sleep in the one room – even if reality may have been different. (It is not communal principles, for instance, that the tourist finds in the hierarchy of the 'bench', or built-in table. Here, the farmer sits at the head, in front of a painted panel; the men occupy the comfortable seats on one side of the table, sitting with their backs against the wall and in order of prestige; the women are relegated to backless stools on the other side – if they are not standing to serve the men more efficiently!)

The search for simple life-styles of the past can also take the tourist to the 'picturesque quarter' of a city, where one can discover the natural and the communal – even if the preservation of 'simplicity' now requires continuing contrivance. Anthropologists study the Alfama, Lisbon (perhaps the most successful picturesque quarter of any city in Europe), as archaeologists study the Acropolis – to keep it alive; there is an Executive Commission for the Divulging and Upkeep of the Tradition and Character of the Alfama.

Tourists may also seek the authenticity of old ways in traditional dance and song, whether or not they understand them. The most famous tourist dance in Europe is the flamenco, but it is done with such disdain that it excludes the tourist from its meaning; in Dublin's ballad clubs, ballad-singers, pipers, accordionists and flute- and whistle-players play traditional music, preserving sentiments of rebellion and melancholy failure – but the visitor is often lost among many of the regional and historical allusions.

Desire to find the authenticity of the past in 'the people' can take the tourist to flower markets, flea markets, or, most successfully, food markets. In the latter, in some countries, the tourist can still participate in a continuation of one of the first developments in European economic and social order, and in one of the most enduring symbols of interdependence and community. Failing these excursions, the tourist may look at past artifacts of past peoples, unspoiled, behind glass in an ethnographic museum. No matter how much goodwill might be aroused towards evidence of a lost peasant culture, however, the non-expert might yet feel some bewilderment: what is it all about? These costumes and their decorations meant that people were different from each other – differences of region, age, sex, season and social class were embroidered into the costumes, and stressed again by tassels, ornaments, and the use of colour – but, as tourists, we can look at folk-dress and imagine a past when people shared a common culture.

Marie Antoinette might be seen as an early tourist. In a corner of Versailles, she built her *hameau*, a replica of a Norman dairy farm, and here she amused herself with the simple life. She was seeking the authentic in the winding paths and clumps of trees of the natural *jardin anglais*, and in the simple styles of country folk. When tourists visit the *hameau*, they are visiting one of the most famous beginnings of the modern tourist experience: the appeal of the Swiss Alps, the folk museum, the picturesque quarter of a city – all come from the same impulse that produced this mock dairy farm set in a mock English garden. Now, it develops new meanings; we know that this is where she was when 'the mob' came looking for her, from Paris.

2. Appropriating the past

Tourists' geometry

We stand in an old building and imagine we are reconstructing its past. Can we? According to the eighteenth-century Neapolitan philosopher Giambattista Vico, whose *Scienza Nuova* did not get much recognition until the twentieth century, examining the monuments of a past age, and knowing something of its myths and rites and art enables us to reconstruct what that age meant to itself – what it saw itself as, what it wanted to be. From this reconstruction the age then becomes different from all other ages. It is an age we cannot understand, except in its own terms. All we know of that era are relics of what has survived, and these may be false clues; in any case almost certainly what is left will be predominantly relics of contemporary ruling groups. As with social groups, so with whole civilisations: at the time when Greeks and then Romans were colonising the Mediterranean, the dominant civilisation in Europe was the aristocratic society of the Celts. The Romans, however, built in stone, and what they built lasted; the Celts built in wood. That does not make the Celtic civilisation as insubstantial as it now seems; from the little that has been found from excavations in burial sites or hilltop citadels and even from what the Romans said about the Celts, there are hints of an alternative European culture. Even more seriously: how can we contemplate so many different 'ages' and imagine that, in one lifetime, we can understand even one of them in the same terms as those who lived in the time itself? Their views of reality and values *may* be represented in these surviving fragments – or may not be represented in anything that survived.

What can we do? In trying to reconstruct the past, we merely make the best we can of it. If we see an assembly of stone and plaster and paint it evokes images in our minds of an 'age'. Those images come from our preconceptions – whether the preconceptions arise from a lifetime's scholarship, our general reading, a quiet look at a guide book, or even if they are of the most puerile and anachronistic kind, an expression of our inability to imagine any way of life other than our own and our subsequent interpretation of all past life in terms of the present. Except in the last case, we react as if what Vico believed were true: we react as if what we are seeing are manifestations of a distinctive collective consciousness, and from these stereotypes of the past – necessarily imperfect and sometimes ridiculous – we continue our equivocations with the present.

But in seeking the past one must, in a sense, have already discovered it, in existing stereotypes. Tourists can glance over an 'Old Town' as if at a geometry textbook: one recognises the stereotypes. Salzburg, for example: it has dignified *squares*, surrounded by *baroque churches* and *palaces*; it has quiet *courtyards* and *narrow*, *winding lanes*, a *town gate* and part of a *town wall*. It has a river and a steep hill, and on top of its steep hill, it has a *citadel*, with rooms that appeal to the romantic imagination – a *golden chamber*, a hall of justice, and a *torture chamber*. It even offers a ride in a *funicular railway* and a ride in a *drosky*. An old town with castle above and river below, it tells us what we know: but the more we already know, the more we may find out.

The approach to tourists' geometry is even simpler with the town square. Even a run-of-the-mill square like Munich's Marienplatz is useful revision for those who have learned their geometry lessons. It was established as a *market place*, as most town squares were; it was a place of punishment – the *pillory* stood here – and sometimes of execution; it bears witness to the catholic church – the city's oldest *parish church* is here, and a slender *votive pillar*, honouring the Virgin for preserving the city from the disasters of plague, war, hunger and heresy during the Thirty Years' War; it was a scene of aristocratic *tournaments* and also of popular *festivals*; and its two town halls, old and new, celebrate civic virtue – the new one in the most florid of nineteenth-century revival styles. We can stand in it and imagine we are reconstructing its past.

Nevertheless, this can be intellectually satisfactory only if we can move beyond the stereotype. How can we do that? The two most defined stereotypes of the 'medieval' – the castle and the gothic cathedral – can, except to specialists, become the most boring. The medieval castle has become too familiar a symbol for the tourist to bother looking at it in any detail. It can no longer be experienced for itself. When tourists buy admission tickets and souvenir postcards at the sales kiosk near the portcullis of an old castle, they are buying a reminder of the most universal of the European concepts of social class and the most universal concept of a fortified building. But many cannot see the stones for the concept of the 'castle'. Even gothic cathedrals can be reduced to the level of obituary notices as the tourists, having looked at the most advertised special feature, wander around the sepulchral monuments, staring at the names of the dead. The ironies of reductionism are profound in the case of these edifices which symbolised the most ambitious of human demands – to grow a little nearer heaven – and which could take up to a century to build (in the case of Köln Cathedral, 600 years). Most tourists learn merely to register a symbol of the *gothic cathedral*. The wholeness of the symbol blinds them to its parts.

In Florence, we see a business palace, solid with rusticated stone blocks, reasonable with symmetrical windows, its columns light and graceful, legitimising power with architectural proclamations of order and appeals to antiquity – and we say 'renaissance' and pass on. Equally, if one sees classical forms thrown about as if in a high wind – dramatically, sweepingly and ornately, with some hope that they might come together in some rational conclusion – one can say 'baroque'. A Rubens figure, which is at once serenely still and yet vibrating with colour to the point where skin appears to quiver, can be classified – 'baroque':'Rubens' – and, once it is named, the tourist can stop seeing it. Abrupt contrasts of light and shade – 'baroque'. Violent action frozen into marble – 'baroque'. Across Europe one can follow the style and name it without looking at what one is naming: in Spain, gothic churches smothered with a froth of stone – 'baroque'; in Stockholm, the 700 pieces of sculpture and ornament found on the *Wasa* – 'baroque'; in Moscow, the icon stand and belfry of the Novodevichy Convent – 'baroque'; in Istanbul, the Nuruosmaniye Mosque – 'baroque'. And the classical statue can provide the ultimate tedium in stereotypes. Like butterfly-collecting, tourism is a mere matter of classification unless we can learn how to 'read' at least some of the stereotypes.

Would we admire the Parthenon if it still had a roof, and no longer appealed to the modern stereotype taste for an outline emerging from rough stone? If we repainted it in its original red, blue and gold, and if we reinstalled the huge, gaudy cult-figure of Athena, festooned in bracelets, rings and necklaces, we could not avoid the question that threatens our whole concept of the classical: *did the Greeks have bad taste?* When, in the 1950s, the American School of Classical Studies at Athens spent $1,500,000 building a copy of the Stoa of Attalus in the old market place they were faithful to every known detail except one – they couldn't bring themselves to paint it red and blue as it had been in the original. To have been authentic would have made it seem untrue to the modern stereotype of the classical.

Inventing the past

In the sacral festival of tourism we turn inanimate matter into 'monuments', and whether it is the Winter Palace or the Eiffel Tower, the ruins of Herculaneum or the reconstruction of Old Warsaw, the *Night Watch* or *Our Lady of Vladimir*, the objects are given meanings that would have astounded their originators. Anachronism (using the word in its original sense) is the very essence of tourism: the present is used to explain the relics of the past, and then the meanings given to the past are used to justify aspects of the present, or to justify beliefs about how things should change.

So, as we walk on guided tours through old buildings or inspect relics in museums, we are contemplating objects transformed into 'monuments' – they commemorate persons, social classes, events, epochs, styles, ideas. Now, though, they are like dead coral that has been painted: they have become something else. When we visit a palace we may do little more than register the stereotype 'palace' and buy a postcard as warranty that it is authentic: we pay our respects without thinking about what we are doing. But we may, instead, study it as an example of art and architectural styles;

alternatively, we may moon around it with nostalgia, regretting lost aristocratic elegance; we may even despise it and see in its discomforts new proof of modern efficiency; we can perhaps exult over it as a symbol of how power can be overthrown. We use the palace for our purposes, and, given that we may have travelled hundreds or even thousands of kilometres as tourist–pilgrims to have this kind of experience, and that the experience has been gven extra significance by its place on a ceremonial agenda and as part of the cult of the authentic, the affirmations we make when we pay respect to the relics of the past may stay with us. None of the meanings we give these relics, however, were meanings the relics had when they were 'alive'.

The huge appetite for monuments as a source of enlightenment and perhaps of regeneration has created an overwhelming transformation of objects – never intended to commemorate anything – into monuments of meaning. When the exhibits in museums were made, they were made for purposes unrelated to their present functions as objects standing for something else. The Parthenon was not built as a ruin celebrating western civilisation; the aqueduct at Segovia was not built as a monument to Roman power any more than Haghia Sophia was erected to commemorate byzantine culture; Cologne Cathedral was not built to commemorate the middle ages; the Palazzo Medici-Riccardi was not built to commemorate the renaissance; the Winter Palace was not built to commemorate the baroque; London's Trooping the Colour ceremony was not designed for tourist 'pageantry'. Outside the Hofburg, Vienna, a bronze statue of Prince Eugene on his prancing charger rises above the parking lot; Eugene was victor over both the Turks and the French. Now, the statue also celebrates the fall of an Austria whose entire capital city, like London, has become a monument to the collapse of imperial ambition.

Even if the word 'monument' is used in the narrow sense, meaning structures specifically erected to commemorate persons, events or ideas, these monuments can also become more general symbols of a way of viewing the world. Nelson on his column in London's Trafalgar Square affirmed Britain's right to rule the seas, and Napoleon on his column in the Place Vendôme affirmed France's right to reorder Europe; but both on their columns also affirmed the more general legitimacy of imperial domination. The statues, plaques and museums which commemorate orthographers, artists, historians, folklorists, philologists and educationalists in the 'new nations' of Europe, honour them as great nationalists – but these monuments, by their very style, also symbolise the bourgeois leadership of the nationalist movements.

The intentions of those who erect commemorative structures have nothing to do with the subsequent meanings of those structures. In Communist countries, nineteenth-century monuments to bourgeois nationalists now bear meanings that would have been unimaginable to those who put the monuments up: they can be seen as assertions of the right to separate nationhood amongst Communist states, or of the legitimacy of the present regimes in those states, or as symbols of dissidence against those regimes.

Consider the stereotype western European tourism throws up in the two words 'byzantine' and 'renaissance'. An important function of western European art museums is to demonstrate the uniqueness of western European civilisation and its superiority over eastern Europe. In this cultural chauvinism, what is most bold is a tendency to speak of medieval civilisation as if it were a purely western European phenomenon when, by the tests of western civilisation itself, the Byzantine empire (that is, the medieval Greek empire centred in Constantinople before the Turks overran it) would, for the most part, score ahead of the west – as would, in their shorter seasons, the Serbian and Bulgarian empires. Yet the word 'byzantine' is likely to have as its first meaning the idea of trickiness and deceit, and, as its second, a strange art of mosaics and icons, unnatural, over-stylised, over-ornate, the part of an art museum the western European tourist can skip, not true art at all, an obsolete model. Westerners can learn a history of medieval art that simply leaves out byzantine styles, even though they formed the basis of western styles.

In the Soviet Union there is an ambivalence about the Russians' byzantine and Orthodox past: the art of superstitions might impair the Soviet programme. In Romania, Bulgaria and eastern Yugoslavia, on the other hand, the byzantine past is a matter for national assertion. Part of the national definition that followed liberation from the Ottoman empire came from a pride in a 'golden' byzantine age; to ordinary Greeks it is more likely to be the byzantine than the classical that seems distinctively Greek. It is not a reproduction of a classical statue that a Greek taxi-driver carries in his cab, but a reproduction of an icon.

To western and central Europe, there is the prestige of the 'renaissance': what we have at stake here is a claim to have been 'in' early on the processes of modernity. At Mainz, the replica of a printing press, as solid as a gentleman's wardrobe, recalls Gutenberg and the beginning of the media revolution. In Krakow, a statue of Copernicus, idealised as a thinker, recalls the beginning of the scientific revolution. In Barcelona, a cast-iron column rising above Puerta de la Paz, with triumphant lions at its base and, at its top, standing on a globe, a statue of Columbus, recalls 'discovery'.

Sometimes an historical figure is defined as a 'renaissance prince', thereby bringing a nation into modern history: Francois I, celebrated in Fontainbleau and the châteaux of the Loire; Rudolph II, recalled in the arcaded galleries and copper roofs of Prague Citadel; Christian IV, remembered in Denmark's famous tourist castles; Gustav Vasa, with his 'renaissance tomb' in Uppsala; and Sigismund III with his 'renaissance tomb' in Krakow. In Budapest, in the National Museum's Renaissance Hall a few fragments of glass, tile and marble recall Mathias Corvinus, Hungary's 'renaissance prince', conqueror of Prague and Vienna. It was he who brought skilled workers from Italy to turn a gothic castle into a renaissance palace of red marble, bronze statues and coffered ceilings – a palace which he stocked with art treasures, humanist intellectuals, artists and a renowned library.

Individual nations can also use Old Masters to claim a place for themselves in the 'renaissance'. In the art museums of Flanders and the Netherlands, it is the Flemish, not Italian, Old Masters that encapsulate painting's renaissance; and in the great German art museums Flemish Old Masters are joined by German Old Masters to project what can then seem the really significant part of the renaissance, adding sombre, enchanted landscapes and portraits of strong-souled men of determined purpose. In Serbia and Bulgaria, too, cultural patriots turn towards 'renaissance paintings' to demonstrate early modernity. After the Second World War, the credibility of claims to a Serbian 'Golden Age' before the Ottoman conquest could, to Serbian nationalists, seem substantiated when

6,000 frescoes in medieval monasteries and churches in the mountains of Serbia, Montenegro and Macedonia were catalogued. The thirteenth-century frescoes (especially those from Molŏsevo and Sopočani) provide Yugoslavia with an audacious ploy against the pride of western Europe: these are 'renaissance' paintings, done some decades before the renaissance in painting began in western Europe. Luminous and elegant in green, blue, purple and yellow, they are humanist, realist, classical, intimate and, with portrayals of court life as well as familiar Christian themes, they make up one of the largest collections of medieval secular painting. Bulgaria's strongest claim to early humanism, as bold as that of Yugoslavia, is found in the cycle of thirteenth-century murals in the little church of Boyana, on the fringe of Sofia. Painted in 1249 with a laconic realism whose observation of court dress and jewels and general milieux equals the Serbian murals' ability to 'report' on aristocratic life, the paintings also show an individualistic portraitist's eye for character: the 22 different studies of the life of Christ, for example, seem 'drawn from life'. In *Bulgaria's Share in Human Culture*, Kirk Kructev, a Bulgarian art historian, writes that these murals 'effected the greatest revolution in art history: they were the first to adopt the pictorial style in painting which was to become typical of all renaissance European painting during the following centuries.'

With these scraps of mosaic and peeling frescoes, the nations of the east challenge the whole prestige of the west as moderniser, so that it can seem that only the bad luck of the Ottoman conquest prevented them from leading Europe. But in the west, progressives now give renaissance paintings a reactionary meaning and bring them as evidence against the bourgeois order. Once it was a pleasurable and relaxing climax to reach the sections of an art museum where, according to modern convention, painting really began. The paintings seemed 'real'; the bodies looked like bodies that could breathe and move; the objects seemed something we could touch and own; the clothing was something we could wear; the techniques of perspective and of light increased this impression that we were in an objectified world, and that our own eyes were at the centre of it. Now that this 'realism' is recognised as merely one construction of reality among many others, it is criticised as one suiting the individualism of a modern competitive world in which painting is no longer co-operative and public, but part of a private world – framed, transportable and privately owned and available to the public only via the munificence of the owner. Even the sense of individuality of characterisation is taken as a reminder of how art is now produced not by anonymous and co-operative craftsmen, but by individual 'geniuses', who move from place to place, accepting the highest offer, determined to defend their individualism.

Whether they are relics or newly created, in the uncertainties of the modern age, 'monuments' can acquire a special glamour that gives them a respect not given to ordinary objects. This magical glow can illuminate meanings that justify power or claim prestige. Power continues to have imagination as its servant: over the centuries a single esteemed artifact may serve, in differing ways, a number of different social orders.

Power is the particular aspect of tourism with which this book is concerned as we pass and repass between the 'dreamlands' of past and present. As tourists, we are haunted by the old ambitions and the old justifications of those who have been masters of Europe. These shadows of past ambitions make up an important part of what is, in any serious sense, the European imagination. But each generation turns the monuments of earlier generations to new purposes and creates new monuments out of what had previously seemed everyday objects, thus creating a new 'dream' to match the world view of a new social order.

Part two

Fragments from the wreckage

3. Power from birth and from God

Power from birth

In understanding how European architecture can glorify the power of princes, Europe's best example is the vista of squares and palaces that make Leningrad the most aristocratic city in Europe. Leningrad's Nevsky Prospect, nearly five miles long, is one of Europe's most celebrated nineteenth-century avenues, and the most punctiliously preserved. As well as its palaces and churches, it has book shops and fashion houses, theatres and libraries, boutiques and clubs, offering images of refinement from the period before the First World War. But if after a stroll on the Nevsky, tourists following a ceremonial agenda go along the curving carriageway that passes through the mighty yellow building at its end, they move into another world, one of regularity and lavish space. They walk under a triumphal arch with a victory chariot on top into a stupendous square, with, in its centre, a red granite monolith, one of the world's highest victory columns. Extending across the whole far end of the square is the green-and-white baroque façade of the 1,000-room Winter Palace; behind it curves one of Europe's greatest colonnades; on either side are vistas of strong buildings constrained into simple neoclassical forms, painted yellow and white or pink and white, set beside wide avenues. When tourists walk to the embankment, the Neva River becomes part of this disciplined display; a gold spire glitters barbarously, but otherwise the river's opposite bank shows the same emphatic world of classically conceived balance and order, underlined by pink and yellow and white, as in a set of framed watercolours. Avenues lead from the first vast square to the second, which is dominated by the august assertion of white porticoes, white pilasters and yellow calm, overriding with a sense of absolute order. At the other end is the bombast of St Isaac's Cathedral, with its marble and granite, Roman portico and gilded dome. Beyond the cathedral is another square, quietly proportioned, where at one edge the restrained *art nouveau* of the Astoria Hotel returns to early-twentieth-century attempts at a new refinement. Nowhere else in Europe is so much masonry deployed with such restrained strength over such vast spaces to convey, with such delicate beauty and assured power, the autocracy of princes.

Also on the tourists' agenda, to be reached by road, electric railway or, in one case, hydrofoil, are the clusters of palaces the Romanovs left in the countryside around Leningrad: half a dozen (baroque, neoclassical, rococo) at Pushkin, Pavlovsk and Lomonosov; and at Petrodvorets the Summer Palace, set in Versailles-style gardens littered with gilded fountains – one of the most famous sets of fountains in Europe. All these palaces and their surrounding gardens, statues, pavilions and grottoes were devastated, or destroyed by the Germans in the Second World War, sometimes by the chances of battle, sometimes from vindictiveness – before the Germans left Petrodvorets they set fire to the Summer Palace and blew up all the fountains. The Soviets have restored all the buildings, sometimes building them again, and recreated stucco, gilding, niches, marble work, crystal and bronze chandeliers, tapestries, frescoes and painted ceilings.

For more than a generation whole institutes of Soviet scholars and ateliers of Soviet craftsmen have been working at meticulously restoring the greatest monuments of tsarist autocracy – the palaces of the tsars themselves and their families, and the great palaces of state through which they controlled army and navy, church and nobility. Yet these palaces – and most of the other palaces built in Europe – were a reminder that what should prevail in the conduct of human affairs was not justice, nor reason, nor efficiency, nor equality, but the right to power by *birth*.

When the only claim on loyalty was that of dynasty, the central political institution was the princely court. In the palaces of the ruling princes courtly displays were elaborated that, from the rising of the prince in the morning to the retirement of the prince at night, daily asserted that what dominated existence was the power, prestige and wealth of ruling princes. These daily rituals were supported by the regular spectacles of hunting and of balls and by music and drama, and by the occasional spectacles of the funerals, weddings and baptisms of the dynastic family. In such circumstances the building of a new palace, or the redecorating of an old one – even the ordering of new paintings or new music – was a political statement.

The role of art was also important in justifying the rights of the nobility who 'served' the princes – that nobles should monopolise the land, enjoy exemptions from tax, exact tribute from peasants, command the positions of wealth, power and prestige given by the ruling dynasty and defend their special attribute, their honour ('born of the desire to distinguish oneself', as Montesquieu put it), as more valuable than life. The portrait galleries, the manor houses and palaces, the precious objects in the jewel chambers are among the reminders of how, until the First World War, relations between dynasty and nobility decided the nature of the state. In Russia, the tsarist autocracy used the nobility as its bureaucracy. In Prussia, the nobles became agents of the crown on the understanding that they kept their privileges on the land and held the important offices of state. In Austria, where nobles held the main positions in the army and the imperial administration, it was said, 'The human race begins with barons': no one was to be allowed at court unless all 16 of his or her great-great-grandparents were noble – except once a year, when otherwise disqualified army officers were invited to a ball (at which they were forbidden to dance and where they were separated from the impeccably noble by a scarlet cord). In Britain, the hereditary landed classes overrode the monarchs and dominated the state themselves, controlling almost all seats in parliament – but they paid taxes and opened their arms most generously to the new rich. In France, the resistance of the nobles to royal power precipitated a revolution. In Poland, the nobles were so many (10 per cent of the population), so powerful and so jealous that, lacking strong central government, Poland fell apart.

In most princely states the richest of the new rich were assimilated into the nobility, if with some friction, as were successful military adventurers and civil administrators. The principal justifications of power, however, remained those of tradition and birth. When men gained wealth and power, their children were given the prestige of birth. Nobility was a matter of 'blood'. People were born noble, and set apart by the wisdom of centuries that had uniquely accumulated in the experience of ruling dynasties and noble families. The few were born, uniquely, to rule. It was the duty of the many to show their loyalty and obedience. By their birth and their necessarily base nature, obedience was their special talent.

It is the new 'aristocracy' (a seventeenth- and eighteenth-century idea) rather than the nobility (a military administrative class going back to the middle ages) that is usually being honoured in the tourist experience. By the eighteenth century, everywhere except in Britain, many of the old nobility were too poor to leave objects valuable enough to become exhibits in a twentieth-century art museum. In France before the 1789 revolution, there may have been 400,000 members of noble families, but in the provinces only some were well-to-do, and in Paris only a few hundred families (*Les Grands*) occupied the main positions of power and fortune-making. It is the relics of the various *Les Grands* of Europe, the rich ruling classes with their claims to excellence by birth, which provide much of the substance of European sightseeing.

A ticket into a baroque palace buys entry into the heart of the tourist image of the aristocratic. The baroque was the aristocratic style *par excellence*. No doubt about its meaning. It was intended to display such triumphant opulence that opposition would shrivel away. Thus, when in 1714 the time came for a palace (the Belvedere) to be built in Vienna for Eugene, the adventurer–prince, victor over both French and Turks, his importance was displayed by two palaces which balanced each other across a terraced French park with fountains, statues, ponds, pavilions, and yew trees put in their place by topiary. Inside both palaces, marble, glass, stucco, gold leaf and paint present Eugene as a great commander and as a great patron of the arts. The upper palace, built on a hill to recall Olympus, has copper roofs on its wings that are reminiscent of the military tents of the vanquished Turks. A painted ceiling shows Eugene, a bright knight of Christendom, rising to heaven in triumph; trophies on the walls proclaim military victories; allegorical reliefs praise an Apollo of the arts. The ceiling fresco in the marble hall has the prince on his throne receiving the wreath of Victory and the hand of Justice while Fame blows her trombone and History records his deeds.

The coming of the modern

After the triumph of the baroque the tourist can see, in fragments of the art and architecture of the aristocrats, the first of the art-symbols of their decline, in the brief, frivolous adventure of the rococo, when the aristocratic style proclaimed its playfulness too indulgently. The gold-edged panellings, the gilded mirrors, the flowing arabesques of Versailles, repeated in many of the palaces of Europe, seem to us now to be signs of self-indulgence before its fall. The sense of Nemesis increases when the adventure of the rococo passes into the neoclassical, the last aristocratic style. The green-and-white Winter Palace in Leningrad is ornate baroque, but is surrounded by the balance and order of pale-coloured buildings in neoclassical styles. Throughout Europe the neoclassical style was to speak the language of clarity, simplicity and purity, and to appeal with the power of enlightened reason. When Greece was liberated from the Turks and Prince Otto of Bavaria became King Otho of the Hellenes, he restored some dignity to what had been a small Turkish outpost by putting up buildings in an elegant neoclassical style: the 'Othonian' style is now seen as the authentic style of Athens. Nevertheless the style of clarity and reason did not remain an aristocratic style. It also proved to be, in France, the style of revolution. With its insistence on the spirit of reason, harmony and enlightenment it can be seen as an early sign of those forces that were to engulf the dynasties and the aristocracies.

It was the first modern republican style as well as the last aristocratic style. With some exceptions (such as new dynasties' attempts to legitimise themselves in new nations – Bulgaria, Serbia, Romania, Belgium, Norway as well as Greece – and the activities of *arrivistes*), from the middle of the nineteenth century the upper classes were giving up new building. When they did build, they merely revived the styles of their predecessors. The ruling classes remained, but in the long counter-revolution carried out in the nineteenth century, most of the aristocrats had no new faith to inspire new building: in a retreat from the threats of the present, they found comfort in a well-authenticated architectural nostalgia.

Now, it is the monuments of the industrial society which are everywhere – the model factory buildings, the great office towers, the terminals of the transport systems, the palaces of mass culture, the showy apartment houses; and (if more patchily in the Communist countries) the display architecture of the big department stores. And almost all the pageantry of belief in Europe, apart from the pageantry of the churches, is also now found in the great mass affirmations of industrial society: the grey rituals of the commemoration of the tens of millions of the war dead that give meaning to the comradeship of soldiers and the massacre of so many innocents; the devoted bustle of the major shopping festivals, affirming money as a measure of value; the celebrations of revolutions and the martyrs who laid down their lives so that others might be free; the collective delirium of the big sporting events when the self is surrendered to the side; the celebrations, mainly in eastern Europe, of the liberating role of the workers; and the celebrations, in the extravagances of 'celebrities' in the west, of the saving graces of wealth; the self-definitions of national days, expecially of those whose nationality is in danger; the military parades of conscripts and weapons; the controlled excitements of the conventional holiday seasons, and the many rituals of tourism.

Of the great shows of the princely courts, once the prime symbol of earthly power, only a few of the surviving pageants of 'royalty' remain. The most commercially successful example is in London where what were once the symbols of entrenched imperial power – the royal guards, the state coaches, Buckingham Palace – are now assets helping tourist promotion. Evzones outside the Parliament House in Constitution Square, Athens, Gardes Républicains outside the Elysée Palace, Paris, troops in nineteenth-century uniforms outside Dimitrov's Mausoleum, Sofia, and the other wearers of old-fashioned dress in the European republics are worth a photograph – but they don't seem as authentic as Beefeaters or Welsh Guards. Nor do the display pieces of the other six remaining monarchies. Only Denmark makes any play with its monarchy on the tourist posters, but the palace guards in toy-soldier dress are put into the Copenhagen sales promotion material with the delicate irony of a country that has had almost 200 years of recognising that it is no longer a great power. Even when marching through the streets of Copenhagen, the Danish royal guards can send themselves up: they know they are an adjunct to the amusement park of the Tivoli Gardens. What gives gravity to the British show is the enormous personal wealth of the Windsors and the vast public cost of maintaining them as the last family in Europe to live in the grand aristocratic style. No other ceremonial soldiers in fancy dress have the same meaning as the Guards in London because no other soldiers owe allegiance to the head of a family with one of Europe's largest fortunes, its own aeroplanes, its own small passenger-liner, five tons of gold plate, the world's largest collection of jewellery, 2,000 authentic Old Masters, a variety of palaces, castles and rural estates, somewhere between 400 and 500 courtiers and retainers, dozens of ceremonial horses and coaches, a famous racing stable, and so many antiques that the catalogue of the furniture in Windsor Castle alone takes up 75 volumes.

Royal pageantry is, for most tourists, exploded of old meaning, except the meanings of nostalgia; it has some of the functions of Disneyland. People are still born to privilege – of wealth or expertise or political or bureaucratic connection – and, through education and wealth, they can maintain privilege. Nowhere, though, remains what until recently was universal: a dominant and public justification of power by the hereditary principle. Instead, to justify power, we now have the legitimations of reason, of class, of nation, of race, of political faith, or of the faith in economic efficiency. The old theatrical roles of the dynasties and the aristocracies are taken over in the public drama by politicians and, in the west, by those peculiarly modern creations, the 'celebrities' – entertainers, sports stars, intellectuals, a few flamboyant rich, with an occasional aristocratic group (the English royal family or the princely family of Monaco) still performing.

Yet sightseeing in Europe is largely a journey past the fragments which have survived of the aristocracies. Whether these fragments are palaces set among gardens and fountains or jewelled snuffboxes set in glass cases, they have been transformed in the same way that makes every museum piece, to some extent, false: they are objects removed from their social context. In being confronted by aristocratic objects without aristocrats, we are presented with an aesthetic view of the aristocratic past that is as false as if we judged modern capitalists by looking at a Mies van der Rohe building or a boardroom Picasso. In this sense, tourist sightseeing can represent something of a crisis in modernity and (whatever meaning you give to it) democracy. Guides in the Soviet Union take care to point this out: it is not obvious, however, that they are successful.

Power from God

If we are not inspecting the relics of aristocratic life, we may be looking at churches and religious art, sometimes another expression of the same thing. Baroque cathedrals exulted in the power of God and bishops as much as baroque palaces exulted in the power of nobles and kings. The Karlskirche, Vienna, showed this confidence by appropriating ancient symbols of empire: under its dome is a classical portico and on either side an imitation of Trajan's Column. Inside, among the white, pink and gold, frescoes commemorate the victories of the counter-reformation as if they were victories of Roman emperors. All the elements of this and other baroque churches that engage the tourist's gaze – painting, sculpture, architecture, music, costumes, incense – came together in an operatic presentation of the unconquerable glory of God.

But the most ambitious claims for God came earlier, with the gothic cathedral, a style invented when a new choir for St Denis Abbey was consecrated in 1144 by ten prelates in the presence of the French king. The suburb that surrounds St Denis, on the edge of the metro system, used to be one of Paris's most run down; as well as clearing up the basilica, the council has set to work on the area around it. Pamphlets from the information kiosk now suggest tourist trails around the suburb, as well as the main attraction – a guided tour of the royal tombs where for hundreds of years the kings of France were buried. But the pamphlets don't tell tourists how to get to see the choir which began the most monumental period of display that the church was to know. Initially it was French ostentation – by these prestigious engineering works, the small new kingdom was convincing itself that it might matter – but the desire to build such glorious projects spread across Christendom. From a balance of thrusts and counter-thrusts from pointed arches, flying buttresses and ribbing as complex as a medieval motet, stone vaulting was pushed several metres higher towards heaven than it had been before. Many of the new cathedrals were not finished and some new churches were so ambitiously built that they fell down. Such accidents did little to impede the dissemination of a style which put ordinary people in their place by mathematical aloofness and a vertical scorn for what was merely on the ground, and which reminded them that all life was lived under the hand of God. Now the gothic cathedrals are the most obvious of all reminders to tourists that, for most of Christian Europe's history, the greatest legitimation of power – legitimising even the claims to power of noble birth – was the will of God, and that for some Europeans it still is.

Art museums and tourist churches continue to celebrate that triumph of Christ that was the permanent reminder of God's might and the permanent justification of the powers of popes and patriarchs, abbots and bishops, monks and priests. Although there can also be images of humility and agony, Christ stares in majesty from the vaults of every Byzantine church; his sitting in judgement in the Sistine Chapel is one of the climaxes of the tourist itineraries. And while the cycle of the Virgin Mary was presented in byzantine and earlier western paintings in a simple background of gold, with a spiritual rather than a physical meaning, as the renaissance plunged on to its excesses, Mary became more gorgeously clothed, her gestures became heavily theatrical and the settings changed from simple gold to Florentine palaces, chambers in the court of Burgundy, elaborate Venetian courtyards, marble halls and aristocratic gardens. As painting moved towards and into the baroque, her bodily rising into heaven became a greater and greater material spectacle, with angels piled on angels, and larger orchestras. Her crowning was most usually an ornately organised tableau of golden joy. Once crowned, she sat in majesty on a golden throne, with regal accoutrements, receiving pleas from sinners. She was the centre of the church's power, the Queen of Heaven.

What we are seeing in the tourist churches and the religious art in the museums is the wreckage of what, until the protestant revolts, was the dominant 'language' of Europe. Europeans were not 'Europeans'; they were Christians. Though there were power struggles, rackets, cynicism, anti-clericalism, indifference, neglect, schisms, heresies and subversive preaching, Christian intellectual concepts, Christian art and Christian ceremony dominated public views of the world: even when there were differences, they were differences within a Christian context.

Made more or less coherent by doctrine and ceremony – the true cements of the church – Catholic and Orthodox churches were custodians of fact, as well as of conscience. Secular people might engage in intellectual life only if the church didn't condemn them: if the church did condemn them, their work might be suppressed and the authors executed. The plastic arts were almost exclusively at the service of the churches; display architecture and the performing arts mostly so; almost all ceremony – state and folk, as well as religious – was conducted or influenced by the churches; almost all scholarship and speculation were carried on within church institutions and all education was performed by the clergy; and churchmen reached out into daily life through their unique command of preaching, and of the confessionals. The churches provided dominant views of what life meant and their monopoly outdid that of even a modern one-party state.

That church views of the world were dominant does not mean that other views did not exist; they were, however, publicly invisible, or almost so. Even the word 'church' can suggest an exaggerated idea of narrow manipulation: a broader view is that the Catholic and Orthodox faiths were the main bearers of the repertoires of European public culture – acted on, as well as acting. Nonetheless, church was the only place where humans could get the chance for salvation offered them by the sacrifice of the son of God on the cross. Grace could be obtained only through church sacraments. The church provided access to the saints whose holy relics could be so usefully invoked in conducting earthly affairs. And the church provided the only route to the Madonna, who, in her crowned majesty, interceded for sinners.

Christianity has now become an object of tourism. The first art institution established after the 1789 revolution in France was the Musée National des Monuments Français. Set up in 1790 in a seized Paris monastery, it became a repository for works of sculpture confiscated from the church or saved from vengeful vandals. The sculptures were arranged in historical groupings and soon became objects of interest for sightseers, thereby beginning that process in which religion is primarily respected for its physical artifacts, its leftovers; by becoming 'art' (which was never intended) those artifacts are transformed into something quite different. Tourism can become, in effect, a celebration of Christianity's fall from dominance.

The church as alternative culture

Although the pageantry of the aristocrats and the festivals of the people may have declined into design ideas for tourist posters, what still survives with meaning if sometimes with a sense of siege – are the ceremonies of the Christian churches. Sometimes they are strong – as in Ireland, where people pour in and out of Sunday mass like shiftworkers; or in Poland, where in the main churches at any hour of the day people are on their knees while confessors sit, hands over eyes as if asleep, listening to penitents whispering their sins, and where coachloads of tourists pray before they photograph the altar.

The Pope is Europe's greatest single tourist celebrity. Tours of Rome on Wednesdays and Saturdays include him as the climax of the city's attractions. On Wednesdays, the Pope now holds audience in St Peter's Square (the 8,000-capacity of the New Audience Hall proved inadequate), where he tours among the crowds in a white jeep. On Sundays, thousands again wait in the square, looking up to a high window on the top floor of the Apostolic Palace: some hold balloons; some hold up signs telling the Pope or the television cameras who they are. There is a rustle of clapping: a small, distant, white figure has appeared. Through the excellent public-address system, the voice is both loud and intimate. For ten minutes, he warns, extols, praises, jokes, between further rustles of clapping – then the tourist coaches quietly move up into position as he leads the people in prayer and then blesses them before the coaches take them off to lunch.

The ceremonies of the Orthodox church also continue to speak with intimacy and compassion. At Easter, the Alexander Nevsky Cathedral in Sofia puts on one of Europe's finest theatrical performances. It has a slow start: beautiful singing from the choir, one of the best in the world, a procession of men in gold and red, black and green through the church and then behind a curtain. The lights go out. The patriarch emerges, ablaze, a human candelabra. The clergy light their candles from the candles he holds and, as they move among the people, there is a spreading of fire as the congregation light their candles from the clergy's. The full spectacle begins, with the lovely voices of the choir, the chanting of the clergy, the clashes of red and black, green and gold, the theatricality of hundreds of movements, co-ordinated, with walkings on and off, gestures with hands, with the cross, with candles, and with the surges among the people. Character interest develops: the Patriarch, old, white bearded, benign; a bishop, ascetic, tortured; a bishop, plump, content; a priest, confident, refined; a monk, quietly zealous. The service lasts nearly four hours. The choir is in the special care of a Bulgarian international opera star; the performance is seen as a significant musical occasion and cultural enactment. Many of those who attend the service (admission by invitation) also believe in God.

It's not only that the Christian church survives. Its past – which is the past of Europe – is so complex that parts of it can be plundered to give meaning to almost any new development, including those unsettling to a social order. In the nineteenth century, some of the Christian denominations were summoned to the aid of the old order, casting prophetic rage on the secularism and materialism of the new capitalism (as they may sometimes still do); others enrolled themselves directly in the service of capitalist order, preaching what became an increasingly secular religion of respectability, family and hard work. Right-wing cultures in all liberal-democratic countries still call religion to their side; but religion can also be used subversively. Here we come to one of the contradictions of tourism, as in expressions of public culture generally: the very 'monuments' that are part of the dominant culture can be seen, by others, as symbols of a counter-culture.

Take, for example, two modern uses given to the Virgin Mary, whose worship began in the fifth century when she was proclaimed the Mother of God and became a figure of unsullied authority, enriched by various powers transferred from pre-Christian deities. To non-believers in her cult, hieratic and courtly scenes from the Mary cycle in art museums can seem mere expressions of the hollow arrogance of the church; what may interest them more are the renaissance paintings of Mary in the naturalistic studies of Madonna and Child, The Adoration, The Holy Family, and The

Flight into Egypt. These can be interpreted as an exaltation of love between mother and child, or even a glorification of the privatised nuclear family of modern industrialism. But to Catholic and Orthodox believers it is the theme of compassion which is central to the cult of Mary. This is a faith possible only in a church of sinners; modernisers in the church can now explore the theme of compassion and give it secular meanings – the church can thereby change its association with pomp that sustains a ruling class and become, again, a church giving refuge to the common people, and especially to the poor and oppressed. For those who reject the determinism and self-righteousness of marxist and protestant faiths, the theme of a compassionate church of sinners can suggest a more complex and generous world where there is room for human will and for the acceptance of human failure.

The modern imagination can also find (as so many earlier generations have also found) a sense of an alternative way in the communality and simplicity of the church. This is why modern taste can find relevant modern meanings in the romanesque. For generations the romanesque was seen as an inferior, crude style. Since the 1920s, however, beauty and meaning have again been found in it: there has been a fashion for uncovering romanesque frescoes, for exploring foundations and cellars of existing buildings for the remains of romanesque structures, for displaying romanesque sculptures and fragments dug out by archaeologists or construction workers, and, in the guide books, for indicating what romanesque elements were retained by the improvers of subsequent periods.

In the market square in Krakow, despite the splendour of the many other buildings, the eye can still be caught by an irregularly shaped little church, hunched in a corner, under a green cupola that in the summer is partly hidden by trees. It is shabby, patched, big enough only for a handful of people. This is what is left of St Adalbert's, a fortified, eleventh-century romanesque church which, though savagely remodelled in the seventeenth century to give it baroque meaning, still remains an exemplar of the intimacy and simplicity of the romanesque. Patches of the original stone of the walls, a portal and a few windows quietly rebuke the violent changes that came later. In the romanesque galleries of the Museum of Catalan Art, Barcelona, is Europe's best collection of romanesque murals, gathered from rough, remote, lumpy little stone churches in the Pyrenees, loosened off the walls in strips, then put together again on reconstructions of the round stone apses and rectangular stone walls on which they were painted, with their edifying cartoons still telling simple stories.

In a romanesque church, power is expressed in the outside walls, built tough and squat to signify God's castle defending the faithful from devils. Within, the space is more rounded and compact, like a community hall. This impression of communality can demonstrate a different power from the imposed power of the gothic – it is the power of agreement and participation. Friedrich Herr, in *The Medieval World* presents the romanesque period (in particular the twelfth and early thirteenth centuries) as one of participatory folk religion at a time when Europe was an open and expanding society, with a liberal tolerance of intellectual and religious diversity and a sense of wide community passing beyond national boundaries; by the mid-fourteenth century – a time symbolised architecturally by gothic predominance – he sees the barriers going up. Nations, states, churches and intellectual systems began to confront each other with familiar modern intolerance.

Along with the romanesque revival goes the view that the monastery was more characteristic of the middle ages than the cathedral. This view can extend to idealising the monastery into an exaltation of a simple communal life lived next to the common people, a life where, saved from the temptations of the world, it was possible to be good. Now this view of the monastery as alternative society can be related by the modern imagination to the commune, the hippy colony, the miniature counter-culture, or other contemporary aspirations to simplicity ('the cell'), goodness ('the cloister') and communality ('the refectory').

The idea of the monastery is successfully idealised in the partial ruins of the Carthusian monastery at Villeneuve-lès-Avignon. Covering three hectares, it was once the second-largest monastery in France. To walk through it is to evoke the contemplative life. With the plainness of their crumbling stone, the beautiful vaulting of their arcades and their sheer survival, the two large decaying cloisters, surrounded by capacious cells (each with its own walled garden, a downstairs room for study and contemplation and an upstairs room for sleeping), offer dreams of solitary peacefulness, and of the possibilities of retreat and self-renewal to be found in a quiet motel.

The revolutionary Christ

One of the great symbols of European revolutionary faith is the memory of the clandestine church, persecuted, but soon to triumph. Maxim Gorki tells in his autobiography *My Universities* how, when he went to his first revolutionary meeting, he thought of 'catacombs, the first Christians'.

It is part of what was later to become the democratic charm of the Christian story that the life of Christ should, according to Luke's version, begin humbly: he was born in a stable, because in Bethlehem there were more travellers than lodging-rooms and the first people to acknowledge him were a group of shepherds. When backgrounds in paintings were all gold this was of small significance. When naturalness came in, however, some painters gave the story that charm of simple humanity that was later to appeal to protestants, and subsequently to socialists. One can see the process in the Alte Pinakothek, Munich. In the delicate and intimate fifteenth-century wooden devotional panels of Stephen Lochner and Martin Schongauer, compositions of ass and ruined stable project, for the religious, the warmth of a personal piety rising beyond worldly pomp, and, for the modern egalitarian, a pride in the dignity of the humble. In the sixteenth-century painting of Hans Baldung Grien, naturalness has proceeded so far that it could be a twentieth-century representation of a family comforted by devotion in a shattered world, refugees sheltering in a bombed building.

However, it is in his sufferings and death that Christ becomes most human. We don't know when the emphasis on the crucifixion began. It wasn't a feature of the early church. The British Museum has an ivory plaque, perhaps from the fifth century, that shows the crucifixion, but it is presented as a triumphant formality: a classical athlete, naked except for his loincloth, is going through a necessary ceremony; the suffering is reserved for Judas, who has hanged himself from a tree. Even when the crucifixion began to dominate, it was at first a crucifixion of kingly triumph. In romanesque art, Christ is on the cross, crowned, a sleeping king confidently performing one of the familiar rituals of his triumph; in late gothic style he becomes a young man of the people, tormented, suffering on their behalf, awash with blood.

For several centuries painters who used the drama of the crucifixion spoke with enormous complexity, and provided many images that were later transferred to secular martyrs. When the byzantine and earlier western conventions of presenting Christ's death as a harmonious ballet of sadness and steadfastness in brown and gold gave way to naturalness and a more human grief, humans could seem to be mourning a fellow-human as wildly as the stormy sky that swept across the background. Or, conversely, depictions of the crucifixion could demonstrate how, in their petty absorption in ordinary affairs, people were unable to understand great events: richly dressed idlers strolled by the cross; horsemen on expensively caparisoned horses rode up and stared; onlookers brawled and gambled; the background landscape showed people getting on with their own business. Naturalness raised the question of how uniquely Christ's death should be presented. Was he a man dying amongst men, or a god dying amongst thieves? The convention was to show him quietly dying, with a more noble body and with halo glowing, while the thieves – their coarser bodies twisted in paroxysms of death, heads thrown back or flopped down, their mouths open – abandoned themselves to pain. But in Cranach's *Crucifixion* in the Alte Pinakothek, Christ, bloodied and dying, shares a common humanity with two other bloodied and dying men; Altdorfer in the Dahlem Museum, Berlin, shows him nobler-bodied than the other two, yet still presents all three as innocent children; in Ruben's cruelly stark *Three Crosses*, all three bodies hang in a stormy landscape like equally dead meat.

In the Rembrandt House, Amsterdam, are two etchings of the crucifixion that came from the same plate, but with the second significantly changed. The first gives a conventional view: the light falls on the dead Christ, on his mourners and on the two symbols of hope – the repentant thief and the converted centurion, who kneels. In the second etching, Rembrandt has changed Christ's face to capture the moment before death: he is in a state of desperate fear, for God has forsaken him; the converted centurion has gone; Christ's mother has fainted; St John gestures hopelessly. The darkness falls more widely and indiscriminately: it loses meaning.

Painters painted episodes from the crucifixion for purposes ranging from experiments with pigments to experiments with new faiths. Nevertheless when it became fashionable to show Christ as man, not God, all these paintings were necessarily concerned with exalting the subversive element in the crucifixion and the whole Christian story: the exaltation of suffering and failure as a preparation for success – and the understanding that what can now seem large on earth will be small in heaven, or will be small in that secular heaven, the future. This exaltation and understanding were later to be transformed by the modern mind into secular faiths that were also to make claims of liberation through sacrifice, and that could find in today's victim tomorrow's hero.

In the art museums this powerful idea of the victim god is supported by paintings of the martyrdom of so many saints. St Stephen, the first Christian martyr, kneels and prays while the stones crack through his skull. St Lucy stands delicately in the burning pyre while the executioner runs a sword into her throat. St Andrew is spread-eagled with great agony along an X-shaped cross. St Judas Thaddeus is crying and twitching and spouting blood as the almost naked executioner positions his club for the death blow. Her face wet with tears, St Agatha holds a blood-stained cloth to her chopped breasts with one hand and raises the other in supplication. St Foriana, a youth in a doublet as golden as his halo, lies on his back while men beat him insensible. Thus, the church is presented as having its foundations in implacability and blood. Its growth is seen as a success story of fanatical opposition and violence – of a zealous policy not to compromise and so to force the authorities into increasingly unacceptable acts of torture and death, and its adherents into inviolable faith – the policy of modern revolutionaries.

The potential explosiveness in the mystical side of Christianity with its allowance for individual conscience and claims to individual revelations showed a god of judgement, but also a god in people's hearts. Alongside the jealous father was the son who could consort with the poor and with the sinners. And revolution was almost guaranteed by the apocalyptic elements in Christian teaching, with their lurid and ambiguous forecasts of how in the future everything would be turned upside down so that the rich and the wicked would be punished and the poor and virtuous would be rewarded in a thousand years of happiness for repented sinners, on earth itself, in a community ruled by Christ and his saints.

It is not possible to 'prove' it, but it is hard not to believe that Christianity gave secular faiths their creeds of progress and perfectibility, of heroic sacrifice, and of a paradise on Earth in which humanity, once perfectible only in heaven, could now be made perfect in this world. Paintings of Christ's sacrifice provide some of Europe's strongest images of how betrayal, doubt, mockery and persecution can be suffered at the same time as faith in ultimate triumph is maintained.

The theme of betrayal is recurrent in the Passion – and betrayal is also a vibrantly modern theme. In the Agony paintings, there is usually a glint of armour in the background where Judas and the soldiers wait; in the Betrayal paintings, Judas is usually the second most central figure, the kissing betrayer. Christ's can seem the calm face in a storm of fear and hate. The theme of betrayal – this time by the manipulation of the powerful or the fickleness of the people – resurfaces when Pilate, recognising the malice of Christ's accusers, offers to reprieve him; the crowd, however, cry 'Crucify him'. In the Zwinger, Dresden, Aert de Gelder depicts most of the people as uninterested: they are not looking up at the balcony where Christ has been displayed; the street is half-empty. However, the small, noisy group which presses round the balcony and calls for the death sentence falsely claim to speak for 'the people'. In the National Gallery, Oslo, a wooden carving shows the learned looking down their noses at an impostor while the people (one of them holding Christ by the hair to see him properly) mock a clown.

Renderings of formal confrontations with authority – Christ's appearances before Caiaphas, the high priest, and Pilate, the governor – also seem to prefigure modern, secular messages. In the Christ before Caiaphas paintings, lawyers, elders and priests try to frame Christ by trick questions and false evidence; they seem malicious know-alls, who use their learning as a weapon of terrorisation. Gerard von Honthorst's seventeenth-century *Before the High Priest* (in the National Gallery, London) presents the modern stereotype rendering of a frame-up: light is thrown by a single candle, like a modern interrogator's lamp; the high priest, a book in front of him to prove he is right, raises an executioner's finger at Christ to make the final damning point; his associates stand by him, absolutely sure that their rigged case will stick. While the interrogator–scholar seems to command the painting, one look at the calm intelligence of Christ's face as he gives his laconically ambiguous answers shows that the accused is the accuser.

4. The voice of the people

Using the people

At the very time of eighteenth- and nineteenth-century challenges to old justifications of power – the legitimations of God and of birth – it became common for those who sought a new order in society, whether bourgeois, nationalist or socialist, to draw on the authority of 'the people' to legitimise their actions. The name of 'the people' was beginning to replace hereditary right as a principal justification of power, even if inferentially and deviously. If it suited the masters of the people, the voice of the people could even be presented as the voice of God.

When the time came to go back to the past for 'monuments' of the people – relics of their early boldness or goodness – there was the problem that, for most of Europe's history, it was the culture of the ruling class that dominated public display. The folk culture, the culture of 'the people', the 'alternative cultures', had been almost completely suppressed from public celebration – or, if expressed, expressed within the language of the dominant public culture and to the advantage of those who benefited from it. The peasantries of Europe followed ways of life that were inward-looking, changing very little over hundreds of years, and these were of small account for the rulers. Yet almost all that survives are ruling-class depictions of the peasants, and usually these are instructions about how peasants should behave rather than descriptions of how they did behave.

Some of our best guesses about these alternative cultures may come from times when the rulers recorded their loathing of the peasants. These occasions were most often prompted by the peasant uprisings that occurred thousands of times from late medieval to modern times. Most historians do not convey their frequency, yet in some ways these risings were rather like industrial strikes in some of the liberal-democratic societies, although with the violence characteristic of almost all political action in most of Europe's history. From what we are told of these risings, we see not a happy, loyal peasantry, but peoples who, when their real faces are revealed to an otherwise contemptuous world, show a rebellious and levelling spirit – apparent particularly in their belief that the land was theirs by right, the most challenging of all beliefs to societies based on the power of landholding. Even if these alternative cultures supported the church, they could claim its authority for their own ends, reappropriating the church as a church of the people; even when they might respect the authority of birth, they could see existing power-holders as usurpers.

But in some of the liberal-democratic societies, peasants' uprisings remained the property of radicals. Therefore, they do not receive public (or tourist) celebration. In England, there is no official sympathy towards popular risings unless they were led by nobles or gentry; thus, although the Peasants' Revolt of 1381 is in all the history textbooks, there is no monument to this series of insurrections, which destroyed castles, manor houses, prisons and merchants' houses, and was accompanied by lootings, a few beheadings and some of the rougher kinds of murder. The peasants' arrival in London (60,000 to 100,000 of them, according to records) produced some of the most memorable tableaux of the hopes and the despairs of a people's uprising – yet the only public monument to these events I could find was a half-timbered pub in the High Street, Dartford, opposite a branch of Lloyds Bank and a Wimpy Bar. The inn-sign showed Wat Tyler attacking a tax-gatherer (he could have been a free-enterprise man in Margaret Thatcher's England); beneath were the words 'Wat Tyler' and, above, 'Courage' – the name of the brewery company now owning the pub. Lettered on the white wall was the bold claim: '1377, Home of Wat Ye Tyler'; but a large explanatory notice only claimed that 'Wat Tyler and several of the commons called at this ancient tavern (so it is said) to quench their thirst with flagons of ale.' The use of Wat Tyler, even as patriotic tax-evader, was abandoned in the middle-class atmosphere of the saloon bar, a 'captain's cabin' decorated with the gleaming brass of ships' bells, rails, steering-wheels and lanterns.

But in those liberal-democratic countries where a leader of the people was already venerated, modern democratic uses could be found, and new monuments could proclaim these new uses. Thus, in Sweden new uses were found for the uprisings led by Engelbrekt, the Swedish popular leader. Almost nothing is known about Engelbrekt, except that he was a small mine-owner swept into leadership of the great Swedish Insurrection of 1434, in which a rebellious army of peasants took their spiked clubs, poleaxes and crossbows, burned down the timber forts of many of the bailiffs, were welcomed as liberators by the people and forced themselves onto nobles and clergy alike. The following year, after a second campaign of liberation, Engelbrekt was martyred: weakened by his campaigns and accompanied only by his family, he hobbled on crutches towards a noble he trustingly believed to be a friend – and was axed, his skull split open, and his body shot through with arrows. At once he became a secular saint: only four years after Engelbrekt's assassination, a bishop wrote 'Song of Freedom', which eulogised him as God's instrument on earth. By that time pilgrims were already going to his tomb and his relics were recorded as effecting many miracles. In the nineteenth century he was canonised in the cult of Swedish nationalism as a great nineteenth-century patriot: he became the 'first Swede'. Nineteenth-century painters, nationalist poets and writers of historical novels fed on him; with the coming of parliamentary democracy, he became the 'father of the Swedish parliament'. He continues to be reinterpreted, to suit the twentieth-century mind. Strindberg wrote a play about him, Natanael Berg an opera; he was sculpted by Bror Hjorth as a people's leader, painted by Sven Erixson as a people's martyr. There is a statue of him in the Swedish Riksdag; the twentieth-century sculptor has given this fifteenth-century leader features of strength, force and integrity; his fist is clenched and raised in the fashion of a modern labour hero.

Most famous of all is the mythic figure of William Tell. Sightseers on guided tours can see, on the underside of the great dome of the Federal Palace that houses the Swiss parliament, the main scene of Act III of Schiller's *William Tell*. A replica of an old Swiss village has been built outside Interlaken for open-air performances of *William Tell*. Reminders of Tell are in all the folk museums and souvenir shops. For some modern Swiss, the fiction of William Tell has become tourist-worn: for political myth, they prefer another fiction – that a famous oath of confederation was sworn by three prototype patriots at the end of the thirteenth century in the meadow of Rütli, near the Lake of Lucerne. The National Council in the Federal Palace is dominated by a mural of mountains and water, symbolising Rütli, and under the great dome three monumental figures, their hands stretched out in steadfast purpose, also symbolise the oath of Rütli. However, the scepticism about William Tell seems only a thin, and rather sensitive skin: in 1971 a satirical version of the Tell story was done for schoolchildren and created a scandal. Before he became a figure of state, William Tell was already a cult-figure of people's rebellion. Peasant risings in Switzerland, such as those of the mid-seventeenth century, were sustained partly in his name; what legend took to be a copy of his hat was hung on a liberty tree in an uprising inspired by the French Revolution. He became a centrepiece in the displays of the new Swiss nationalism; his name was then used by the socialists and invoked in the general strike of 1918. Amongst modern Swiss radicals, he is now appropriated as a prototype guerilla freedom-fighter. In 1977, a monthly journal of the new Left was founded; it was called *Tell*.

It is in the Communist countries that relics of peasants' uprisings are as prized as saints' relics. In their museums and monuments, Communist nations portray people's uprisings as precursors of the proletarian revolutions to come. The uprisings are presented as peasants' movements (sometimes ignoring the presence of other classes) that came from class conflict; their failure is described through historical circumstances helpfully listed in marxist analysis on the explanatory cards in the glass cases.

They take their place in the tourist business. For example, in summer the Yugoslav village of Gorja Stubica with its surrounding districts is a place for the citizens of Zagreb to enjoy a day out of town. It is also a reminder of the history of class struggle. On a hill near the castle, a big statue stands in front of a vast stone semicircle; its arms are outstretched in what at first sight appears to be one of the stereotypes of welcome. But the arms are not raised in welcome to holiday-makers: they are raised in revolt. Barefoot, in ragged clothes, the statue represents Matija Gubec, the most heroicised of the leaders of peasants' uprisings in Croatia. Behind him, on the stone semicircle, is a huge bronze mural showing both the gallantry and the hopelessness of the peasant cause.

The castle (built on the site of the earlier castle of the Hungarian lord against whom Gubec first raised the revolt in 1573) houses a restaurant specialising in local dishes, and a museum typical of those celebrating peasants' uprisings. In the first room of the museum the simplicity of peasant life, symbolised in household goods and tools, is set off against a map, emblazoned with colourful coats of arms, showing the landholdings of the feudal magnates. In another room, under a glass case, on a simulation of the countryside, are red and blue lights. As they wait for their lunch, tourists can push buttons, from left to right and watch the movements of the peasants' armies and magnates' armies in what became a general rising against the economic privileges and oppressions of the rich. The simulated battle maps end with the lights representing the peasants' armies going out. In the next room, slides and tapes present the floggings, mutilations, bone-crushings, impalements, disembowellings, beheadings and the tearings-apart. The museum's entrance ticket has, on its back, a reproduction of a nineteenth-century nationalist painting, the *Execution of Matija Gubec*, that hangs in the Modern Gallery, Zagreb, and illustrates how a peasant leader could be used in the mythology first of the bourgeois nationalists, then of the Communists. The painting is set in the square, now a car park, outside St Mark's Church where Gubec, known as the 'king of the peasants', waits while the executioners prepare to bring to red heat the crown of iron they will mockingly place on his head. This painting is of a different Gubec from the barefooted revolutionary done in brutalist bronze at Gorja Stubica: he is one of nature's aristocrats – well dressed, mourned by a finely clothed lady and gentleman as he waits patiently for the executioners to prepare their fire. Gubec has become a prototype revolutionary leader: his name was evoked by Tito's Partisans during the resistance against the Nazis.

In the opening hall of the Revolution Museum, Bucharest, are marble statues of two of the most famoust Romanian peasant leaders; one of them, Tudor Vladimirescu, leader of the 1821 uprising, is given the place of honour opposite a statue of Marx.

The 'peasant uprisings' are taken as such a serious part of Romanian history that they are treated in each of four different museums in Bucharest. The first of the four main uprisings, the Transylvanian peasants' revolt of 1437, is displayed in campaign maps, contemporary parchments and glass cases of exhibits that contrast the luxury of nobles with the poverty of peasants; it is described as 'one of the greatest social movements in medieval Europe', in which 'the exploited masses' reaffirmed through class struggle their 'unity and fraternity'. The Romanian authorities treat the third great revolt (1784–85) as such a significant period in their history that Horia, one of its three leaders, is also given a statue in the entrance hall along with Marx. Beneath portraits of the leader-heroes, maps show the movements of thousands of peasants and record the destruction of 200 castles and manors; documents recall the peasants' demands to end the nobility and divide the land among the people. Then an engraving shows the martyrdom of two leaders: the naked body of Horia, already beheaded, is about to be split in half, from crotch to collarbone; Closca, also naked, is spread-eagled on a wheel – his body will be broken, and then disembowelled. Over 2,500 peasants have been brought to the execution scene to watch, and learn. As a reminder, the naked bodies will be dismembered and the parts distributed on pikes throughout the land.

The Museum of History in Moscow's Red Square gives three rooms to the greatest popular uprisings in Russian history before the 1905 uprising. The museum has arranged exhibits and explanatory material with the logical exposition of a book; between them, these rooms of insurrection provide the museum's first sense of historical climax in the development of class conflict. There is no reliance in that museum on the mere authenticity of objects. A didactic story runs through every showcase: thus, from the usual Neolithic, Bronze- and Iron-Age relics, the first seven rooms show 'the growth of forces of production and production relations in tribal society' that then produced 'the erosion of primitive tribalism and the formation of social classes'; then, with birch-bark scrolls, fragments of stone carvings, coats of mail, spiked helmets, gate bars and some more paintings 'the growing exploitation by the feudal class' is demonstrated, along with 'deterioration of the serfs' condition and increasing class antagonisms'. The tourist has now been prepared for Room 16, with its weapons and drawings and maps, and its engravings of executions; these show how 'the crystallisation of an autocratic form of government' produced the 'popular uprising' (1606–7) and the 'peasant war' (1667–71), led by Stepan Razin. Room 23, devoted to 'The Peasant War 1773–5, led by E.I. Pugachev' comes as no surprise: the faded, tattered remnant of a peasant standard rises above a portrait of Pugachev. On the other side of the room are the engravings of punishments and executions. In reprisal for the maraudings and the atrocities of the uprising itself (scalpings, stranglings, drownings, impalings, burnings, hangings of several thousand landholders and officials), whole villages were razed and ploughed under; peasants were broken on the wheel and hanged by hooks stuck in their ribs; some were let off with a flogging, a nostril-slitting and a forehead-branding; the lucky ones got only a beating. Pugachev himself was taken to Moscow in an iron cage too small for him to stand in, put on display like a wild animal, and then, beneath a Kremlin wall, beheaded and quartered; the parts of his body were displayed in various quarters of Moscow.

These messianic Russian insurrections, among the greatest social upheavals in European history, produced ballads and epics glorifying past, and therefore future, rebellions. There was a particular cult of the martyred messiahs Razin (spoken of by Pushkin as 'the one poetic figure in Russian history') and Pugachev (Pushkin wrote the novel *The Captain's Daughter* about him). Legends developed foretelling their second coming. With 1,500 or so separate peasant risings in Russia in the first 60 years of the nineteenth century, populist intellectuals could wait for the day when the fury of the people would burst over Russia like a liberating storm: on May Day 1919, in a speech made on the site of the Kremlin execution-block, Lenin, speaking of 'the struggle against slavery and exploitation', claimed succession from Razin.

The end of the peasants

In the twentieth century, peasant discontent made possible the Russian, Chinese and Spanish revolutions. But now Europe is urbanised and farms have become factories, and in the old sense of the word, there are no peasants left. However, nothing much in the way of monuments marks the nature of the peasants' passing. To celebrate the agrarian revolutions that began the destruction of the peasants, one needs the eye of a John Berger who, in *Ways of Seeing*, can take Gainsborough's *Mr and Mrs Andrews* and turn it into an historical statement. The painting shows a delicately coloured eighteenth-century landscape transformed by profitable agricultural improvement and, in front of it, posed with absolute sureness, the gentleman who owns the land; beside him is his wife and, under his arm, his gun – a reminder of his exclusive privilege as a gentleman to shoot game. The atmosphere of the painting suggests the sympathetic proprietorship of the new wave of gentry who wished to be intelligent in the managing of farming. Mr and Mrs Andrews may also share some sense of beauty in what they own; but there is no doubt that they own it. The painting reflects the eighteenth- and early-nineteenth-century British ruling-class revolution that, in a series of three thousand six hundred local coups called Enclosure Acts abolished the peasants' commons and wastelands and also, as it turned out, in effect abolished most of the peasants as a class. Yet presumably because it was a revolution of expropriation, the agrarian revolution receives scarcely any mention in England – except occasionally in a village museum, in the old spring guns and man traps used against poachers. All that these now evoke, however, is a pleasant *frisson* as tourists may congratulate themselves on having avoided the barbarities of the past. (In Ireland and Scotland, though, there are memorials to those who starved to death in the service of English landlords.) Not even the rational aspects of the agrarian revolution are celebrated, although the halls of the older Agricultural Societies in Britain could be turned into a monument to the efficiency with which the survivors extended to Britain the improved farming methods introduced in Flanders and the Netherlands in the late middle ages, and then added to them with such high spirits that, for continental Europe, British farming became a symbol for rationality and optimism. Some of the most significant aspects of tourism can be found by looking for those elements in a country's history which are *not* celebrated.

An appropriate monument to the comparatively peaceful disintegration of peasant discontents in western Europe might be the

Frihedsstotten, the Column of Liberty opposite the main railway station in Copenhagen, put up to celebrate the Danish peasants' 1788 liberation from restrictions by landowners: as the Frihedsstotten announces, the peasant became a 'free citizen'. The Frihedsstotten might also now be taken to celebrate a process as important as the English improvements in farming techniques: the policy of an autocratic but enlightened Danish ruling class in setting up a state-supported system of freehold farming dedicated to producing cash crops. The most appropriate monuments of a century later, the nineteenth, are remains of the early buildings, marked by commemorative plaques, of the first farmers' co-operatives in Denmark and the Netherlands, celebrating democracy as well as farming improvement.

Substituting ballot boxes and parliamentary procedures for improvised weapons and revolts, farmers formed political parties in the Scandinavian nations and Switzerland. Elsewhere in western Europe (apart from the south) farmers got so much of what they wanted that Europe's greatest potential force for social explosion became one of the great forces for conservatism.

But in Russia, emancipation of the serfs was so unsatisfactory that it helped produce the 1917 revolution. The last of the peasant risings in Europe were the many revolts against collectivisation in the Soviet Union.

In the rest of eastern Europe, the nations liberated from the Habsburg, Romanov and Ottoman empires, had, during the 1920s, dreams that have left a few sediments in Communist museums of revolution – the dream of a 'Green International' in which, with land reform and government by peasants' parties, Poland, Czechoslovakia, Hungary, Romania, Bulgaria and Yugoslavia would become democratic peasant republics. The peasants' parties that, for seasons of varying length, came to political prominence in these countries are celebrated in inverse proportion to their political success. In Czechoslovakia, the Agrarian Party was a constant element in government and successful land reform programmes were carried out. The party, therefore, is denigrated among the sets of colour slides running over two walls of Room D of the Klement Gottwald Museum and exposing 'the social contradictions of the bourgeois republic'. In Hungary and Romania, the Smallholders' Party and the National Peasant Party respectively were for a while influential in government; they are presented in the museums of the revolutionary movement as being at best 'liberal–conservative' compared with the fascism that followed. In Warsaw, because Wincenty Witos, leader of the Peasant Party, was overthrown as prime minister in the military coup of 1926, the Museum of the Revolutionary Movement presents him as a victim of militarism. In Zagreb, a long street and the principal square in the upper town are named in honour of Stephen Radić, leader of the Croatian Peasant Party and supporter of a peasant republic, who was fatally shot in the Yugoslav parliament in 1928. In Bulgaria's Museum of the Revolutionary Movement is an act of public contrition towards the Bulgarian Agrarian Union. Dedicated to a peasant republic and brought to power in Bulgaria, the Agrarian Union was thrown out in a military coup in 1923; its leader, Alexander Stamboliiski, was executed. The cards identifying the relics of this coup in the museum admit the mistakes of the Bulgarian Communist Party in 1923 in dissociating itself from the Agrarian Union, a decision that had come from 'the party's unsatisfactory ideological reorientation, stemming from its earlier incorrect concepts about the role of the peasantry'. The Bulgarian authorities need to present the Agrarian Union as having played a useful part in history because the Agrarians are part of the 'Fatherland Front' that set up the people's republic.

Part three

The revolutionary
landscapes

5. The tourism of the 'bourgeois revolutions'

There were many possibilities for conflict within Christendom. The church exalted both majesty and humility; its central divinity spoke in puzzles and was both helpless and yet strangely powerful; its holy scriptures could be quoted to support both obedience and rebellion, church authority and individual conscience, or, indeed, almost anything. When the church began to disintegrate it marked one of the beginnings of the revolutions of 'modernity' that were to make Europe unique – leaving behind new monuments which continue to have new purposes. These are the monuments of the protestant reformations. They are tense with double meanings. In theological terms, they are reminders of God's will; they are, at the same time, reminders of Europe's faith in revolution and, as such, amenable to other secular purposes: nationalism, socialism, commercialism. When the principal religious upheavals subsided, overtly political revolutions – the so-called 'bourgeois revolutions' – became a feature of Europe (although marxists and some others see the earlier religious revolutions as part of the same process). The old order in Europe put up such a fight against new challenges that, from the end of the eighteenth century, Europe became a continent obsessed by politics, as we now understand that word. Like frozen rivers of lava and escarpments of rock, many of the buildings and art works of Europe can be seen as thrown up by the eruptions of this revolutionary restlessness. From these violent political changes came new political modes for Europe, and for most of the rest of the world – and many of the 'monuments' of tourism, were interpreted and reinterpreted to meet shifting demands about how things should seem.

The great religious revolutions

One can make a case for considering the early-fifteenth-century

Hussite revolution in Bohemia as the first modern revolution. When virtually the whole Czech people seceded from established Christendom and, for 15 years, defied both known civilisation and five papal crusades with a revolutionary army, they became, as it were, the first Bolsheviks. In celebration of their revolt, both Czech nationalists and Czech Communists have used monuments to Hussitism for their own purposes, in a way entirely characteristic of the secular use of reformation monuments.

In the nineteenth century Czechs were again learning how to be Czechs and John Huss became one of the symbols of Czech nationality – the nationalists made a holy place of the Prague hill where the great Hussite general, Jan Žižka, defeated the first papal crusade with what we would now think of as a 'people's army'. In 1915, on the five-hundredth anniversary of Huss being burnt at the stake, nationalists put up a Huss monument, which itself seems to capture the sheer weariness of his martyrdom and the later rebellion. Erected in the square outside Prague's Old Town Hall, scene of many melancholy defeats, the monument's characters emerge from the stone, but also seem to be part of it, pulled back into it, incomplete. With independence from the Austrians, the Czech government put up a National Memorial on the Prague hill (now Žižkov Height), in front of which Žižka, in statue, rides on his charger.

The Communist government inherited, and exalts, these monuments: in the period of radical Christian communalism that followed the burning of Huss, there was enough rebellious speaking of the language of equality ('Everything must be common for all, no one must possess anything in private – otherwise they are guilty of mortal sin') for new monuments to go up. A radical Hussite priest is now also celebrated, on a wall plaque on the Old Town Hall, and from 1948 to 1954 a replica was built of the Bethlehem Chapel, where Huss became resident preacher in 1402. The National Memorial itself is now a Communist mausoleum, where the red marble tombs of the 'worker–presidents' dominate the white marble of the central hall.

In the Luther Monument at Worms, John Huss is among the figures shown as the forerunners of Martin Luther's mythologised defiance there of an Imperial Diet in 1521. Put up in 1868, the monument commemorates the last act of what had become his three-and-a-half-year revolt against the old order, begun, according to legend, with the nailing of 95 theses to the door of the castle church of Wittenberg (the normal method of attracting debate). Although there is no hard evidence that Luther in fact used this customary device, a replica of the church door (although not the church) has been reconstructed at Wittenberg which is now part of the German Democratic Republic. A Museum of the Reformation has also been established at Wittenberg; and at Luther's birthplace the authorities have provided further celebrations of this conservative radical whose defiance at the Diet of Worms was followed by the largest popular uprising ever to occur among the German peoples, an uprising which Luther himself denounced in his pamphlet 'Against the Murdering, Thieving Hordes of the Peasants'.

Despite the considerable tolerance of the Lutheran church in the GDR, it was more difficult for Luther himself to be tolerated; Frederick Engels sympathetically presented the uprisings as a 'peasants' war', and that is how they are shown in the museums of the GDR, which link the people's armies of the 'peasants' war' with the People's Army of the German Democratic Republic. The problem of Luther has been tackled by labelling him an early leader of the 'bourgeois revolution', a type of person essential to progress. In 1983, the five-hundredth anniversary of his birth, ambitious arrangements were accordingly made for the tourist pilgrimages.

Lutheranism itself does not offer notable tourist monuments: the true monuments of the Lutheran reformation are the pulpits of the reformed churches and, in glass cases, first editions of Luther's translation of the Bible which can become as much symbols of nationality as of protestantism. The same applies to all those other protestant-inspired vernacular translations of the Bible – from Poland (1542) to Iceland (1584) – that now cluster under glass in museums and libraries, and epitomise one of the great secular movements in the disintegration of Christendom: the development of national languages. More attractive to the sightseer of a Lutheran tourist church, though, is whatever has survived in it from when it was part of the Church of Rome.

Lutherans are more likely to be celebrated when they can also be turned into important figures in a nationalist movement. Thus, at the entrance to the Tivoli Park in Ljubjlana in the Yugoslav Republic of Slovenia, is a statue, put up in 1910, representing a man of great character, with a neat, long bob and a full, but neatly shaped, beard: an epitome of both force and reason. This is the Lutheran Primož Trubar, whom Slovenes describe as 'one of the great figures of the protestant reformation' and who became, in 1561, the superintendent of the Slovene Protestant Church. There is also a bust of him in the National Library. The latter commemorates him not as protestant, but as one of the patriot–philologists who pioneered the Slovenian written language. Slovene protestants preached in Slovenian, rather than in the German of the occupying Habsburgs – Trubar first preached in Slovenian in 1530; then the Bible, catechisms and hymn books were translated into Slovenian and a Slovenian grammar and a Slovenian dictionary were produced. First editions of these are displayed in glass cases in the library, along with illuminated books from medieval Slav scriptoria, and newspapers and pamphlets from the wartime underground presses of Tito's Partisans. The juxtaposition with the Partisan press is apt: when the catholic counter-attack began in the Austrian lands, both protestants and the Slovenian language were forced underground; protestantism was banned; the property of the protestants was confiscated; their books were burned; the Slovene grammar was prohibited as a subversive publication.

In Sweden, Gustav Vasa, who founded the Reformed Swedish Church in 1544 (and later extended it to the Swedish territory of Finland), is more celebrated as the founder of Sweden. His portrait appears on the five-Kroner note and is a popular trademark; his name is on more streets and honours more voluntary associations than that of any other Swede; there is a Vasa Park, a Vasa raincoat, a Vasa bread, a Vasa biscuit, a Vasa ski race. At the height of his cult in the nineteenth century, Uppsala Cathedral was redecorated, as was Vasa's tomb. Paintings glorified him as the young patriot-warrior who, after many daring adventures, led a revolt against the Swedish union with Denmark, and, a new Moses, brought his people out of Danish captivity. Beside a painting of Luther in Uppsala Cathedral is a portrayal of Vasa as protestant, holding the first Swedish translation of the Bible.

Even Bulgarians, whose predecessors knew nothing of the

reformation, can nevertheless make a retrospective claim. In Bulgaria, followers of the heretical sect of the Bogomils are presented with pride, both as predecessors of the reformation and as progressive fighters for social justice, fraternity and equality. A tenth-century anti-Bogomil stone inscription and a document reporting to the Bulgarian king on the heretical priest Bogomil are museum reminders of the spread of Bogomilism, with its contempt for feudal and church authority (based on the belief that all earthly institutions were the evil inventions of the fallen son of God) and its preference for an ascetic communal life. These museum objects are also reminders of the importance of medieval Bulgaria: maps show how Bogomilism spread to Byzantium, Serbia, Bosnia and Kievan Russia, and, in the form of the Albigensian heresy, to northern Italy and southern France. Bulgaria can be presented as a harbinger of the reformation, as well as of the renaissance.

For tourists, Geneva notes itself as a protestant centre by the International Monument of the Reformation, unveiled in 1917 and nearly 100 metres long. Against an austere wall are set reliefs of important incidents and statues of leading figures, both theologians and defenders of the protestant reformation. These are accompanied by significant quotations in French, English, German, Dutch and Hungarian, the four language areas where the Calvinists had their greatest successes. But there is no statue of Luther. The message is clear: the reformation began in Geneva, in 1536, with John Calvin's *Institutes of the Christian Religion*. In Zurich, however, there is a different message: the reformation, or at least the Swiss reformation, began in 1519 when Huldrych Zwingli began preaching a more radical doctrine than Luther's. A statue of Zwingli stands guard, Bible and sword in hand, beside the river, and the Grossmünster (whose austere romanesque towers are mocked by fancy gothic toppings and eighteenth-century copper cupolas) is presented as a founding centre of the reformation. There is no mention of Zwingli in Geneva's International Monument of the Federation.

Of the Calvinist martyrs, the most celebrated are the Flemish. When Belgium became a nation in 1830 and a sense of nationality had to be found for it, those Calvinist Flemish nobles who had been killed by the Spanish Duke of Alba more than 300 years before, were easy to turn into national heroes. They are celebrated even though, partly as a result of Alba's Edict of Blood, Belgium was to remain catholic. The insult the Spanish terror offered to one of the most lively and ordered centres of civilisation in Europe is brought out, with calm understatement, by the arrangement of the Place du Petit Sablon, Brussels. Formal gardens, bronze statuettes representing the 48 medieval trade guilds and a semicircle of statues of famous sixteenth-century Flemish humanists are reminders of the flourishing society Alba terrorised. In the centre of the semicircle of humanists are statues of Egmont and Horn, the one with his arm on the shoulder of the other. The whole thing might seem a celebration of the cultivated life, except for the words lettered on a gilded background recalling that these two nobles, so affectionate to each other and part of an assemblage of such decency and cleverness, were taken by the Spaniards and beheaded in the Grand Place, the main Brussels square, and now the central spectacle in Brussels tourism. There is no reference, however, to their Calvinism.

In the Northern Provinces of the old Spanish Netherlands, where the Calvinists won, and created the modern Netherlands, there is scarcely any Calvinist boastfulness. The Dutch doctrine of *verzuiling* (toleration of the divisions of society between Calvinists, catholics and secularists) does not allow for boasting. Edinburgh is more of a Calvinist capital than Amsterdam and John Knox, the catholic priest who turned Calvinist theologian, is part of its tourist projection – perhaps because, despite Scotland's many catholics, Knox can be seen as a national, as well as a religious figure. He can also be reduced to reassuring tourist cosiness. Bible in hand, his statue is set against the wall of St Giles and portrays him as the founder of Scottish presbyterianism. His image is rather different in the souvenir shops and even more so in 'John Knox's House', further down the Royal Mile from St Giles, which offers sixteenth-century half-timber quaintness – but in reality has no connection with Knox apart from the fact that it is shut on Sundays.

Calvin Square, Budapest, is a reminder of Calvinism's defeat in Hungary, despite opening victories; in France, however, there is mainly silence on the defeat of the French Calvinists, the Huguenots. The statue opposite the Louvre of Gaspard de Coligny, the first of the thousands of Calvinists killed in the St Bartholomew's Day Massacre, is more that of a grave-faced admiral of France than of a religious martyr. The dispersal of the Huguenots following their final suppression more than 100 years later, is celebrated here and there. There is a Huguenot Museum in East Berlin and where St Stephen's Green joins Merrion Row in Dublin, there is an old Huguenot cemetery dating from 1693. The most the passerby is likely to glean from its lichened slabs and shattered tombs, though, is a story of age and decay, rather than one of religious persecution.

The most famous Calvinists of the British Isles were those who left it, the 'Pilgrim Fathers'. On the stone wall that reaches to the small entrance of the old harbour at Plymouth, a classical arch has been erected, bizarrely, to stand above the simple Devon stone. British and United States flags fly on either side and, at the base, a tablet commemorates *Mayflower*'s departure in 1620. At Plymouth, the Pilgrim Fathers have become an attraction for United States tourists – while 'Elizabethan seadogs' are used to attract British tourists. Thus, the high, modern hotel which overlooks Plymouth Hoe is called the 'Mayflower'; the cinema on Royal Parade is called the 'Drake'. A hotel down from the Mayflower uses seadogs, pirates, pieces of eight and the Spanish King Philip to promote its restaurant; the Mayflower writes *its* main attractions on a menu held up by a cut-out of a jolly, fun-loving, gourmandising Pilgrim Father.

For tourists with guide books which tell them what they are seeing there are many reminders of the religious divisions of Europe. In the ostentatiously baroque chapel of St Januarius in Naples Cathedral, a fresco shows the Virgin, in blue, in the pose of a soprano about to sing an aria, interceding with Christ for Naples, while on the ground, stripped of their clothes, the naked bodies of the overthrown Luther and Calvin are trodden down by a happy warrior. One above the other in Westminster Abbey's Chapel of Henry VII lie the remains of two queens, Elizabeth I and Mary I, whose juxtaposition dramatises the uncertainties of sixteenth-century dynastic interventions into religion. Mary ('Bloody Mary', to the protestants) had disestablished the church of England, formed by her father Henry VIII, as a challenge to papal supremacy; her successor, Elizabeth, restored protestantism when she came to power and Mary's grave was dishonoured by being piled up with stones from 'papist' chapel altars destroyed in the Elizabethan backlash – and when it came to burying Elizabeth, her marble tomb was put above Mary's grave. Bohemia, too, bears witness to the slaughter, plunder, starvation and pestilence occasioned by the Thirty Years' War, when Spaniards, Austrians, French, Germans, Danes and Swedes fought in various religious factions. In the Gesu Church, Rome, the Jesuits' triumphs against heresy in Poland, Austria and the southern German lands are celebrated in coloured marbles and bronzes, which undulate with the sombre luxuriance of satin.

What is lacking are monuments of toleration. They should be looked for above all in the Netherlands. This was the first protestant society to achieve the manners of toleration. According to a Dutch theory put forward in the 1960s, this tolerance was acquired in the seventeenth century because the collective consciousness of a class (the Dutch upper class) took on an entirely secular aspect. Spinoza, writing in Amsterdam in 1670, declared that there should be freedom of conscience in religion and that the liberty of the individual should be the basis of the state. Religious sectarianism could impede trade, and Amsterdam was the trading centre of the world. The Amsterdam guide books recommend the Amstelkring Museum as a monument to toleration, since it preserves a clandestine catholic church – Our Lord in the Attic – which was built into the upper floors of adjoining houses, while preserving their exteriors so that they looked like dwelling places. This common habit was accepted by the merchants who ran Amsterdam as a way of overcoming the edicts against the catholic religion. Most tourists, however, schooled in the expectations of tourism, will tend to see the Amstelkring Museum less as a monument to Dutch toleration than to the elegance of classical seventeenth-century Dutch living-room styles, with their fine walnut furnishings and magnificent silverware.

The first two anti-dynasty revolutions

In the Netherlands History section of Amsterdam's Rijksmuseum, a large painting by van der Venne shows two rival fishing parties in boats, each supported by hundreds of partisans on opposite banks of a stretch of water. On one side, the partisans are all sombrely dressed in black and white, and hold up Bibles; these are the Calvinist Dutch. On the other side, the black and white are interspersed with the reds and yellows of priests and courtiers; these are the Spanish catholics and the catholic Netherlanders who supported them. Both fishing parties are netting the water: what they are catching are small shoals of people. *Fishing for Souls* recalls the religious drives of the Twelve Year Truce (beginning in 1609) in the Eighty Years' War fought between Spain and the 17 rebel provinces in the Low Countries. At the beginning of the war, the Low Countries were the richest, most urbanised and industrialised and, in our sense, the most 'modern' part of Europe; the northern provinces, re-formed victoriously as the Dutch Republic, were to dominate world trade for most of the seventeenth century.

The Eighty Years' War was the first great successful rising against the hereditary principle of dynasty and, as with so much else in the Low Countries, one of the beginnings of modernity. It is celebrated as a war of liberation in the Rijksmuseum, in paintings showing sea battles, land battles, sieges, stormings of ramparts. From the roof hang flags seized from Spanish ships. Opposite a glass case displaying the armaments of pikemen, cuirassiers and musketeers, is a large-scale model of a siege, complete with spyholes through which the tourist can look as if through field glasses, and, stage by stage, see the Dutch win. A painting of the Battle of Lake Haarlem (1573) seems merely to depict an over-crowded regatta, until one sees the flashes and sparks; beneath it are displayed relics of the battle itself, dredged from the lake. Generals, admirals and merchant–politicians look out over the carnage, steady-eyed.

What was the victory of the Dutch Republic to mean? The answer comes in the paintings galleries of the Rijksmuseum, in the work of Johannes Vermeer and Pieter de Hooch. Here is a beginning of bourgeois art. The Dutch are to be a neat, clean people who eat plenty of wholesome bread for breakfast, enjoy snacks of herring during the day and worship in plain, white churches that are as uncomplicated as themselves. In their high, narrow houses and little streets, they are to be a people who understand the virtues of smallness, an industrious people, happy to relax over simple country pleasures. In their spotless, shiny interiors with doors or windows opening out on to placid views, they are to be a domestic people, to whom the important part of the house will be the storage cupboard, replete with the material good things of life.

The northern provinces' victory against the Spanish can be seen as Europe's first triumph of a 'middle class' that then became a ruling class (the term 'middle class' does not lose significance simply because it has almost as many meanings as the word 'God'). In the new Dutch Republic, the legitimation of the dynastic principle was replaced by the legitimations of the commerical efficiency of the ruling merchant class, whose tall houses are now admired on the canal tour of Amsterdam. These old houses of the urban patricians are as much symbols of power as castles, cathedrals and palaces.

Fittingly, it was when the Netherlands was becoming the world's greatest maritime power that Amsterdam domesticated renaissance styles for a new bourgeois world. Dutch architects perfected a classical style in brick with stone trimmings (and gables for individualism) for a new-rich society, and this style in brick spread to the new bourgeois societies in Scandinavia, the Rhineland and Britain.

In this seventeenth-century 'social dictatorship of the merchant class' that replaced the rule of the dynasts, power was no longer justified by birth, but as Johann de Witt argued in his *The Interest of Holland* (1662), by the way in which the enterprise and skill of the rich sustained the prosperity of the whole state. This was exactly the argument to be used by successive business classes up to the present day. It meant that wealth could still be inherited – it did not take the Amsterdam merchant–patricians long to see themselves as commercial dynasts – but wealth and power were no longer justified by inheritance. What was now to justify power were arguments of an efficiency that created the prosperity of all. The age was beginning in which part of a tour could be of a shopping plaza or an office tower, a factory or a stock exchange.

Two contradictory ceremonies take place in London each year within a few hundred metres. At one, outside Westminster Hall, wreaths are laid and psalms sung beside the statue of Oliver

Cromwell, Lord General in the Free Commonwealth of England, and then Lord Protector, who, following the restoration of the monarchy in 1660, was disinterred and subjected to the humiliation of having his head displayed on a pole near Westminster Hall for 23 years. The other ceremony takes place at the Banqueting House in Whitehall, whose ceiling Rubens painted in celebration of the Stuart reign. Here, annually, a wreath is hung above the entrance beneath a tablet that probably marks the place where Charles I emerged and walked to the scaffold where he was beheaded.

The English have never been able to agree on how to remember their revolutionary civil war. Similar contradictions are found at Westminster in the paintings hung in the peers' corridor of the Houses of Parliament. On one side, paintings celebrate the Calvinist puritans, parliamentarians and 'roundheads' who fought Charles; on the other side, Charles himself and the 'cavaliers' who supported him are celebrated. Like so much else in the Houses of Parliament, this shows a useful accommodation of opposites, but it also shows the ambiguities in the two seventeenth-century English revolutions – the Civil War, and (despite its name, for it was merely a coup) the much lesser 'Glorious Revolution' of 1688. The English had astounded Europe, first by their civil war, then by putting a king on open trial, executing him, and replacing him with a 'Protector', and, finally, in the Glorious Revolution of 1688 when they dismissed another king, imported a new one and tamed him by putting him on a salary. Although the revolutionary armies in the Civil War may have had an enormous potential for more egalitarian change, the change did not come. We know the potential was there from extraordinary occurrences such as common soldiers and their officers debating in a parish church what mattered in life, how the state should be ordered, and even contemplating what it might mean if 'the poorest he that is in England hath a life to live, as the greatest he'. And there were times in the religious struggle when Calvinism seemed ready to carry the day. When it was all over, though, hereditary legitimation still prevailed. The basis of privilege may have been different and revised to favour those who, in continental European terms, were the nobility (including the gentry), but the right to rule by birth remained unchallenged. Rather, it was now a question of determining which kinds of birth should give the right to rule. Even the

Netherlands-style, bourgeois justifications of commercial efficiency did not come to the top in England, although, by the eighteenth century, the clandestine organisation of England for the benefit of private profit was well under way.

The great democratic questions and their echoes of the language of people's uprisings flickered briefly to the surface in the first English revolution, but were then to sink back into the minds of the dispossessed. The second ('glorious') revolution, whilst producing nothing analogous to the Dutch Republic's bourgeois legitimations of efficiency, did, however, spawn some new ways of looking at power. These were most forcefully articulated only a year after the Declaration of Rights in John Locke's *Two Treatises of Goverment* (1689), which were to be among the founding doctrines of liberalism. Optimistic and rational, they declared a belief in three natural human rights – life, liberty and property – which were more important than the power of the state; if a regime threatened those rights, it was proper that it should be replaced. These views of liberty were taken up by both French and American political thinkers and had some influence in shaping the ideals of those countries' revolutions. However, in Britain the aristocratic principle remained entrenched, strengthened by the comparative ease with which *arrivistes* could work themselves, or their children, into the upper classes. To Montesquieu it was the aristocracy of England that was the basis of liberty, defending liberty not only from king, but from the people.

As in the Netherlands, these changes in Britain can today seem to be symbolised in the design of houses. The merchant–patrician style of Amsterdam migrated in the eighteenth century to Britain as Georgian. It found its finest expression in 'New Edinburgh', which, though established 100 years after Amsterdam, showed that renaissance architectural principles were still lively enough to play their historic role of housing business families and their offices in buildings that helped 'explain' their power by associating it with strength, elegance, reason and the antique. What makes 'New Edinburgh' a marvel of reason is its domestication of the classical style into Georgian – in large, beautifully proportioned squares, circles, crescents and streets, hectares of them, now skilfully conserved in one of Europe's largest survivals. There is rationality in symmetrically arranged grey stone and stucco, plain and controlled, but also large-mindedness in set pieces such as the palace fronts of Charlotte Square; as in Bath, the palatial is made ordinary in what can seem a logically arranged world.

The French Revolution

In one of Paris's less distinctive squares, part of it now a car park, a brown line marks the grey pavement. The square is the Place de la Bastille and the brown line indicates the outline of the walls of the Bastille – a building whose iconography is essential to that part of the European imagination which trusts that the people can rise against repression ('To the Bastille!'), and prevail. It is one of the most effectively established symbols of tyranny ever thrown up by events and glorified by myth-makers – just as the French Revolution as a whole provides a theatrical spectacle almost as great in the European imagination as that of the crucifixion.

How the iconography of the Bastille developed is shown in the Room of the Bastille in the Carnavalet Museum in Paris. There are contemporary paintings of the attack on the Bastille, its capture and then its demolition (regretted in the Carnavalet guide as a loss to tourism). In one painting, the Spirit of Liberty is high in the heavens and presides over the storming. Probably all that had been intended when the people moved on the Bastille was a display of force impressive enough to persuade the garrison commander to hand over a store of gunpowder, but one accident led to another, producing an heroic event and its souvenirs: the Carnavalet has models of the Bastille that were prepared for the souvenir trade soon after it fell, and representations, in stucco, porcelain and faience of the assault on it; there are paintings on commodes of its capture, mementoes made out of the stone of its walls, commemorative medals made out of its chains. The next paintings, medals and flags are of the commemoration of the first anniversary of the fall of the Bastille when, in a fête on the Field of Mars, 14 July became a national day.

The half-million spectators celebrating the rise of liberty on that day included Louis XVI, greeted in one painting as 'father of France and king of a free people'. This first great fête of freedom also has its great iconographic paintings in the Carnavalet. The revolution was precipitated by an attempt of the nobles to extend their privileges. This had caused such reactions that Louis seemed to be presiding over what we would see as the modernisation of France into a property-owning bourgeois state where rewards would go not to birth, but to initiative, talent and energy: documents in the Carnavalet record how titles were to be abolished and the nobility were to lose their rights; careers were to be opened to talent, taxation equalised, justice made free and equal for all, the rights of property guaranteed, administration rationalised, weights and measures standardised, religious toleration established, and the church to become part of the civil service. The lawyers, functionaries and other middle-class people who were then giving the revolution its meaning spoke the language of the Enlightenment; they believed in progress in all rational fields of human endeavour, in a secular state. The museum then records how, in 1791, Louis proclaimed a new constitution and declared 'The revolution is over.' Publicly, he sent letters to foreign courts praising the revolution's 'destruction of a multitude of abuses accumulated over the centuries', but privately he was conspiring with foreign courts. When he tried to escape and raise the banner against the revolution, by the standards of revolutions he justly precipitated his own execution.

In the Carnavalet's next room the Republic is declared and symbols of democratic and republican hope proliferate. For most of the eighteenth century the enlightened had looked to absolute monarchs to carry out their programmes; now they speak in the name of 'the people'. On the walls a large, illuminated poster of the Declaration of the Rights of Man and the Citizen, with its expressions of individualism, has now become a sacred text, but it is joined by announcements of the democratic Jacobin constitution with its declaration of universal suffrage. The display cases present those romantic symbols of revolution that have become standard decorations of protest movements for the next 100 years: flags proclaim Liberty, Equality, Fraternity or Death; tricolours and liberty caps are glorified; in glass cases, buttons announce new slogans. Plaques, insignia and miniatures publicise revolutionary themes; so do cups, saucers and plates. Candelabra are supported by allegorical representations of Reason, and of the authority of the people. A sculpture shows a woman in a flowing dress (Liberty) crowning a naked man (France); there is a painting of a fashionable opera singer posing in the radical chic of a *sans culotte*; in a warm, harmonious painting, three hopeful members of the cultivated bourgeoisie are gently singing a patriotic song; in a painting glorifying the new constitution, the emblems of monarchy are abased before a statue of Liberty; in a painting of the funeral of the assassinated Marat, his body is arranged as that of an heroic Roman, a stoic martyr; there is a painting of the fête of unity in the Place de la Révolution and a painting of the fête of the Supreme Being in which a tree of liberty was planted on top of an artificial hill.

The revolution that is being celebrated is that of the enlightened middle class; there is no celebration of the revolution of the peasants (who ceased being revolutionary when they got what they wanted), and the revolution of the *sans culottes* (who remained revolutionary because they didn't get the social justice and direct democracy they wanted) is represented only at second hand, as interpreted by the middle-class revolutionaries.

There are also souvenirs of the guillotine – models of it, a painting showing it standing in the Place de la Révolution under the gaze of the statue of Liberty; a dinner-plate showing the executioner holding up the head of a tyrant; these are presented as symbols of Reason and Hope. Then comes the anti-climax that will haunt all future dreams of revolution: a bas-relief shows the apotheosis of Napoleon, classically nude, a gold crown held over his head, riding to the heavens in a chariot.

The spirit of liberty

The mythologising of revolution is weak in the Place de la République, where the statue of the Republic shows her as an overdressed bourgeois cousin of Queen Victoria; weak, too, in the Place de la Nation, where a bronze group, *The Triumph of the Republic*, is framed between two columns with a king on top of each. But 52 metres above the traffic in the Place de la Bastille, on top of a column too wide for its height, stands a naked man, his gilt now turned to green, expressing the Spirit of Liberty. Louis Philippe, the citizen king, erected the July Column to offer glory to those citizens of Paris who put on their tricolours and fought behind barricades for three days in July 1830, imagining it was a revolution; 615 of their bodies are buried in the vaults below. When, in 1848, it was Louis Philippe's turn to be overthrown in a drama of the streets, his throne was burned beside this column erected in the name of liberty.

It is in the Louvre, in Delacroix's painting *Liberty Guiding the People* (1830), that the romantic idea of bourgeois revolution receives its most celebrated icon. Painted to perpetuate the July days of 1830 ('even if I haven't fought for the country, at least I can paint for her') it provides the world's most idealised symbol of the spirit of the barricades. Bare-breasted and barefooted, tricolour in one hand, rifle in the other and the bonnet of revolution on her head, Liberty advances, leading top-hatted bourgeois, worker–patriot and heroic youth out of the smoke and dust of the old order, over the bodies of martyred comrades, towards the freedom of the new.

The Parisians had been building barricades since the sixteenth century, but engravings of barricades are to be found in the nineteenth-century sections of almost all the history museums in Europe. They became one of Europe's political forms. At their most complete, as in Paris, they were built of pavingstones, or omnibuses and waggons weighed down with pavingstones, strengthened with iron railings, lamp posts and trees. The 1,500 barricades of the 1848 revolution denuded Paris boulevards of 4,000 trees. Barricades would run right across streets, perhaps up to the second storey, and in the main squares they were built as small forts. In cities less practised than Paris in building barricades, carriages, food stalls, sentry boxes, shop counters, sacks of flour, beds and bedding, sofas and even pianos were piled high. While the barricades were being improvised, tocsins would sound continuously from the churches, drums would roll, chemists would make gunpowder, printers cast shot and women bring food and drink; women and children might mount to the roofs with cauldrons of boiling water. When all was ready, a tricolour would be raised (the colours varying with the nation): later in the century, a red flag might also be unfurled.

As one wanders around the museums, one can see the anatomy of the revolutions of enlightenment. *Act one*: large assemblages of people, some chance shots, a small slaughter. *Act two*: the rush to the barricades, the seizing of canon or arsenals, the failure of the army to retaliate, the temporary victory, the wall posters, the provisional decrees, the celebration of the glorious dead. Sometimes this is then followed by *Act three*: the reprisals, the defeat, the revenge shootings.

By now, the cult of the massacred secular martyrs had arisen, although it was not to reach its full expression until meaning had to be given to the dead of the First World War. The idea of political martyrdom reached its most memorable expression in the image of the firing squad, which at this time became an essential part of the European imagination – most memorably celebrated, in Goya's *The Shootings of May 3, 1808, in Madrid*, now in the Prado, a painting of an execution by one of the firing squads used in reprisal for the uprising against the French. In this famous work, the riflemen-executioners are anonymous parts of an efficient machine; each of the persons facing their guns, however, is an individual. Goya has caught their diverse personalities at the very moment before their death; they are not heroes, but humans, about to be destroyed. At the bottom, the painting seems smeared with fresh blood, as if the canvas had been wiped with a murderer's hands.

Goya's painting captures horror and death in a people's rising. Perhaps more relevant to some other moods of revolutions of enlightenment is a painting in the Museum of Spanish Nineteenth-century Art in Madrid, *The Execution of Torrijos and His Comrades* by Antonio Gisbert, showing the shooting of liberals who had planned a revolt against Ferdinand. They are worthy citizens, cultured men of gravity and enlightenment, thoughtful but steadfast as they stand, blindfold, while the firing squad waits. At their feet are the bodies of those already executed, also worthy men, respectably dressed, bloodstained and dead. Beside one body is a top hat.

Apart from an occasional painting of *The Massacre of Ten Thousand Christians* or of *The Massacre of the Innocents*, painters before Goya – or those of them whose works have survived in the art museums – did not concern themselves with the torture or execution of ordinary people, except to frighten them, in *Last Judgements*, or in the kind of admonitory engravings that now get into history museums to show the failure of a peasants' war. In his *The Disasters of War*, Goya democratised massacre, so that it could be the fate of everyone. Dismembered bodies are sketched with the dispassionate care of a botanist; acts of violation are recorded with a dreamlike realism. His etchings are the first famous celebration of the modern 'atrocity'.

The first great celebration of an individual political martyrdom is David's *Marat Assassiné*, in the Brussels Fine Arts Museum. The inkwell and quills recall that Marat was writing down his thoughts for the people's salvation; his nudity recalls the classical and Christian traditions of death and martyrdom; the mood is one of great seriousness and dignity, and, at the same time, of finality. It is a painting demanding reverence, so simply and starkly presented that from the paint comes an impression of eternal silence.

The year of revolution

In Romania, statues are still going up, paintings are still being painted and publications are still being produced commemorating the heroic days of 1848, the year of most widespread revolution in Enlightenment Europe. In Bucharest, three different museums have maps with lights showing the revolutionary uprisings of 1848 in the Romanian lands against the Turks and the Austrians; there are portraits of heroic leaders, and the proclamations they issued, the chairs they sat in, the pens they used, the new flags they raised, the rosettes they wore – before their uprisings were suppressed. In Prague, one of the many memories of failure in Wenceslas Square is that, ten days after it had been the setting for the inaugural mass of the Slavonic Congress (called in June 1848 for Slavs throughout the Austrian Empire to meet in their national dress and discuss Slavic culture), an Austrian general bombarded the city into silence. Among the patriotic memorials in O'Connell Street, Dublin, a statue of a statesmanlike figure, arms folded in composure, represents William Smith O'Brien, leader of 1848's quickest fiasco, the failure, in a country desolated by the Great Famine, of the Young Ireland movement's brief attempt at uprising. In front of Budapest's vast revival-gothic parliament building, a monument erected by the Communist regime in 1952 shows Louis Kossuth, who chaired the Committee of Defence in Hungary's 1848 revolt against Austria and in the war that followed, dressed in a braided Hungarian gala coat, calling to arms a statuary group of peasants, students and workers. In the Hague and Copenhagen, documents in glass cases are reminders of how easily the Dutch and Danish kings gave in. In Vienna, only a plaque or two can be found to commemorate the 1848 uprising which twice led the emperor to leave the city and, later, to abdicate, and which was overcome only when imperial troops shelled and shot their way back into control. But in Italy, five cities have statues, embellished by winged lions, laurel wreaths, palms of triumph, raised swords and unfurled tricolours, commemorating five of the seven 1848 Italian risings. In the Friedrichshain People's Park, East Berlin, among the hills made from bomb rubble, there is a cemetery to the martyred dead of March 1848, whose corpses the Prussian king was forced to honour. In history museums in both Germanies, there are drawings of buildings in flames, guns smoking, crowds with battering rams. Lights flash to suggest gunfire. Posters and proclamations acknowledge the winning of the liberal demands in most of the 30 or so German-speaking states. Then paintings of heroic deeds, triumphal processions and allegoric figures lead the tourist on to a last section, labelled 'The Reaction'. Lights flash again. This time they are flashes from the victorious guns of the princes and kings.

The first outbreaks of 1848 had begun in Paris, in February, when the people seized the royal palace of the Tuileries, and a government of intellectuals appointed itself, with the novelist George Sand helping to produce *Bulletins*, and the poet Alphonse de Lamartine, as Minister for Foreign Affairs, apostrophising revolution ('We are making the sublimest of poems'). But Paris does little to commemorate 1848, beyond adding a footnote about it to the July Column – perhaps because fiasco so quickly followed the revolution, when the elections, the first ever held on a universal (male) suffrage, produced a conservative assembly only two months after the revolution. George Sand, who had said, 'I have seen the people grand, sublime, generous, the most admirable people in the universe,' now attacked them as 'blind, credulous, ignorant, ungrateful, bad and stupid'. Two months after the election, government forces were shooting the workers.

The perplexities of bourgeois revolution

The magic of the nineteenth-century revolutions of enlightenment comes together among the heavy carved furniture in the Victor Hugo Museum in the Place des Vosges in Paris. The museum is in the apartment Hugo rented for 15 years before the revolution of 1848. Here is the tricolour he wore, and manuscripts containing some of the originals of the cascades of words he poured out to greet the false dawn of 1848. There are also mementoes of his long years in exile under Napoleon III, when he became that heroic nineteenth-century figure – the liberal patriot who, though exiled from his own land, sustains a rhetoric of liberty and justice and sympathy for the poor that makes him a hero amongst the disappointed. These are followed by mementoes of the salvoes of liberal and patriotic dogma ('O city you will make History kneel down before you') that he fired off in honour of himself and of France when he returned to Paris after Napoleon fell, and the Prussian siege began. His face, now no longer high-domed and weak-chinned as in earlier caricatures, is bearded and venerable; a head sculpted by Rodin portrays him as philosopher. Remaining a symbol of democratic hope, Hugo survived with dignity even the disappointments and insipidities of the Third Republic.

The museum has a reconstruction of the room in which he died in 1885. It then tells the story of one of the nineteenth-century's most spectacular funerals. The funeral car in which his body lay in state under the Arc de Triomphe was almost too high for the arch; on the funeral day, to commemorate a lover of the poor, his body was carried on a pauper's hearse through crowds of 400,000 people to the Panthéon, which had been restored as a hall of fame to receive him. In the museum there is a sculptured relief of his apotheosis: surrounded by classical figures, he rises to Olympus, naked except where his horse's wings cover his genitals.

That the state should so honour Hugo, as ideal representative of liberty and of the people, was partly because such a funeral was a snub to the French royalists. But its symbolic meaning was wider: it was an example of how the French had developed a talent for accommodating leftovers of the idea of revolution while remaining socially stable. One of the main results of the first, and great, French Revolution was that it had established a conservative society of small proprietors – of satisfied peasants and of comfortably-off property owners in towns. For them, the revolutionary tradition meant accepting limited violence as a useful way out of a crisis:

short, sharp shocks could shake away a government, or even a constitution, or bridge some other social landslip, while leaving the rest of the landscape much the same. The Paris revolution of 1830 put the *haute bourgeoisie* in charge of affairs in France. And that was that. There were no more real bourgeois revolutions in France. The dramas of 1848 were merely a masquerade, although a masquerade deadly to some of those with the highest hopes: after the excitement, much the same people prevailed.

The perplexities of the European secular faith of revolution, romanticised and idealised, is an essential part of the European imagination. Some maintain a permanent hope that action in the streets will right wrongs or even that 'the people' will prevail. Some even hope that, through the sacrifices of revolutionary martyrs and apocalyptic change, society will be cleansed and humanity saved. Other reformers see all revolutions as necessarily false dawns, provoking fine hopes but inevitably failing and then provoking bitter reaction; or, if they succeed, the radicals of yesterday become the reactionaries of tomorrow.

There remains a special feeling of authenticity about action in the streets. Like nature, or the picturesque quarter, it can be seen as the true reality, the ultimate sincerity – the occasion when the artificialities and frauds of official political life fall aside to reveal the final truth; the people speaking with their authentic voice. But can 'the people' be trusted? In the fusilade of insults she fired when the French voted the wrong way, George Sand found them not only blind, credulous, ignorant, ungrateful, bad and stupid – they were also *bourgeois*. She had posed the problem: in a France already more bourgeois than aristocratic, whence would come a revolutionary force? One answer was in the red flags now found among the tricolours on the barricades. Some of the lower classes, even if they did not provide leaders, were rebelling (if in an unarticulated way), not just against dynasty and the hereditary rights of aristocratic birth, but also against existing rights of property – or at least how that property was being used. That is why some of those who defended the barricades in Paris in February were executed in June. If the rights of property were to be at risk, however, why should the bourgeoisie support revolution? Except as part of nationalist revolts, or from the disasters of war, the bourgeois revolutions declined as a political form. But their monuments remain, and pose problems in presentation.

In Communist countries, monuments to the bourgeois revolutions are both laudatory, in that they are presented as part of a process that has culminated in the 'people's democracies', and didactic, in that they display characteristic bourgeois faults. In capitalist countries, those who gained most from these revolutions (the owners of capital) can be among those least likely to respect the revolutionary monuments as having any contemporary relevance: when people have got what they want out of revolution, they abandon it as a political form. There can be no monuments to revolution in general, only to particular revolutions.

In the second half of the nineteenth century, no revolutions could be expected from the *haute bourgeoisie*, who now showed off their jewels in the red plush and gilt of the Paris Opéra, or put up their extravagant mansions in the Kurfürstendamm, or sent their sons to good schools in England; neither could they be expected from the many other people who aspired to these goals. But there were were still to be many individual bourgeois who dreamed of revolt or planned it. (Sometimes they seemed the main people who did so, as if articulating ideas of revolt were a bourgeois speciality.) They were intellectual heirs of catholic humanists, Dutch toleration and eighteenth-century Enlightenment – and these represent programmes that always raise more hopes than they fulfil. Even more particularly, as new classes of owners developed new powers against old dynasties, they were forced to adopt the style of speaking not just for themselves, but in the name of 'the people' – creating a language of disinterested and universal concern.

At this point, the word 'bourgeois' is getting in the way. Its connotations are too diverse: solid citizenry, stifling mediocrity, petty proprietorship, merchant–patricians, industrial capitalists, bold entrepreneurial owner-management and huge bureaucratised corporations. To explain why so many different types of people came out into the streets in 1848, and, for that matter, in 1968, we need some other term. The types of middle-class people most evident in the 1848 revolutions were not capitalist-owners; they were lawyers, journalists, government officials, educators, intellectuals, students. With the slow disintegration of the old ruling classes over several hundred years – in some countries earlier than in others – there had been growing what one might call the 'deciding classes', people who, in increasingly complex societies, engage in, or are directly related to, the rituals of decision-making (even if they are operating in a power context greater than themselves). And it is a split among these people that provides a kind of 'critics' culture'. On the one hand, there are those who appear to run things – nowadays, as well as owners, they include officials of the great bureaucracies of business or political parties or governments, professionals, technicians and other experts, teachers, journalists, artists, intellectuals, performers, promoters and students – and they are given greater social bulk because the 'white-collar workers', who do less interesting work, also tend to identify with them. They are the main support for things as they are, perhaps providing the principal reason why there are no more revolutions in liberal-democratic advanced capitalist societies. But, on the other hand, some of them, in the sheer *élan* of imagining better decisions, become the most bold and guileful enemies of the system – because, in ways that range from reform to revolt, they have their own ideas of how things should be run. Sometimes, they will still speak mainly to each other, seeking action in political or administrative coups; at other times, they may have programmes that depend on mobilising 'the people'.

6. The tourism of reaction

The golden past

The potential conservative function of sightseeing that can come from nostalgia for the past can be accompanied by specific regrets for the destruction of hereditary privilege. Thus, tourists who visit monuments of the revolution in Paris may be moved not by the cult of liberty but by the cult of reaction. Of this cult, the patron saint is Marie Antoinette. In the Carnavalet Museum's reminders of the 1789–95 revolutionary period, a special room, the Salle du Temple, offers relics from the cult of the royal martyrs. Objects displayed include some used in the Temple prison (later destroyed by Napoleon lest it became a royalist shrine): a spoon, a plate, a laundry list. Nearby are documents of the Terror: 'Comité de Salut Public', 'Commune de Paris', 'Ordre d'exécution'. The tour of the Conciergerie (the passage through three superb gothic halls built by Phillip the Fair in his extension of the palace in the fourteenth century) can seem to tourists just a teaser: the real moment comes when the guide raises one hand and says, 'And now to the prisons!' In fact, the three large halls were also used as part of the prison during the Terror, but the story seems better if all the condemned were crammed into the few small rooms now described as the 'Prisoners' Gallery'. On the tour, special attention is given to the novelty of the Salle de Toilette, where hair was cut so that the guillotine's blade would chop more cleanly. The centrepiece of sentimentality, though, is Marie Antoinette's cell – as if the climax of the revolution was the death of this Austrian princess, executed because, at a time of war, she passed military secrets to the enemy.

Marie Antoinette became the greatest martyred secular saint of nineteenth-century political reaction. Other regimes added martyrs of their own: in Austria-Hungary it was Count Latour, the Minister for War, whom the mob killed with hammers and iron bars before stripping and hoisting him to a lamp post, where women dipped their handkerchiefs in the blood of some of his 43 wounds. To some, the French Revolution is a symbol of some of humankind's greatest depravities: the rattle of the tumbrils, the roll of the drums, the thud of the blade. How important this was in symbolic terms can be seen in the 130-year confusion over the statuary, paintings and declared purpose of the Panthéon, which was alternately controlled by conservatives, who wished to celebrate a Christian and royalist France, and by radicals, who wished to celebrate a rational and liberal France. The result: ambivalence. Outside, in its pediment the Panthéon proclaimes that it celebrates great men and has the *Patrie*, assisted by Life and History, distributing laurels to jurists, generals, scientists, writers, artists and other secular celebrities, conveniently grouped to fit into the two sides of a shallow triangle. Inside, an enormous complex of murals celebrates catholic France in episodes from the life of St Geneviève, St Denis, Clovis, Charlemagne, St Louis and Joan of Arc. A cupola painted with a glorification of the continuity of the monarchy rises above marble groups aggressively honouring the revolution.

There had been no more ambitious proposal for a temple to commemorate the secular saints of progress than the Constituent Assembly's 1791 decision to convert into a temple of fame the newly finished church on the Mont de Paris, originally intended as a shrine for St Geneviève. It had been under construction for 30 years, partly on the proceeds of lotteries, and was conveniently designed in a neoclassical style that lent itself to a civic purpose. As the revolution's most famous orator ('Go and tell your master that we are here by the will of the people and that we shall not budge save at the point of a bayonet'), President of both the Jacobin Club and the Constituent Assembly, Mirabeau had become a cult-figure worthy of secular sainthood: his tomb in the Panthéon was to be an altar of liberty. Accompanied by suitable theatrical ceremonies, it was soon joined by the tombs of Voltaire and Rousseau. Later, Mirabeau's reputation was revised and his body was reburied in a pauper's grave. A new favourite, Marat, became a cult-figure whose Roman funeral ended at the Panthéon:

five months on, with another change in mood, his body was buried elsewhere. Napoleon ordered a tarpaulin put over the secular pediment that had been put up, and re-established the Panthéon as a Christian church. With the restoration of the Bourbons, the pediment was destroyed and replaced with Christian symbols. In the wake of the 1830 revolution, the Panthéon was again secularised and the present secular pediment designed. Napoleon III again gave the building over to religious purposes – but the Commune revolutionary uprising of 1871 saw the crosses being sawn off and the hoisting of the red flag. One of the icons of the failed revolutionaries is now in the Carnavalet Museum: it shows the martyrdom of a Communard – he has been forced to kneel on the steps of the Panthéon . . . the sleet falls . . . the execution squad aim their rifles . . . the officer raises his sword to give the signal. In the 1870s, a 'moral order' government commissioned the Panthéon's great murals to honour catholic France; in 1885, to find a resting-place sacred enough for Hugo's body, a radical government again secularised the Panthéon. In 1913, another government ordered statuary to honour, amongst other matters, the revolution.

Throughout the nineteenth century similar symbolic battles were fought in most countries of Europe. It was the century when ideologies rather than Christian faith became the prime languages of power, both justifying power and explaining it. Liberalism, radicalism, socialism, nationalism, imperialism and conservatism came to be the creeds used in attempts to mobilise mass support in emergent industrialised societies. There were many religious revivals. Whatever new forms Christianity took – from the doctrine of papal infallibility to the forming of the Salvation Army – they shared in common a reaction to social change. As a justifier of power or as an explainer of events, Christianity was now most significant in the ways in which it could be used to support, or contest, one of the new secular ideologies. Romantic yearnings for a golden, aristocratic past were fundamental to the new moods that helped resist social change. They gave emotional content to the newly created ideology of 'conservatism' and to tourism, its principal glamour. This form of romance was part of the stuff of those conservative doctrines that aimed to mobilise mass support behind what could survive of the old order. Scott, Novalis and other European writers invented a mythic middle ages of organic stability in which the church and hereditary right were presented as the proper bases of human society. In Britain, France, Prussia, Austria-Hungary and Russia theorists of power wrote books which were to become famous; they delivered lectures praising the experience of the past, the stability of village life, the virtues of the peasantry, the wisdom of serfs, the craftsmanship and comradeship of the guilds, the wonders of the Christian family and the freedom and strength of ancient institutions which stood as a bulwark against the despotisms of the mob. The conservatives had become 'tourists' of the past, seeking justifications in history. In doing so, they set some of the most important bases for the modern tourist experience.

Nostalgia for the aristocrats

Perhaps the painting which best symbolises the reality of aristocratic life is Goya's *The Family of Charles IV*, in the Prado, Madrid. It has the rich, shimmering colour and brilliant light of courtly confidence; the people, though, are given meaning purely by the clothes they wear, by their sashes, ribbons and medallions, and by the children they display. In the treatment of their faces and poses, however, there is no pretence that these people, in themselves, possess aristocratic virtues. They are very ordinary looking, and wear the symbols of privilege not because they have earned status, but because they were born to it.

The aristocracy most usually presented to tourists rarely carries a face of such sober realism. More usually, we are left to admire the luxurious artifacts left behind by defeated nobles and overthrown dynasties. Now that it is an empty shell, Versailles can seem a greater glorification of the dynastic principle than when it was a monument of discomfort and overcrowding and stank of urine. Since so much sightseeing is given over to admiring the relics of hereditary privilege, one result of tourism – not least in the palaces and treasuries of the Soviet Union – can be highly conservative: it can become a way of glamorising and applauding past privilege, for the objects have become so sanitised and decontextualised that their presentation can give a false impression of the realities of a society dominated by dynasties and nobles.

Consider the contributions made to the Bavarian tourist industry and to tourist vision by the Wittelsbach family. From 1180 until 1918, when it was deposed by a soldiers' and workers' revolutionary council, this family were dukes, then prince-electors, and, in the end, kings of Bavaria. They have left behind an enchanted trail for the tourist industry. In the Treasury of the Residenz Museum, Munich, there are more than 1,200 of their precious objects, displayed behind glass with concealed lighting and unobtrusive curtains to set them off – from an amphora engraved with mythical scenes in rock crystal, to all the insignia and garnitures of the two Wittelsbach family orders. Built around seven inner-courtyards, the Residenz is a palace whose construction over 500 years faithfully records a family's quest for self-definition through new halls, new arcades and gardens. Here, a tourist interested in silver will find 3,500 pieces; a tourist interested in china will find 19 rooms displaying porcelain. Eight suites of opulent courtrooms are smothered in tapestries, frescoes, bronzes and marble sculptures. In one suite, the Halls of the Niebelungs, dozens of murals and ceiling paintings mark the first large-scale illustration of the Niebelung epic. An eight-room suite in early rococo celebrates the emperors of Rome and the Wittelsbachs of Bavaria; in another, a Wittelsbach ordered allegorical paintings on coffered ceilings to record his views on the world and on eternity. In the glitteringly ornate Ancestors' Gallery, portraits of 121 Wittelsbach ancestors (only one mythical) stare from between gilded carvings, demonstrating a lineage that descended from Charlemagne.

If tourists want more Wittelsbach display, an S-Bahn ride takes them to the Nymphenberg Castle, a palace of pavilions linked by arcaded galleries, elegant in white and pale green and fanciful in frescoes and stucco. There are four other tours. At Schleissheim there are two Wittelsbach castles – one built in the sixteenth century as accommodation and the other, built in the eighteenth century, to house paintings. Further away, in one of the forests of the Ammergav Alps, is the cream-coloured Linderhof Castle, richly built in Grand Trianon style, remarkably luxurious inside, and with a jet in its formal garden that shoots higher than any fountain at Versailles. Part of the summer tourist programme is a coach tour to Herrenchiemsee, a Wittelsbach palace built in the style of Versailles – but on its own island, in a wide, blue lake, so that the king would not be bothered by the people; the summer tourist season offers chamber concerts in a hall lit by candelabra as part of an inclusive tour. The grandest coach tour is into the tourist land of the castles of Hohenschwangau and Neuschwanstein, built by Wittelsbachs in the richest nineteenth-century fantasy of the middle ages. Hohenschwangau becomes an operatic set, with the fables of Lohengrin and Tannhaüser on its walls, although its architectural style is that of the English gothic revival. Neuschwanstein is incomparable. Built partly on the basis of some sketches by a theatrical designer, its true comparison is not with any other form of architecture, but with the fairy-tale castles in the illustrations of children's books. The absolute culmination in ivory-coloured towers and pinnacles of nineteenth-century romanticising, it might be too inauthentic for Disneyland; it does, however, make one of the Federal Republic's more striking travel posters. Ludwig II, builder of Linderhof, Herrenchiemsee and Neushchwanstein and once regarded as a selfish madman, has become a romantic cult-figure in Munich, where he is seen as patron of the arts without parallel. Others have shared his imagination – Sam Goldwyn, for example, or Cecil B. de Mille.

The very layout of a museum can give souvenirs of aristocratic luxury a glamour they did not have when they were in use. In what used to be the riding school of Lisbon's Summer Palace, two large halls glow and glitter with the world's largest collection of aristocratic carriages and coaches, 74 altogether – miniature palaces of gilded carving, flamboyant paintings and sculptures. The three triumphal cars of a Portugueses ambassador are like floating baroque fountains. There is red plush inside the gilded coaches, appropriate for aristocratic cheeks, and finery in leather and velvet, lace and pearls, appropriate to aristocrats' horses. Livery is provided for the coachmen and postillions, and silver trumpets to proclaim honour.

In the Historical Museum, Dresden, the German Democratic Republic preserves the hunting weapons and weapons of pomp which the Electors of Saxony began collecting in the sixteenth century. It now offers the most impressive display of sporting armour in Europe, with matching sets, shining with gold and jewels, for horse and knight. It also offers a conspicuous display of gold-embroidered horse saddles, covered in silk and strung with pearls; hunting weapons, gilded and enamelled and set with emeralds and turquoise; firearms with handles of stag horn inlaid with silver; and rapiers and daggers so elaborately embossed, enamelled and bejewelled that they could never have been used – even if use had been their purpose. Despite the cards that explain these objects' socio-economic significance and relation to the class struggle, what can come through is not the pushing and shoving of aristocrats showing themselves off by the use of such flashy, costly instruments, but images of expensive 'beauty' detached from historical reality.

Even the treasures of a religious house, if divorced from use and meaning, can become primarily a glorification of past privilege. In the Descalzas Reales, an aristocrats' convent in Madrid founded in a palace by the daughter of a Spanish king, the second cloister has become a sumptuous gallery of art objects – displayed in chapels where Christ lies naked and dead in every alcove, surrounded by luxurious display. Beyond the cloister are stores of treasure viewed by tourists on guided tours – the gold and jewels of crucifixes and chalices and precious secular paintings, displayed in rooms with painted ceilings and silk-covered walls. In a T-shaped hall built as a nuns' dormitory, Rubens tapestries give the impression of a tented harem.

Concentration on these palaces and treasures can help the sightseer understand the promptings of those who, when the old hegemony was threatened, began to write as if art would not be possible without an aristocracy. This was to be a continuing nostalgic theme. Intellectuals who found modern industrial societies distasteful, or inexplicable, built new theories out of selected passages from famous past defenders of the old order. Using the word 'aristocrat' in its etymological sense of 'the best', they implied that most aristocrats of the past really were 'the best', and that walking through the museum–palaces to admire the gilding and the stucco and the painted ceilings was to have the opportunity of recalling a time when art was still possible. For them, art became identified with luxury and conspicuous display. Tourists can also see it like this. So many of the European art museums are either palaces or imitation palaces that art itself can seem palatial and this impression can be strengthened by rumours of the enormous costliness and evident inaccessibility of art objects.

There may be another confirmation of the view that art, or in this case 'true art', is aristocratic. The kind of sniggering that used to go on in front of museum nudes is now very largely aimed at modern art: one of the effects of a coach-tour visit to an art museum is to confirm some tourists' impression that modern art (a non-aristocratic art) is not really art at all.

If one painting were to be chosen as a symbol of the aristocratic nature of art, it might come from the republic of Venice: Francesco Guardi's *Gala Concert*, now in the Alte Pinakothek and painted in 1782 to portray a gala concert for a visiting Russian grand duke, shows a vast, gilded reception room where a women's orchestra and choir wait on the platform for the guests. The floor is awash with jewels and powdered hair and rustling silk, and from the ceiling hang the spangled dream of rich chandeliers. The painting seems to appropriate all art and all pleasure to those uniquely born to them.

And what important effect is there in the method of display chosen for some of the treasures in the Kremlin's Armoury Chamber other than to dazzle the tourist with costly symbols of power? The chamber's Regalia Hall displays Russia's ancient thrones, greatest of all symbols of a ruling class in their ability to remind us that all power – whether making, interpreting, or administering laws, as well as society generally – could come from one person who sat in an expensive chair. Behind glass are the ivory throne of Ivan the Terrible, with its golden eagle, and the oriental throne of Boris Goudonov, with its low back and armrest and its stamped gold leaf and jewels. There is the first throne of the Romanovs, studded with turquoise, rubies, pearls; a silver-and-gold throne inlaid with 900 diamonds; the silver double throne of Peter the Great; and, in a showcase opposite, among the brocade court dresses, four more thrones, upholstered and made more comfortable for the industrial age.

Nineteenth-century chivalry

In the Groeningemuseum, Brugge, the central panel of Lancelot Blondeel's *The Legend of St George* shows a familiar scene: the busy, successful knight in armour is about to drive his sword through a dragon that already has a broken lance in its throat. The emphasis is on a well-dressed, courtly success. The surrounding four panels show scenes of this fashionable young man's coming martyrdom. In one panel, he is strung up and tortured; in the next, he is boiled; legs scarlet from the boiling, face smashed by pain, he is pulled through the town by a horse in the third panel. In the final panel he is beheaded: his legs are still scarlet, but the expression on his face is now one of peace. St George is one of the most frequently painted Christian martyrs to be found in the art museums, but to show him like this, in the agonies of his complex martyrdom, is rare. Accepted as the patron saint of chivalry, he is almost always shown as a Christian knight, combating the dragon which threatened the life of a king's daughter. (It is one of the roles of women to be threatened; the chivalric concept of womanhood reached one of its heights in the First World War, when patriotic posters defined one of the great purposes of the fighting to be the protection of mothers, wives, sisters, sweethearts.)

The archangel Michael sometimes also became a Christian knight – even Christ was occasionally shown as a knight, leading a crusade. St George, however, was the Christian figure most frequently used to glorify knighthood and Christian battle. As with the figures of Christ and the Virgin Mary, he could be adapted to any artist's purpose. In the Louvre, Raphael shows him engaged in knightly exercises in a nobleman's park; in the Rijksmuseum, Luca Signorelli has him performing in front of a courtly assemblage, as in a tournament. To Dürer, he is a thoughtful, mature protestant, important in himself, with much administrative experience behind him and a useful eternity ahead of him. To Altdorfer, he is a lonely man, almost unobserved, overwhelmed by surrounding circumstances, engaged in a testing encounter that no one sees.

Paintings are only one of the art forms in which St George was represented. In Leningrad's Winter Palace, a gilded sledge is modelled into the St George and the dragon legend. In the central lobby of London's House of Commons, a mosaic shows St George with the dragon at his feet, while, to his right, Fortitude holds his banner and, to his left, Purity holds his helmet. A tourist 'must' in Stockholm is a large wooden sculptured group, in three parts, of St George, dragon and princess, described as 'one of the greatest sculptural monuments from the later middle ages in northern

Europe'. The Treasury of the Residenz, Munich, boasts a light-hearted statuette: St George, in full armour of diamonds and sapphires, kills a dragon of emeralds and rubies.

Central to the nostalgia for the cult of chivalry, itself central to the conservatives' golden age, St George became one of the heroes of the nineteenth century. The institution of knighthood had developed in the eleventh and twelfth centuries as a way for warrior-landholders to do their fighting and control the countryside. In the nineteenth century, hundreds of years after knighthood had lost its original purpose, it was revived in a proliferation of new secular Orders as one of the reaffirming legitimations of the aristocrats. Orders of knighthood were established in every petty court in Europe, although without the old meanings. Within the British empire, seven new Orders were introduced. There were increasing numbers of admirals, generals, governors, statesmen and officials to 'decorate'; there were Indian and other 'native' princes to be bonded into collaboration with the imperial rulers (an extremely ambiguous business, with hypocrisies on both sides); there were the new businessmen to honour and tame; and after the Order of St Michael and St George was extended to the colonies in 1869, it became the most glittering prize for those who sought entry into the Government House circles.

Accompanying the nostalgia for chivalry was a new glamorisation of the crusades: in 1848, the Belgians put up a statue to Godfrey de Bouillon in Brussels, where he now raises his standard above the traffic of the Place Royale; in 1860, the British erected a statue to Richard the Lion Heart, who now brandishes his sword over the car park of the House of Lords. In a more general reinvention of medieval chivalric ideals, artists, poets and composers pillaged the songs of the troubadors, the great Arthurian cycles, the cycles of the Cid and Nibelungenlied to create new forms of nineteenth-century art, and to attach to the aristocracy – with varying credibility – chivalric ideals of Christian faith, altruism, and bravery in the defence of justice and the protection of the weak. There were many new representations made of St George. Some of the favourite posters of the First World War showed Christian knights in armour, defending right against wrong; all the belligerents had posters in which, as a symbol of the just nation destroying evil, a St George slew his dragon. And when the millions of conscript dead were honoured, they were honoured partly in the language of revival chivalry.

The Cervantes Monument in the Plaza de España, Madrid, pays tribute to Cervantes, the most famous scoffer at knights. Indifferent to all the allegorical figures around him, he sits half-way up a high, fat column, while in front of him bronze figures of Don Quixote and Sancho Panza seem to be tempting him to some ridiculous expedition. But some of the ideals that Cervantes saw as laughable still survive in Spain. In Madrid's War Museum, an oil painting of Cervantes is surrounded by knightly suits of armour, swords, lances and heraldic flags. The novelty shops have metal souvenirs of Don Quixote and Sancho Panza which are surrounded by souvenirs of earnest knights in armour, and hundreds of knightly swords, from exact replicas to souvenir paper knives.

In the late 1970s, London's Imperial War Museum devoted a special gallery – about as big as the gallery given to trench warfare in the First World War – to the glorifying of one man by displaying his noble garments and his knightly baubles. This display of the garments and honours of a man who had never commanded a military unit nor fought in a war took up one of the seven galleries of the main floor of the museum; the other six galleries were the museum's allotment of space to the world's two largest wars. The man was the Duke of Gloucester, Queen Elizabeth's uncle, a person of great personal insignificance. Under the general title 'Soldier Royal', the museum paid homage to the life and service of 'Field Marshal His Royal Highness the Prince Henry William Frederick Albert, Duke of Gloucester, Earl of Ulster, Baron Culloden'. It displayed his genealogy, his armorial bearings, and his relationship to most of the other royal families of Europe. It then praised him by staging a show of all 14 of the military uniforms he had been allowed to wear as a result of his birth, ending with two uniforms of a field marshal – one for the temperate zone, and one a tropical uniform. Also displayed were the insignia of the 27 Orders presented to him by his relatives in Britain and Europe, and in other countries he had visited on state business. The display included, in gothic lettering, a quotation from Chaucer: 'He was a verray, parfit, gentil knyght.'

The victories of the conservatives

As democratic demands grew, the old order tamed them – so far as it could – by maintaining some of the symbolic language of the hereditary principle, or, more generally, of 'tradition'. In Britain, Europe's greatest living museum of the hereditary principle, this conjuring still goes on. An example is the complex of images of the British parliament. At its least, the British parliament is 'Big Ben', the Spassky chimes of London, the performing clock which is one of the most widely accepted symbols of a British nation, and was a rallying symbol during the Second World War. Its success as a symbol comes from the broadness and ambiguities of what it is seen to stand for. To traditionalists, it is part of the royal palace of Westminster, a prime symbol of Britain's regal and aristocratic past; to a chauvinist, the very height and strength of the Victorian gothic clock-tower and its sombre bells can be reminiscent of British greatness; to followers of the cults of parliament, it stands for 'the Westminster system', a symbol of what they think of as British pre-eminence in 'parliamentary government'; to democrats, it can seem a symbol of British democracy; to populists, it can symbolise the British people. But to tourists inspecting the Houses of Parliament, what can dominate the tour is not that these buildings are a parliament house, but that they are a palace. The actual chamber of the House of Commons may turn out to be one of the less impressive parts of a tour in which the main sights are a medieval hall, a gothic chapel, the aristocratic splendours of the chamber of the House of Lords with its royal throne and suite of royal rooms, the royal staircase by which the monarch enters the palace, the royal robing room, the royal gallery and the princes' chamber where the monarch meets the leading nobility before entering the House of Lords to sit on what can appear to be the throne of England. At the tourists' sales desk at the end of the tour, the books most featured are not on parliamentary democracy, but on Queen Elizabeth and Big Ben.

Seeking an ideology designed to mobilise the masses in an industrial age, many conservatives chose to use some of the new political languages. Napoleon III in particular was adept at speaking some of the languages of democracy: he discovered mass voting could be a profoundly conservative device and became a master at holding plebiscites ('Other French governments have ruled with the support of perhaps one million of the educated masses: I have called in the other twenty-nine million'.) Bismarck was one of Europe's great pioneers of state welfare. He gave the German regime extra authority by introducing social welfare schemes, and part of his success came from a talent for making accommodations with liberals. Throughout Europe, from time to time, the old authorities would rejuvenate themselves with a reform programme. With the emancipation of the serfs in 1862, even a Russian tsar, Alexander II, could shine, for a season, as a light of progress in the modern world.

Where it was possible, the easiest means to refurbish the authority of the old rulers was to take over the progressive, secular faiths of nationalism and provide a conservative version of it – most effectively, by turning it into imperialism. Nationalism became the last refuge of the aristocrats. This happened even in France, where nationalism had been one of the doctrines of revolution. In the second half of the nineteenth century, the nobility began to reoccupy the French army, with the blessing of the church: the right, if it was to appropriate nationalism, needed strong, simple symbols. The Left had Marianne, the revolutionary personification of French liberty. The Right claimed Joan of Arc. After their success, statues went up in the places of her birth, her victories and her martyrdom; they were also erected in many other French towns and even villages – becoming almost as ubiquitous as the local monuments that were later to commemorate the dead of the First World War. Most of them were of the right; some were of the left. The memorials to Joan are part of the tourist experience in France and, furthermore, are relics of a battle for national definition. In the Second World War, both the Gaullists and the collaborators claimed Joan for their side.

Joan had been a national symbol of some kind since at least the sixteenth century when her birthplace, Domrémy, became what we would now think of as a tourist attraction. Napoleon, too, had used her as a propaganda device – though at that stage she was not specifically the property of the right. When the right did claim her, she was transformed from the child of nature the romantics preferred, or the daughter of the people the democrats imagined, or the simple female knight of the military imagination. She became, instead, a catholic, and, after a campaign backed by conservative Catholics, a saint. In the struggle for symbolic command of the Panthéon, the right won all the victories in the depiction of Joan. In murals celebrated in history textbooks, she is presented as the devout peasant girl of Domrémy, who hears divine voices as she tends her sheep, and accepts her sword from God. Then she is the warrior-maiden, the true and perfect female knight – dressed in armour, her sword raised, she storms the ramparts of Orléans. As kingmaker, she is knight in shining armour, sword ready to defend the faith, eyes to heaven as Charles VII is crowned; divine approval is suggested by the strong rays of sunlight which shine providentially through the glass of Rheims cathedral and strike the crown. At Rouen, bound to the stake as neatly as a parcel, she is no longer heretic but saint; as the soldiers pile up the firewood, she seeks hungrily for the cross.

But the right does not always achieve this monopoly or this complete synthesis of piety and patriotism. In the Place des Pyramides, Paris, in a memorial that is an object of an annual pilgrimage, Joan is presented as a gilded youth, with gilded armour, on gilded horse and with a gilded face. The peasant girl has gone. This is a Joan for the rich. At Compiègne, the scene of her capture and one of the important sites of her cult, a statue erected in the town square in 1895 portrays her as all peasant maid – big-breasted and heavy-legged, she stands with her standard held high, her sword on her hip, and her strongly armoured thigh thrust out. But on the other side of the river ('on the exact place of her capture') she is not of the right at all; she is a Joan of the resistance – her face is remote, selfless; feminine physical attributes are irrelevant. At Domrémy, in one statue, she is still a secular patriot, the nation's defender, with the spirit of France inspiring her. But a rival statue shows her as servant of God, a simple girl kneeling before three catholic saints. The piety of her home life is such a feature of the Domrémy presentation of Joan that part of the legend becomes the story of her obedience to her mother. Perhaps the most devout of all the Joan statues is the memorial put up in Domrémy in 1961. It is not to Joan, but to her mother. It is dedicated 'à la gloire des mamans'.

Nationalism is in itself a neutral instrument. It can mean anything.

Part four

Industrialised Europe

7. Industrialism: The greatest revolution

The way we live now

In the museums of revolution in major Communist cities, industrial investment can seem the principal purpose for having a proletarian revolution. After the legitimacy of a country's revolution is established in rooms of photographs, flags, rubber stamps, documents and other relics, the stress is on plans for industrialisation. In the Moscow museum, the climax of the civil war victory is marked by a great painting of Lenin standing in front of a map of the Soviet electrification project. The Prague museum has a tape-recording of the opening of the first blast furnace of the Klement Gottwald Iron Works. In Bucharest, a large, beautifully crafted representation, coloured and illuminated, of Romania, shows the main industrial plants as if they were jewels. In all these museums, successive five-year plans have become principal demonstrations of faith.

When representatives of capitalist and Communist societies meet across a conference table, they are in a situation familiar to both – they are in committee. They both live in cities where the office block and the factory, the sports stadium and the assembly line, the clock and the public transport queue are dominant contemporary symbols; for both, the spirit of industrialism is in the care of great bureaucracies, with the rules made by members of the 'deciding class'. One way to distinguish between the two types of society is to compare not their forms of ownership, but their degrees of bureaucratisation and their styles of bureaucratic control. To both sides, the *prie-dieu* is the desk, the Mass is the committee meeting, and the cathedral is the office block.

Industrialism – which sees society as a factory and humanity as the means of economic production – has now taken Christianity's place in providing the official meaning of life in Europe. It does so in both capitalist and Communist countries which organise society so that capital can be centrally accumulated and allocated and humans can be organised into a workforce. In both countries, progress is seen as the great justifier of events, and 'the economic' predominates as an explanation of human conduct and as the basis of social programmes. It is not God's intervention but economic growth which will provide protection from disaster and distress. The people in these new societies know how to read the instructions and follow the rules and have learned how to adapt to change. It is commonly believed that material reward is justly related to the work people do, and that 'work' itself (which usually means only paid labour) provides one of the central meanings of life: neatness, punctuality and obedience are prized, and people learn the disciplines of the mass logistical movements that take them to and from their employment.

The tourism of industrialism

Where is the tourism of industrialism? At first glance the answer may seem obvious: it lies in visits to plants, tours of old industrial sites, visits to technology museums and science museums. Yet these can be ways of avoiding what is most significant in an industrial system. For instance, among the glimpses of the past now offered to tourists in Britain are industrial archaeology trails – some run as packaged tours, some only for people with a stout pair of shoes and an Ordnance Survey map. The Wales Tourist Board has produced a booklet which suggests 15 tours (including the *How Green Was My Valley* coalfields tour), and describes several hundred 'industrial archaeological' sites. Tourists can go on train rides through the tunnels and chambers of old slate quarries; they can photograph winding houses and shaftheads in old copper, gold, silver and lead mines; they can picnic beside spoil heaps glamorised as 'lunar landscapes'. At Swansea, they can see Europe's first reinforced-concrete building, and, at Penydarren, patches of the tramroad where, in 1804, Richard Trevithick drove the first steam locomotive. They can buy stone-ground wholemeal flour from old water-powered corn mills; at old steam-powered woollen mills, they can buy fine quality Welsh weaves. They can inspect towering stone railway viaducts and iron bridges, go for canal trips, or walk along towpaths through nature reserves. They can photograph ruins of engine houses and blast furnaces of what, for a season, were some of the world's largest ironworks. At Nantyglo, there are views from a bridleway of the fortified round houses built by two ironmasters as protection against workers' uprisings.

These archaeology trails tame the industrial revolution by reducing its relics to quaintness. An old industrial site comes to have the charm of a picturesque quarter in an old town, or the 'authenticity' of a famous old village. Similarly, tourist interest in seeking monuments to past industrialism can become a simple nostalgia for the 'sincerity' of nineteenth-century industrial architecture.

In cities this nostalgia looks away from the revival architecture of proclamatory buildings to the engineers' glass-and-iron structures which covered railway platforms. In London, the glass and iron of the Palm House in Kew Gardens remains, and some tourists go to Kew not to see the plants, but to admire the functionalism of this historic building: it can mean more than the revival styles of the Bank of England or the Houses of Parliament. In its use of simple materials, it is as sincere and authentic as a peasant's cottage in an open-air museum. A similar interest can take tourists to nineteenth-century factories and dockyard warehouses; although the engineers who put them up may have added modest decoration with brick pilasters, or cast-iron classical columns, simplicity and practicality give these buildings a modern 'honesty', a status as precursors of functionalism. It is one of the paradoxes of tourism that monuments to the most disorderly process in history – the industrial revolution – should be sought in buildings such as these. What is presented is an industrial revolution without the revolution.

In Sweden, an early centre of industrialisation has been turned into a tourist resort. Osterbybruk ('bruk' means 'ironworks estate'), a small industrial town of 3,000 or so people north of Uppsala, now has its own Tourist Information Bureau. It suggests tourist walks that take in reminders of romantic Old Osterbybruk, when the ironmaster in the elegant mansion in its private park controlled his forests, mines, smelters and forges, and the workers lived in small, low, white, plastered cottages with barns behind where the women kept a few animals. Tourists now swim in dams constructed in the seventeenth century to provide water-power to work the hammer mills; they inspect the two streets where the historic cottages that remain have been converted into modern two-storey dwelling units and the barns picturesquely restored; they line up to see an old hammer shop, built at the beginning of the nineteenth century and now restored to its former condition, when it was worked partly by child labour, 24 hours a day. From the manor house, a bust of the last ironmaster, presented as a Roman senator with toga enlivened by a Swedish Order, looks out across a well-kept garden. The old ways of Osterbybruk, going back several hundred years, were ended in 1902, when the Osterby Works pioneered high-speed steel production. But now the emphasis is on elegance. In the ironmaster's house seminar rooms have been installed and the building converted into a conference centre. In paint work and carpentry the pre-industrial past has been restored.

Tourist programmes can pay special honour to a 'tower', or some other construction of strange shape, preferably with a revolving restaurant at its top. This is really honouring the idea of industrialism as a safe and amusing toy, like the museum exhibits in which children are encouraged to push the buttons. In Communist countries, visits to factory plants are one of the necessary rituals of respect the 'delegations' must pay to their hosts. This is mere homage to machines and their products: one learns nothing of the social processes of the factory or of the effects the factory has on people's lives. There can be similar factory tours on the tourist programmes in some of the capitalist cities, but again there is a turning away from the normality of industrialism. Usually the most popular tours are not to factories with high technology, but to a brewery, or to an old workshop where people are pursuing an ancient craft.

Visits to technology museums, like visits to other kinds of museum, can be tributes to the tyranny of authenticity: one can say, 'Here is an *authentic* eighteenth-century English flying shuttle,' as one says, 'Here is an *authentic* eighteenth-century Dutch genre painting.' What the museum has to 'say' may depend on the chance factor of what its curators have collected in the way of authentic machines.

And in emphasising one machine relic rather than another, the museum can imply one historical interpretation rather than the other. Thus, the Science Museum, London, favours steam engines. When tourists move from the vestibule into the museum's East Hall, they are at once among the 'atmospheric machines' that, set in stone, with heavy beams like huge rocking toys, were developed early in the eighteenth century to pump water out of mines. Then come the rotative steam engines, their metal gleaming, their pistons and engines shining, their wheels large and leisurely, and all of them authentic. These are presented almost as if they were the prime movers of the industrial revolution itself, as well as of the early cotton factories where they replaced water-power. The early spinning and weaving machines are put in a side gallery on the first floor: yet the most famous of the early 'mechanical tools' – Hargreaves's Spinning Jenny (shown in the museum in replica) and Arkwright's spinning and carding machines – might be taken as more apt symbols of the industrial revolution because these machines can be seen as creating the beginnings of the industrial working class, the members of which, when their own manual means of production were rendered worthless, were forced to use the 'mechanical tools' of the new capitalists.

Like claims for 'beginning' the renaissance, claims for 'beginning' the industrial revolution can become prestige matters, 'proved' by a display of authentic objects. Birmingham in the Midlands of England provides an example. It was to become, in Tocqueville's words, 'an immense workshop, a huge forge. One hears nothing but the sounds of hammers and the whistle of steam from escaping boilers.' But all this hammering and whistling came mainly from 'small masters' who were making much the same kind of consumer goods that had been made for many years before – only now there were more of them. This does not stop the Birmingham Museum of Science and Industry, laid out in an old factory near a canal, celebrating Birmingham as birthplace of the industrial revolution. Similarly, Coalbrookdale claims honour as 'the crucible of the industrial revolution' because there, at the beginning of the eighteenth century, the ironmaster Abraham Darby discovered how to smelt iron ore with coke, opening the way for cheap cast iron, although making cheap cast iron was not the industrial revolution.

Presenting the early stages of the industrial revolution as 'scientific' can be another way of avoiding the event's realities *as a revolution*. In a glass case in Munich's Deutsches Museum, on one side of a room in the physics section, are models of medieval and renaissance perpetual-motion machines, complex, gracefully finished elaborations of the impossible. On the other side, in an alcove, is a reconstruction of one of Galileo's workrooms. With a crucifix behind it, the desk of the master stands on a small dais on a floor of black and white tiles; the main part of the room, beside the wooden-shuttered, lead-paned windows, houses tools similar to those used in his careful observations – a telescope, a sphere, a wooden bucket on a pole, a long plane and a set of scales, symbolic of the scientific passion for measurement. Similarly, the museum's chemistry section has a reconstruction of an alchemist's laboratory, with beautifully blown, green-glass retorts, copper pots, bellows, kettles and scales. In the alcove next to it, there is a reconstruction of the laboratory of Lavoisier, founder of modern chemistry. But the science and technology that went into the industrial revolution's inception were slight. These reconstructed scenes do not commemorate industrialism. They commemorate the beginnings of science and the secularising of much of European society.

It was not science that created industrialism, even if it was part of the 'illumination' that in the eighteenth century enlightened sections of the 'deciding classes'. Rather, it was the successes of industrialism that enormously increased faith in science. Subsequently, industrialism employed science for its purposes. It is this second stage of the industrial revolution that is fittingly celebrated in the Deutsches Museum, in the originals of the working apparatus used by German scientists at the time Germany began to take over from Britain as Europe's most innovative industrial society. It is equally fittingly celebrated in Stockholm's National Museum of Science and Technology, where turbine dynamos and electrical blast furnaces are exhibited with as much connoisseurship as would be lavished on a display of ancient crafts.

In looking for symbols of the industrial revolution, a belief in 'genius' can be as misleading as a belief in science. James Watt is one of the principal hero–geniuses of the London Science Museum. Around the corner from the hall dominated by early steam engines, James Watt's workshop – the *very* workshop in which the genius worked – is preserved with its 6,000 bits and pieces just as it was when the genius died; the museum's kiosk sells postcards celebrating the genius's inventions, as if they were Old Masters. Yet in looking for symbols of industrialism's dawn, one can move beyond individual genius or old machines and find, in museum printrooms, drawings of early factory floors with their logical layout.

What was of overriding importance was not machines, but the part they played in a social invention – the factory system. This introduced the idea of planning an arrangement of humans and machines so that material would go in one end raw, and come out the other end processed and 'finished'; soon, whole nations would be seen as factories. By concentrating on machines alone, the museums ignore social origin and content; it is as if machines, and not capitalists, were in charge. Reverence is encouraged towards machines for their own sake – as if all machines are necessarily good, and their results progressive: human progress can seem to depend on machine begetting machine, without human agency.

Yet an *accurate* monument of the beginning of the industrial revolution would include more than James Watt in its statuary group. It would represent the kinds of people created by Britain's transition to a profit-oriented society, with agricultural production ruthlessly modernised by expropriation: there would be depictions of the masters of the early cotton mills – and of the Indian manufacturers whose enterprises were ruined by a monopoly that gave Britain assured markets, as well as of the slaves who were bought in Africa and sold in America as part of the trade that accumulated cash in the great slave-trading centres such as Liverpool. In addition to the story of capital accumulation, there would be the story of that general ordering of human beings in the eighteenth century, of bringing them under rational control, that made the factory system possible. As it is, the industrial museums present industrialism without the story of its losers and winners.

The tourism of the modern

Symbols of industrialism are all around us, defining the modern world. The museum itself is one of these symbols, with its encyclopedic vision, its aims of edification, its categorisations, and its precise concentration on *the object* (as the museum experts describe what the tourist calls 'the exhibit'). Concentration on the object is part of the view of the world that produced the modern doctrines of materialism. There is no speculative nonsense about the object. It is made of *matter*. Concentration on the object is part of the world of 'evidence' and 'proof'. There is no denying the truth of the object. It is there for all to see and its authenticity is guaranteed by experts. A visit to a museum is a reaffirmation of the values of the industrial world, values reflected in the organised tour with its imposed order, its planned movement of bodies, its concern with time-tabling. What matters on a tour is not what one sees, but that one should see what is on the programme, at the time stated in the itinerary.

The tourism of 'the modern' is a reminder of the disturbances of earlier ideas of reality that came with industrialisation. The industrial revolution had been in process for almost 100 years before architects began attempting to proclaim what might be thought of as the 'modern' in prestige buildings. And once they turned away from revivals to formulate a 'modern' style, the newspapers and 'public opinion' could react with little more than a sense of scandal. Each act of modernity created a 'sensation'.

Reminders of these 'sensations' of modernity are now on the tourist itinerary. In Paris, there is the Eiffel Tower, the largest early expression of the modern: 300 metres of steel and air, 12,000 metal pieces. Put up in 1889 by a French engineer in that area where the spirit of reason was celebrated during the revolution's most famous festivals, it now provides the model for one of the world's most recognisable souvenirs. In each city of Europe, there is usually at least one building, or street – or perhaps a whole suburb – which is seen as some particularly remarkable expression of the modern, and attacked or praised for it. As years go on, it becomes less noticed. In Vienna, the Hoch Haus – straight up-and-down, early-twentieth-century lumps of grey – forms irregularly patterned courtyards as images of a new rationality and practicality. Copenhagen has the whimsy of Grundtvig Church, done up to look like a pipe organ. Frankfurt has the undulations of concrete and glass of the IG-Hochhaus, an office building in 1920s baroque. Oslo Town Hall's 31 pieces of sculpture and vast murals express a renaissance exuberance in the forms of contemporary advertising techniques. In Moscow, the plain cubes of faith of the Lenin Mausoleum gave Soviet architecture a simplicity it was soon to lose.

For some tourists, there is now nostalgia for the early styles of 'the modern' – those long-delayed attempts of designers to make buildings and objects in a style suited to an industrial age. Beginning with art nouveau, it expressed itself as the *style moderne* in Paris, the *Jugendstil* in Berlin, the *stile Liberty* in Italy, the *Sezession* in Vienna, the *modernista* in Madrid. Whatever the name, each was based on a fundamental need to be different from the past, and therein lies the paradox of modernism: if to be different is the aim, then difference breeds difference, and nothing new lasts. The contradictions of 'revolutionary' modern societies throw taste into permanent revolution, while the past is preserved with increasing diversity; it is only when a 'modern' style sinks out of fashion and then is later rediscovered – as part of the past – that it becomes permanent.

Art nouveau had its run, and shops like Liberty's in London, which lived on it, can remain tourist attractions. But when the sense of design it had given back to the applied arts was mass produced and coarsened, art nouveau gave way to new decorative styles (retrospectively, art deco) with a delight in oxidised metal, plastics, vita glass and the use of a neo-Aztec style. The essence of the new styles was to be found in the luxury transatlantic liners, the public architecture of the Fascists, the League of Nations building in Geneva and the picture palaces of the 1930s. Visiting a surviving 1930s picture palace can be part of the tourist experience; like Moorish, Venetian or Swedish rococo, art deco is itself now a revival style.

Tourists unused to modern painting (and many who are used to it) can find a visit to a museum of modern art one of the most horrifying experiences of modernity. They can stand in the presence of the modern crisis in reality, presented in all its variety in chemical pigments and synthetic resins. In the old Musée d'Art Moderne in Paris, tourists were presented with contradictory creeds of reality in a one-way gallery, room by room, but in the Centre Georges Pompidou this linear tyranny is gone. The centre's gallery follows open forms – there are 'streets' of paintings to move through as one chooses, and 'houses' of paintings with particular themes. In many paintings, reality is no longer framed; in some, 'real objects' are part of the painting. Some exhibits are not paintings at all, but displays to walk into. And this is in a building whose viscera – conduits for air, for electricity, for people and objects – hang out over the Rue Beauborg, demonstrating the building's authenticitiy as honest, 'functional' architecture, holding no secrets. The guide book (called not 'guide book', an authoritarian term, but 'key') begins with a recognition of failure: 'The public's first real look at the Centre is, paradoxically, turned outwards to the city and for some even towards the past. Glorified and challenged once again, the seducing beauty of the past and its radiance becomes a source for comparing, for incomprehending [sic] and, perhaps, for rejecting the present.' This great European centre of modernism can be a way to seek 'the past'.

The great monuments to industrialism are to be found not in the machines and their products, but in new social orders. In this sense, there is a tourism of social class – a tourism of the bourgeois social order in the capitalist countries and, in the Communist countries, the tourism of monuments to the belief that the working class is the prime mover of human liberation.

8. The capitalists

Capitalism of the past

The most complete 'monuments' to pre-modern capitalists are the late-medieval commercial cities of Flanders, the cradle of modern capitalist civilisation in northern Europe. This was the first urbanised area, with a sophisticated pattern of towns linked by markets and smaller settlements. The Flanders cloth trade – highly organised by a few rich men who imported raw materials, employed an urban proletariat, owned the facilities and arranged exports – was perhaps the world's first large-scale system of capitalist production. Flanders had even had its own 'bourgeois revolution' (capitalist owners against feudal princes) and a form of class conflict in which the propertyless could be seen as agents of history: 'the people of God', chosen by destiny to fight a 'war against the rich and the priests'. For a small season in the fourteenth century it was a republic, a curtain-raiser to the successsful Dutch Republic that, 200 years later, was to be so significant in the development of modern Europe. Flanders was the initiating centre in the north for new art forms, developing a modern 'realism' in painting, a great civic architecture and a new music. And it was the first capitalist society to go through the crises of obsolescence.

It was industrial obsolescence that preserved Brugge as the best example of these early capitalist cities. After the decline of its cloth trade, Brugge became something of a ghost town. Most of its old buildings were left alone: there was nothing to be done with them. As a result, it is one of the most marketable concepts in the Belgian tourist trade. The suggestion that it is purely 'medieval' is tempered by the reality that even some of the most famous buildings came later and that many of the 'medieval' buildings are in fact modern. Luck and an eye for unity, however, have kept things matching. The two great squares are dominated by huge halls of commercial and civic power; around them spread cobbled courtyards and narrow, winding lanes; 50 small bridges cross the tree-fringed canals, and, along the routes of recommended walks that give vista after vista in patterns of stone and water, superb small art collections are dispersed like hidden boxes of jewels. In the tourist season, souvenir shops and eating places are crowded, the motor traffic is jammed and, on canal rides, the guides' commentary blares out in six languages. Nonetheless, the turning of Brugge into a monument to the 'medieval' and to 'art' conceals its earlier nature. As a proto-capitalist society, Brugge was *anti*-medieval. But there would be no tourist potential in projecting it as a museum to 'the world's first large-scale system of capitalist production' because that would lack what we are taught to see as the 'romance' of travel.

Monuments of the bourgeoisie

The great bourgeois cities like Manchester, Düsseldorf and Lille which developed in the unparalleled building booms of the second half of the nineteenth century were no longer dominated by palaces, cathedrals and churches. Rather, public buildings of civic or cultural virtue (museums, universities, libraries, colleges, theatres, operas, concert halls, town halls, post offices, gaols) and, above all, department stores, offices and other new institutions of capitalism assumed primacy. Cities became places for factories and business offices. The new temples were banks. Some of the most sumptuous designs went into building stock exchanges. Ritzy hotels were the new palaces; department stores, the new market squares; railway stations, the new gateways of the city.

European nineteenth-century cities are monuments to the new rich. Most of central London now tempts the onlooker with nostalgia for the solid Victorian and Edwardian days of *le confort anglais*, attracting from continental Europe both admiration and envy. Banks and business houses in 'the City' and mansions and town houses in 'the West End' are reminders of the reassurances of material wealth; these are pragmatic dreams in bricks and stucco that only money could buy. For spiritual assurance, the tourist can survey the most grandiloquent vista in London, the Mall (put into its present form in 1911), looking, through the triple gateway of Admiralty Arch (1910), to Trafalgar Square (1841) where four colossal British lions (1868) guard the memory of a great battle, and, the other way, to the Queen Victoria Memorial (1911), with its affirmations in marble sculpture groups of bourgeois virtues. However, it is in the big department stores and in the famous specialty shops that many tourists find most meaning.

A different aspect of the bourgeois triumph can be found on a walk through the complex of museums, educational buildings and halls in London's South Kensington. All were built during the Victorian heyday and express its most generous face – its belief (assisted by the enlightened gentry) in progress, in the arts and sciences, and in education and emancipation. The five hectares of the Victoria and Albert Museum's courts and galleries provide one of the world's largest displays of fine and applied arts behind a renaissance-style façade. Across Exhibition Road from the Victoria and Albert the terracotta romanesque Natural History Museum, ostentatiously ornamented, provides four acres of halls, bays and galleries displaying stuffed animals, fossilised vegetables and categorised minerals. Nearby are the Geological Museum, the Science Museum and the Science Museum Library. On either side of Imperial Institute Road are the buildings of the Imperial College of Science and Technology, dominated by the copper-domed Queen's Tower, a revival-renaissance campanile. Prince Consort Road has the Royal College of Music, and close by is the Royal Albert Hall, one of the world's largest concert halls, an immense oval amphitheatre under a glass dome and with a terracotta frieze displaying the Triumph of Art and Science. Along the road stands the Royal Geographical Society, and, opposite in the park, is the Albert Memorial where, under a gothic canopy, Victoria's Prince Consort – seemingly representing the finest aspirations of the bourgeois mind – sits in gilt bronze holding in his hands the catalogue of the Great Exhibition of 1851; Albert presides over 178 marble statues of artists, and 4 large statuary groups symbolising Agriculture, Manufacture, Commerce and Engineering.

These South Kensington buildings represent the voice of nineteenth-century capitalism at its most enlightened, buoyant with optimism and reason and a belief in improvement. Education, science, art and technology would bring light. Free enterprise would bring abundance to the world and this abundance facilitate eternal progress.

For the new capitalists of the great bourgeois age, the prime social unit – the family – was the very basis of property and is now celebrated in museums in the furniture styles of the bourgeois home. In their simpler forms – the Bledermeier style in its earlier moods, in particular – these can project to tourists nostalgic reassurances of solid comfort; then, however, a manic self-assertion takes over. Later in the century, one article of furniture with carving and gilt, and brass panels and inlays can contain as many representations as the façade of the museum in which it is now displayed. In the Victoria and Albert, a single mid-nineteenth-century French cabinet – seeking excellence in marquetry, gilt bronze and porcelain plaques – embraces to itself styles covering three centuries of French ornament. Museum displays of the great bourgeois age are littered with gold and silver objects, Sèvres china, stained glass; reconstructed rooms are thick with carpets, and walls are covered in carved panelling, decorated wallpapers or watered silk hangings. Dark polished woods – mahogany, black walnut, rosewood, ebony – bring the forests to join other reassurances that life should be a matter of assertion as well as of comfort.

One of the most bourgeois of all the tourist experiences (in both Communist and capitalist countries) is a visit to the museum–house of a genius. There is the emphasis on genius itself, and on its manifestation in material objects – the actual pen the genius used, the actual chair on which the genius sat – but to these are added the solid consolations of bourgeois domestic comfort. Whether in the Goethe House, Frankfurt, or the Ivan Vasov House, Sofia, the true interest is not the genius or the work, but possessions and furnishings. If, as with Rembrandt or Shakespeare, the genius left no possessions, a house the genius lived in will do. When the Belgians put up a statue to Rubens in 1840 and declared him their 'national painter' the Dutch replied by making Rembrandt 'the national painter' of the Netherlands and designated the 'Rembrandt House' a museum (Rembrandt had lived there until debts forced him to sell up). At Stratford-on-Avon, for the one-day tourist the emphasis can be not on Shakespeare as England's 'national poet', but on the half-timbered house as England's national domestic monument. The Shakespeare Birthplace is an introduction to the English oak experience; his mother's house, the farmhouse experience; his son-in-law's, the Jacobean furniture experience; his grand-daughter's, the formal garden experience. And the importance of the genius is given further proof in the selling of souvenirs. In Amsterdam, there is a brisk selling of Rembrandt souvenirs that encompasses even Rembrandt cakes. Near the Goethe House, Frankfurt, are the Goethe House Restaurant, the Goethe House Bookshop, the Goethe House Café and several Goethe House Souvenir Shops. In Stratford-on-Avon there are William Shakespeare tea towels, Tudor head-scarves, do-it-yourself cut-outs of the Shakespeare family houses, Shakespeare souvenir pens, key rings, sandwich trays and Wedgewood china sets, an Arden Shoe Shop, an Elizabethan Gift Shop and Anne Hathaway's Tea Rooms.

In Communist countries, misery produced by the actions of the new capitalists is an essential part of the museums of history and of revolution; among the capitalist countries, on the other hand, only the Federal Republic of Germany has standard museum displays of the miseries of the industrial revolution. The museums of other nations are likely to present the industrial revolution merely as a matter of new machines. However, such exhibitions as the labour movement provides in the capitalist countries – and there are not many of them – will have contemporary etchings and engravings. These depict gaunt faces – at best overcome by lassitude, at worst exhausted by despair – or maltreated women and children, explosions and maimings, towns clogged by filth from chimney stacks. An engraving of the Black Country near Wolverhampton shows furnaces spreading like an uncontrollable forest fire. Gustav Doré's English etchings present rows of workmen's cottages as variants of hell: in one, *Over London by Rail*, cottages with tiny, teeming backyards seem mere rubbish dropped into spaces left by the railway viaducts.

By hereditary right, the nobility had treated the lower classes arrogantly; the new capitalists also treated them arrogantly – from a belief in their own innate superiority. Masters deserved their positon because they were better people than workers, who were fundamentally contemptible. Like 'natives' in the colonies, they deserved their fate: the language they best understood was that of fear. Human history became a story of necessary progress based on the survival of the fittest: improvement in material production had produced a cult in which human betterment depended on material progress – and material progress depended on the perseverance, energy, moral character and individual willpower of successful businessmen: this approach is not commemorated in the technology museums.

Justifying bourgeois power

Capitalists could not justify their power as coming directly from birth or from God, although the patina of nobility and church, if they could associate themselves with it, could give them a vicarious glow. Nevertheless, social reality began to be redefined in a way to suit capitalism. It could seem natural that society was organised for production, that production was for private profit, and that private profit was for the good of all. The code of the capitalists became the new 'rules', the new 'common sense'.

A reminder of how the power of the capitalists was maintained could be found in the shiny doorknobs and whitewashed front steps of working-class houses in London. The idea of 'the home', reflected in the stretches of terraces in London, was not only the centre of the bourgeois world and the sustaining ambition for the petit bourgeois – it also became the ambition of the new white-collar workers, then of skilled workers, and of unskilled workers . . . until it became one of the principal spiritual cults of modern industrialised society, conveniently combining the ideas of family and of property and, with fear of unemployment, providing a crucial means of keeping people in line. For the mass of people, the interior expression of the importance of the home became the front parlour – spick and span, adorned with the best furniture, and meticulously left unused. The outward and visible signs of grace were the highly polished doorknob and the scrupulously white-washed front step. It was in such value-setting that the capitalists most exercised social influence. But there are no shiny doorknobs and white-washed front steps in the Victoria and Albert Museum.

Where are the monuments to free enterprise, like the old monuments to God or hereditary right, or the new ones to the nation or, in Communist countries, to the idealisation of 'the worker'?

There are not many of them, but opposite the Highland Crafts Centre, Edinburgh, is Canongate Kirk – and in the kirkyard, behind iron railings, a large gravestone set against a wall announces with theatrical flourishes of stone that suggest a billowing hope: 'Here are deposited the remains of Adam Smith, author of the *Theory of Moral Sentiments* and *Wealth of Nations*, etc. etc. etc.' Adam Smith's concept of 'the market' was to become the basic justification for capitalism – and a central metaphor of capitalists' liberalism. In fact, it could seem that if transactions (whether of business, or of politics, or of ideas) were left untrammeled, a natural order would prevail. However, Adam Smith's grave is not revered by capitalists as socialists cherish the grave of Karl Marx. Those who already know something about what they are looking for can go to Manchester for reminders of business *laissez faire*. Perhaps there they will see the statue of Richard Cobden, leader of the Anti-Corn Law League, the world's first great pressure group of businessmen: as the statue rises above the taxi rank in St Ann's Square, one might imagine that the arm stretches out in a gesture of reason, the reason of the 'Manchester School' (*Manchesterismus*, to the Germans) which promoted the idea that if things were left alone, a natural rationality would prevail. But Manchester is not a monument to *laissez faire*; it is a monument to its failure: along one side of St Ann's Square runs the Manchester Royal Exchange, whose vast trading floor – claimed to be the largest in Britain – was once a symbol of the marvellous bustle of business. It is now closed as a temple of free trade and has been converted for use by the state-subsidised Royal Exchange Theatre Company.

Perhaps, to the initiated, what remains of the exchanges of Europe might be seen as monuments to nineteenth-century businessmens' economic liberalism: the Paris Bourse, modelled on the Temple of Vespasian; the Bourse, Leningrad, one of the freest flights of neoclassical fancy and now a Naval Museum; the Stock Exchange, Budapest, decorated with imperial ornateness, and standing next to an equally ornate bank, has now become the Hungarian House of Technology in what has been renamed Liberty Square; the London Royal Exchange, with corinthian columns and steps from which the name of a new monarch is announced. To the tourist, though, they are more likely to be seen as monuments to nineteenth-century architectural revival.

'Free enterprise' must constantly devour its own monuments: all that is permanent about it may be the junkyard and the building site. Although the French Revolution made things easier for the later capitalists, it was not in itself a manifestation of emerging capitalism. Rather, it was a product of the enlightenment of lawyers, functionaries, small owners and minor nobles reacting against aristocratic stupidity and greed, which then found itself supported by both an old-style peasants' revolt and an old-style rising of the city poor. The real 'bourgeois revolution' is the continuing revolution of capitalist change. It is in that area its monuments are found.

Before the 'consumer society' economic progress demanded frugality among the workers. Then, in one of the many about-turns of capitalist societies, if offered a frivolous indulgence in which life would gain meaning by heeding the coaxing voices of advertisements, neon signs, hoardings, shop windows – the icons, slogans and mythic images of advertising, offering a 'competition' which differentiates products that are basically the same, thus casting up a more general shadow-play of freedom and choice.

Capitalist-liberal Europe

Just inside the entrance to the crypt in the Panthéon, Paris, two tombs face each other: one looks like the front of a house, in which, in the opening left by a slightly ajar door, a hand is poised in motion; the other tomb is partly obscured by a sage wearing a flowing robe. These are the tombs of Rousseau and Voltaire whose bodies the Constituent Assembly of France decided would sanctify this new Hall of Fame. Both men were seen as prophets of enlightenment, although neither would have been good liberal candidates for nineteenth-century capitalist-liberal parliaments. Voltaire's enlightenment was too aristocratic, Rousseau's too democratic. But it was because of their enlightenment that the capitalist-liberals were able to fashion a liberalism to suit themselves.

The new forces of the left that were developing in Europe were beginning to see liberalism as a humbug intended to add dignity to the rackets of the capitalists. Although it came from older sources, themselves related to earlier social and economic change, liberalism grew along with the new capitalism. Much of the emphasis on human rights, apart from property rights, however, has not been necessary to capitalism. Sometimes capitalists could be leading opponents of 'rights' (for example, the collective rights of workers). As capitalists became political conservatives, they could become in many ways anti-liberal and support the kinds of regimes that might have gaoled, tortured, or executed Voltaire and Rousseau. Hitler's Germany, Europe's most successful capitalist economy of the time, was Europe's most repressive regime. Nevertheless, with exceptions, European capitalist regimes have usually lived – if in some tension – with varying types of this liberalism, which checks their power, just as it sweetens it. The principal articulators of the 'critics' culture' may not criticise the fundamentals of capitalism. Still, the critics are likely to criticise anything else.

Communist regimes denounce liberalism as a fraud. Nonetheless, aspirations to a broad liberalism are likely to spring out even in their symbolic sculpture and idealised murals. In the belief that humankind was naturally innocent and waiting to be freed from social oppression so that it might flower, even Marx was, in this sense, a liberal, although unlike the others, he did not imagine that human personality would flower merely because liberal constitutions said it would. The naked heroes of Alexander Matveyev's sculpture group *The October Revolution*, could equally well be western European naked heroes celebrating the spirit of liberal-democratic freedom.

Some of the most visible official monuments in the cities of the west are monuments to nineteenth-century liberal aspiration. A classic example can be found in the Colonne du Congrès in Brussels, a gilded column which provides the most ambitious bronze Declaration of Rights in Europe. It was put up in the 1850s to commemorate the National Congress which, after the Belgian revolution of 1830, adopted a constitution professing that all Belgians were equal in the eyes of the law, their individual liberty was guaranteed, and their homes and property were inviolable. They were to enjoy freedom of worship, of speech, and of association; schooling was to be free, and the death penalty abolished. The Colonne du Congrès rises 47 metres, supported by bronze groups representing Freedom of the Press, Freedom of Association, Freedom of Education and Freedom of Religion. For good measure, in the manner of cautious liberals, the column honours royalty at its top, with a statue of Belgium's first king; at its base, it honours patriotism, with the graves of two 'unknown warriors'. This was the liberalism of constitutional guarantees, celebrated everywhere except in England, where the 'pragmatic' mysticism of a belief in an unwritten constitution was preferred.

In the Central Museum of the Risorgimento, inside Rome's Victor Emmanuel Monument, in the room that records the events of 1846–9 with helmets, swords, proclamations and pennants, there is a sudden flourish of constitutions: Naples, Florence, Turin and Rome were all granted constitutions in the one month in 1848 – although they were all later withdrawn. Apart from elements of national liberation, the object of each of the 1848 revolts in Europe was to obtain from a monarch a document which would confer rights and liberties on citizens. The celebration of constitutions even became part of the topography of capital cities, in the form of a 'Constitution Square'. Some of these still have meaning. Warsaw's Plac Konstytucji celebrates a constitution and, since 1981, its signing has been restored as a national holiday. The principal square in Oslo is named after a liberal constitution the Norwegian elites gave themselves on 17 May 1814, and this still has symbolic meaning. But while Constitution Square in Athens may mean something to contemporary Greeks (although that is doubtful, since the Greeks have had so many constitutions), to tourists, it can be best known as the place where the coach tours start. It is difficult to know what meaning continues to be given to Luxembourg's Constitution Square: it is now a parking lot.

The nineteenth-century cult of constitutions also produced veneration of ancient documents. The British enshrined the four copies of their Magna Carta of 1215; the Flemish claimed the van Kortenberg charter of 1312, heavy with seals, as Europe's earliest form of a constitution. Now, the Swedes claim to have had a constitution since the fourteenth century; the Swiss national day celebrates the signing of the 'Bundesbrief', a thirteenth- or fourteenth-century document, seen as the first Swiss Federal Charter, a copy of which was discovered by a scholar who used it as part of a university dissertation. A copy of the First Norwegian constitution is in a glass case in the History Chamber of the Norwegian Storting. The constitution of Denmark is enshrined in a silver and glass reliquary resting on a marble stand in a lobby of the Folketing, the Danish parliament; behind it, in a glass case, also presented with great dignity, are three earlier constitutions, the first of which is celebrated annually on Constitution Day, the Danish national day.

Monuments to liberal constitutions are agenda items for school tours, and adult citizens of a particular nation might feel piety towards those that retain meaning. Foreign tourists are likely to see monuments to liberation as low in spectacle value – in effect, not monuments to liberty, but to discarded styles in statuary. What can have more meaning are the graffiti of contemporary protest movements. And the celebrations of constitutionalism that attract tourists are less likely to be bronze allegorical figures of freedom than medieval charters under glass – of interest not because they were liberal (they were not), but because they are old, and *authentic*.

Among the red and gold of the main debating chamber of Oslo's Storting, one painting makes the most famous political statement in Norway. Behind the rostrum, beneath the painted ceiling and guarded by the Norwegian lion with his battle axe, it shows the founding fathers (elected by the well-to-do at assemblies of the Lutheran church throughout Norway) meeting in the largest room in Eidsvoll Hall, a substantial country house 40 kilometres from Oslo. Norway was about to be taken from Denmark and given by Napoleon's victors to Sweden: in little more than a fortnight these solid citizens wrote, and successfully claimed for themselves, a modern liberal constitution. Eidsvoll Hall has become a museum, with the assembly room furnished as it was in 1814 and the first Norwegian parliamentary chamber, which was in Oslo, has been reconstructed in the Folk Museum. It is a simple school room where the president of the chamber presided like a teacher, at a green-covered desk, and, like students, the members of parliament sat in a semi-circle around him. The very modesty of this room where parliament met for 40 years makes an heroic statement of middle-class ordinariness.

The first concern of liberals in Oslo, and throughout Europe, was to establish the main principle of the new parliamentarianism: that the lower house, not the monarch, should choose and control the government. This meant the monarchies would become 'constitutional' and the liberals would control parliament. These changes were fought for in parliamentary crises, and in elections full of political passion.

For sheer stamina and patience in seeking constitutional change, the Danes established the record. The enshrined constitutions in the Danish Folketing celebrate 71 years of struggle. Beside the first (1849) constitution, sits the second (1866) – which took away what 1849 had given. In 1866 the king put the upper house entirely into the hands of rich landowners to entrench an upper-class government he believed would suit the dangerous times following imperial Denmark's defeat by Prussia. It took 35 years of peaceful attrition by a 'United Left' of the parliamentary parties and by intellectual groups outside parliament to undo this arrangement. From 1876 the 'United Right' lost election after election; its numbers in the Folketing sank to 16 seats in a house of 102 members. Nevertheless seeing themselves as the natural ruling class, and supported by the king, they remained in government. It was not until 1901, when they won only 8 seats out of 102, that they gave in. By then it seemed accepted that parliament, not the king, was master of governments. When a king tried again in 1920 to take over, demonstrations forced him to give in. This time there was also some use of the language of revolution.

The Danish Folketing meets in part of what is officially still a royal palace. They are like a victorious, if courteous, occupying force: only the 'royal state apartments' are left to the monarch – and their main functions are for tourists to view, and politicians to use for state receptions. On the opening day of a Folketing session, the monarch takes no part in the proceedings, apart from sitting in a box and watching what happens.

Parliamentary Europe

The liberals of the nineteenth century were participating in the revival of a unique European political form – the representative assembly – and turning it to new purposes. A.R. Myers says in his

Parliaments and Estates in Europe to 1789 that in the late medieval period it became a unique characteristic of western European nations to have representative assemblies. Beginning in the thirteenth and fourteenth centuries, strongest in the fourteenth and fifteenth, nearly all of them were surviving – although weakened by absolutism – on the eve of the liberal revolutions. As well as the British parliament (falsely seen by the British as the 'mother of parliaments'), representative assemblies – such as the Sejm (Poland), the Rigsdag (Denmark), the Bundestag (Switzerland), the Staten-Generall (the Netherlands), the Parliamento (Italy), the Cortes (Spain), the Sobor (Romania), the Orszagguüles (Hungary) and the Landtag (individual German lands) – were important in granting tax money to the monarch and in approving laws.

The liberal ideal was that government should seem to be conducted not by monarch nor by the nobility, but by representative assemblies devoted to liberal ideas. In some countries, the medieval names of these assemblies were directly revived; in others, French revolutionary or republican Roman names were taken over. It now became important for appropriate buildings to be provided. In some cities, as in Paris and Rome, old palaces were converted; in others, as in London, new palaces were built. In the period of monarchy it had been the monarch's court which had been presented as the centre of legitimacy and government action; now the liberals wanted the new parliament houses to be presented as the centres not only of law-making, but of central authority. Even where the monarch's court was still presented as the centre of authority as in the Habsburg empire, grand new parliament buildings went up, to add extra legitimacy to the court. Budapest got its baroque-gothic palace (where the representatives of the Patriotic People's Front now meet in a national assembly chamber in which one of the two main murals celebrates the coronation of the emperor in 1867); and in Vienna a parliament house was built which now provides the most ridiculous of all the dissonances between the old imperial grandeur and modern realities. Stretching along an enormous frontage, it demonstrates every form of decoration known to the nineteenth-century classical revival, from the Parthenon in its middle, to Pallas Athena where gilded helmet rises high above the monumental fountain at its front; probably more winged victories than adorn any other building in

Europe appear to be driving their chariots all over its roofs.

In some countries, a parliament house is a prime national symbol, but of no tourist interest. In some other countries, a parliament house gets on the itineraries of the coach tours for foreigners, as well as nationals. Normally, though, only some form of architectural grandeur comparable to London or Vienna will attract an independent foreign tourist.

Only the Swiss maintained an official scepticism about the political value of a representative assembly. Right across one wall in the Council of States of their Parlamentsgebäude is a mural which provides a reminder of how the Swiss see a basic part of their democracy – its regional and direct participatory sides – as depending upon the people themselves. The mural, with 180 characters all drawn from life, is of a *Landsgemeinde*, a direct assembly of peasant citizens handling their own affairs. The whole Swiss Parlementsgebäude is a symbol both of a limited political compact in the midst of cultural diversity and of the more participatory aspects of democracy. To the tourist, many aspects of it may seem merely provincial.

The Communist countries also provide the ceremonies of representative assemblies. In Moscow, the Supreme Soviet meets in the modern white-marble building of the Soviet Palace of Congresses, the Kremlin, in front of a fire curtain decorated with a vast icon of Lenin set against a red flag and surrounded by the rays of the rising sun. The ceremony doesn't take long: for most of the time, the Soviet Palace of Congresses is used for other conferences or for opera and ballet performances. Similarly, the Hall of the Palace of the Socialist Republic of Romania, an annexe to the old royal palace where the Grand National Assembly meets, is also used for other conferences, and for concerts and theatre. In Prague, the Federal Assembly meets in a grandiose reconstructed building in Wenceslas Square. Four other Socialist republics have retained parliament buildings of previous regimes: the Hungarian National Assembly still meets in a parliament built in the imperial days; the Polish Sejm meets in a neoclassical chamber built in the 1920s; the Bulgarian National Assembly meets in a parliament building constructed after independence was gained from the Turks; the Yugoslav Federal Assembly meets in the high-domed neo-baroque palace begun for the Serbian parliament and completed after the First World War. In Berlin, the People's Chamber of the German Democratic Republic meets in the Assembly Hall of the marble-and-glass Palace of the Republic; elsewhere in the palace is the Great Hall, for banquets, balls, conferences, concerts, and a number of cafés, milk bars, bowling alleys, exhibition galleries, restaurants, an intimate theatre, lecture rooms, buffets and a disco.

The screen that records voting in some European parliaments is more exact as a symbol of the legitimising functions of parliaments than are murals of events from national history. Parliaments are about voting. The idea that parliaments 'represent' the people is merely a necessary fiction, justifying power. In complex industrial societies, parliaments are necessarily in the control of political parties. 'Representation' other than this is not possible in the central government of an industrialised society. Nevertheless, parliaments are part of the magic of our times: their rituals can hallow the laws and proclaim the mystery that by carrying out these ceremonies the people are 'represented'. And elections are among our most significant festivals: in liberal-democratic societies where choice (however limited) is possible, people assemble in halls or in front of television sets to watch great struggles between the forces of light and darkness; some of them make declarations of faith by displaying symbols on their persons or their houses or their motor cars – or, with spray cans, on public walls; icons and slogans are paraded and there are many affirmations, oratorical and theatrical, of what life is, and should be. With God and hereditary right gone, voting is a new way of binding citizens to the state.

Though representation is merely myth, a liberal can claim that voting provides checks on government and can accompany extensions of liberty in both social conflict and individual behaviour. A museum in Berlin celebrates this belief. It is in the reconstructed Reichstag, one of the most symbolically important of all of Europe's parliament houses. Outside, the Reichstag has been put together again almost as it was before it was burned as part of Hitler's rise to power. Inside, it is a modern building, bland and airy, with a conference chamber that could become a parliamentary assembly hall if the Germanies were ever reunited, and with exhibition space for museums. An exhibition there, 'The Reichstag in German History', gives reminders – in photographs, paintings, posters and cartoons – of the Reichstag's failure. There are scenes of well-dressed, bearded men bustling and jostling in a chamber dominated by gleaming, luxuriantly carved woodwork; then, in November, 1918, a photograph of a Social Democrat, at the base of a pilaster, proclaiming to the people the coming of the German Republic. There are representations of some memories of what are called 'the good, middle years' from 1924 to 1928, when it appeared that the German parliamentary system would work. After photographs about 'mounting crises', Göring's face is pictured rising over the carved wood of the bench of the president of the Reichstag. This is followed by the famous photograph of the Reichstag in flames, which precedes photographs of the gutted building, left as a contemptuous display of power by the Nazis. The final photograph shows the gutted, shell-smashed wreckage of 1945, seen across a field of rubble.

9. The workers

No honour to the people

The Free Trade Hall in Manchester (celebrated now not for its free-trade associations but for its symphony concerts) stands on part of what used to be St Peter's Field, the setting in 1819 for what radical legend calls the 'Massacre of Peterloo', a great historic occasion in the struggle for parliaments to be not only liberal, but also democratically elected by all the people. It was a time of riots, and of movements for political reform. At the beginning of 1819, 'Orator' Hunt, the greatest crowd-raiser among the radicals, had told 8,000 working-class people gathered at St Peter's Field that, 'The only source of all legitimate power is the people, the whole people and nothing but the people.' As the year went on, there were more and more crowds, talk of a national convention, and fears that these protests might make Britain ungovernable. On 3 August somewhere between 60,000 and 100,000 demonstrators, with flags and banners and bands and red caps of liberty, assembled in St Peter's Field to hear Orator Hunt. The authorities arrested him and ordered the crowd to be dispersed by hussars and yeomanry. The latter – businessmen on horseback – used such violence that 11 demonstrators were killed and more than 400 injured. A legend was created instantly. Newspaper reporters used the word 'massacre', and the *Manchester Observer* combined 'St Peter's Field' and 'Waterloo' to coin a telling word: Peterloo. A month later when Orator Hunt rode in triumph into London in a procession waving with emblems and flags (including a white flag inscribed in black to the victims of Peterloo and a red flag inscribed with the words 'universal suffrage'), a crowd of 300,000 watched.

The plaque commemorating Peterloo refrains from reference to 'massacre', or even to injuries and deaths. It says: 'The site of St Peter's Field where Henry Hunt, radical orator, addressed an assembly of about 60,000 people. Their subsequent dispersal by the military is remembered as "Peterloo".' There is now a mural of Peterloo in the Free Trade Hall, but in the nineteenth century when the artist Ford Madox Brown was commissioned to paint some murals on the history of Manchester, he was not allowed to include Peterloo. English liberal historians prefer to present the democratisation of voting as something the upper classes granted the lower classes (when it was beginning to be decided that democracy was harmless) – not as something struggled for: in the cults of liberal as well as conservative views of parliamentarianism, popular agitation can seem a threat to social order.

The Chartist movement was the first of Europe's working-class movements. From the late 1830s to the late 1840s, it was the only sustained working-class movement in Europe aimed at democratising parliamentary elections. Yet in Britain there are no significant monuments to the Chartists. Studying the *absence* of monuments can be as significant as studying what is celebrated.

Were Britain ever to become a socialist country, its museum of the revolution could make an heroic tale out of the Chartists, telling the story of the formation of hundreds of Working Men's Associations, the 'People's Parliament' in London, the three great petitions to parliament with several million signatories to the 'People's Charter', the thousands of arrests, the martyred dead of the 1839 'Newport rising' (when direct action in a Welsh seaport led to the death of 14 and the wounding of 50), the attempted national rising of 1840, followed by sentences of imprisonment and transportation, and then, the processions and demonstrations, culminating in the meeting at Kennington Common in 1848, the year of revolution, when the Duke of Wellington had 150,000 special constables sworn in to assist the police and the military in defending London. Not even on Kennington Common is there a monument to the last mass demonstration of the Chartists.

The frescoes in the display areas of the British parliament honour the nobility and the gentry who fought on both sides in the struggles with the Stuarts. They also honour King Alfred for fighting the Danes, Richard I for fighting a crusade, the English barons for forcing John to sign the Magna Carta, Wycliffe for translating the Bible, Sir Thomas More for resisting Henry VIII, Elizabeth I for sending Raleigh to America, Sir Thomas Roe for establishing British power in India and Queen Anne for signing the act of union between England and Scotland – but nowhere is there any celebration of the common people.

Similarly, most of the other parliament–palaces of western Europe lack symbols of those working-class struggles for the popular franchise that have given them modern legitimacy. Thus, modern parliaments are unable to symbolise the realities of their own democratisation, even though strong working-class organisations – trade unions even more than political parties – are as essential to maintaining aspects of a 'free society' as support for the traditional liberties in the critics' culture.

However, there was some assertion at least of democratic ordinariness when the Swedish Riksdag moved into a new building, planned originally for business offices, which was taken over because the old parliament building was in poor shape. Prime ministers ate in a cafeteria; the entrance was a serviceable escalator; the foyer outside the debating chamber was as functional as a modern theatre foyer and made of simple Swedish materials. All that was retained of the aristocratic past were some paintings showing the four estates of the old parliament, and some chandeliers from the former parliament house. On the birchwood walls inside the debating chamber, the only symbolic decorations were a set of typical regional textile weaving patterns. For session openings, a royal coat of arms was put up – normally, though, the dominating symbol was the screen that recorded the push-button voting. This democratic ordinariness was rejected in 1978 when the Riksdag decided to return, in 1983, to the restored old parliament house at Helgeandsholmen – the one the chandeliers had come from.

Trade unions: peace or violence?

The plaques on the Barbican at Plymouth, England, recall famous embarkations from this old harbour. One, however, celebrates a return: in March 1838, four of the six 'Tolpuddle Martyrs' came back from the penal servitude in Australia to which they had been sentenced – in effect, for forming a trade union. A group of trade unions put up the plaque in 1956: it ends with the proclamation, 'Freedom and justice was their cause.'

The six labourers from the Dorset village of Tolpuddle can be seen as the founding saints of western Europe's trade union movement, not because of their victimisation – all over Britain for decades workers trying to unite had been persecuted – but because of the strength and nature of the protest their sentencing aroused. There is no doubt they were treated unjustly: when they founded their Friendly Society of Agricultural Labourers, they had sworn a secret oath, in the manner of the infant working-class movement which sometimes adopted masonic-type regalia and mystic rituals. The government, ready to make an example of someone at a time of machine-smashing and haystack-burning, used a law passed 37 years earlier for a different purpose: the Tolpuddle labourers were found guilty of having administered an 'unlawful oath', and were transported.

An important symbol in British working-class art is a primitive painting, now held by the Trades Union Congress, of thousands of protesters against the Dorset labourers' sentences assembled behind high pink banners that carry esoterically significant blue initials. They were watching the beginning of an enormous procession of 35,000 or so trade unionists in sashes and top hats; in the centre of the vanguard is a wagon drapd in blue-and-pink calico bearing a huge paper scroll – a monster petition for the release of the Tolpuddle labourers, with more than 200,000 signatures. This was the largest demonstration of peaceful working-class protest the world had seen, and a quarter of a million people watched the procession pass. Several years later, after recurrent protests, the Tolpuddle men were pardoned.

Props were placed to help support the sycamore tree ('the Martyrs' Tree') planted where legend had them holding their meetings; a memorial, put up in 1912 in front of the Tolpuddle Methodist chapel, quoted the words of one of the martyred at the time of his sentencing and honoured 'the faithful and brave men of the village' who had nobly suffered 'in the cause of liberty, justice and righteousness'. In 1934, with much ceremonial singing of the 'Song of Freedom' written by one of the martyrs ('We raise the watch-word liberty; We will, we will, we will be free'), commemorative medals were distributed, prizes were awarded for essays on the social and economic significance of their martyrdom and six memorial cottages, to be lived in by retired farm labourers of good union record, were declared open; a museum arranged in the community hall, and a shelter built near the Martyrs' Tree, were also declared open. Five plays were written and produced by amateurs; the British Broadcasting Corporation put on a radio documentary.

This can seem a very modest celebration of what was, in fact, one of Europe's most significant social creations – the formation of organised working-class movements. This great social transformation first occurred in Britain. However repressed, trade unions existed in Britain decades before they could form in most other European countries – yet even now, the British union movement has produced little to commemorate this social revolution, apart from a bronze sculpture (The Spirit of Trade Unionism) which stands outside the TUC's London headquarters at Congress House. This shows the union movement, personified as a vigorous youth, assisting a fallen comrade. Some private enthusiasts collect badges and emblems as people used to collect matchboxes. In Limehouse, there is a small museum of labour history. The favourite display pieces, sometimes put together as exhibitions, are the union banners. In these, in symbolic association, idealisations of 'the worker' are shown together with personified virtues, sages, goddesses, horns of plenty, wreaths of victory – all in neoclassical settings with corinthian columns, ionic porticoes, statues and busts intermingled with idealised workplace scenes. The banners do not usually call on the workers of the world to unite: they make softer cries – 'All men are brothers. It is our duty to assist each other'; 'One heart, one way'; 'Good will towards men'; 'Defence, not defiance'. The industrial revolution in Britain produced the world's first industrial proletariat, with new forms of social struggle. It also produced ways of muting that struggle.

Britain is not alone in this. The Norwegian trade union headquarters in Oslo has a statue of a toiler in overalls, a sledgehammer over his shoulders and the old cry of 'Freedom and solidarity' inscribed beneath his boots. But apart from an occasional decoration such as this, labour movement headquarters are usually just like any other office buildings. The headquarters of the Danish Federation of Trades Unions, a five-storey office block in rusticated stone and light-coloured brick adorned with classical pilasters and pediment, is the most elegant building in Copenhagen's Rosenorne Street; in its modest presentation even its allegorical representations of the workers are low key, being confined to five small, round reliefs depicting what seem to be cherubs at play. In Frankfurt, the Gewerkschaftshaus (the trade union headquarters) was the first building in that city to be designed in the new commercial style.

Set in opposition to nineteenth-century union hopes of steady gains and increasing reform there also glowed the heroic prospect of proletarian revolution. The proletariat of the first factories was made up mainly of cruelly treated women and children. There were riots, political convulsions, the horrors of damp tenements, epidemics, industrial maimings and poisonings, oppressively long work hours and relentlessly low wages, workers cheated by fines or payments in kind rather than cash. But it could all seem to have nothing to do with skilled workers. The new unionists did not want to risk strikes that might lose them the little they had gained, and early reforms for the provision of sewage, piped water and drainage occurred because the cholera that killed the workers could also kill their masters, or because of campaigns by aristocratic philanthropists. In London's Piccadilly Circus, the cast-aluminium figure of a winged archer is not the Eros of British folk belief and tourist promotions, but the Angel of Christian Charity – part of the Shaftesbury Memorial erected in 1893 to commemorate the earl whose legislation ended some of the worst exploitations of child labour. 'Eros' connotes romance; child labour an unpalatable form of reality. Assignations could be arranged beside a statue of a symbol of love, though not beside a symbol of the exploitation of children.

The two months from the end of March 1871 gave the prospect of proletarian revolution a legendary quality when, after the fall of Paris to the Prussians, revolutionaries of diverse kinds won a Parisian municipal election, called themselves 'Fédérés', raised a red flag over the Hôtel de Ville and proclaimed the Paris Commune. The Commune would inaugurate 'a new political era, experimental, positive, scientific' – and was to become a symbol of all that was hoped for, or feared from, proletarian revolt.

It was not, however, a proletarian revolt, although it had

proletarian elements. Still, there were a lot of red flags and red scarves around; new forms of populist rhetoric ('exploiters of monopoly', 'servitude of the proletariat') were being used; and the mere presence of a number of workers in a town hall could seem a proletarian revolution. 'What is happening is nothing less than the conquest of France by the worker,' wrote the diarist Edmond de Goncourt, who saw the workers as 'the convulsive agents of dissolution and destruction'. And this belief that the workers were madmen at the helm was fed by Communard atrocities.

For those who sought martyrs, however, there were a great many more corpses – something like 20,000 to 25,000 – on the other side. These were the bodies of the Communards executed within a few days of their defeat, at first in summary or random shootings, and then in squads, when captured Communards were lined up in cemeteries, parks, army barracks and railway stations, put into batches of six, and killed. The Paris Commune became one of the great legends of proletarian revolution, so that the Commune and its monuments can seem to dominate working-class aspiration in the nineteenth century. Marx was one of the principal myth-makers: 'The battle must break out again and again in ever-growing dimensions . . . Working-men's Paris, with its Commune, will be for ever celebrated as the glorious harbinger of a new society. Its martyrs are enshrined in the great heart of the working class.' In Père Lachaise Cemetery, the Wall of the Fédérés is now one of the principal pilgrimage places of the working-class movement. It was against this wall that, on the last day of the fighting, to revenge the shooting of the Archbishop of Paris and the mutilation of his corpse, government forces executed 147 indiscriminately selected Communards. Their bodies were photographed, then buried in a ditch beside the wall. Today, it is one of Europe's sacred walls – low, made of stone, vine-covered, with terracotta tiles on top and neat lawn in front, in the most fashionable bourgeois cemetery in Paris. Under the inscription 'To the dead of the Commune', visitors place wreaths, and special ceremonies are held on the anniversary of the execution. As well as the Communist Party pantheon, the graves of French radicals and memorials to Nazi concentration camp victims are placed close to the wall.

Whoever may have 'led' the Commune, there was no doubt that

most of its martyrs were working people and the reaction to it became a symbol of the reservoirs of state violence. Fear of proletarian violence was to become one of the characteristics of modern times, even though most of the violence was to continue to come from the state.

The monuments of the social democrats

In Sweden, Norway, Denmark, Austria, Britain, the Netherlands, the Federal Republic of Germany, Switzerland and Belgium, political parties based on the working class (whether called Socialist, Social Democrat or Labour) have either dominated government, played a strong part in regular coalitions, or had their share of office according to the movements of the pendulum. In other western European nations, similar parties are at least part of the parliamentary system. In France, Spain, Portugal and Greece they have also had their victories. These parties are seen by some as having helped domesticate the labour movement to many of the prevailing liberal-democratic values. But they can be seen in another way: whatever their behaviour in practice, the social-democratic parties are still bearers of principles that are important to the modern conscience – the belief in social justice and in intervention by the state; for some, a scepticism about capitalism; perhaps a special belief in the value of the working class; perhaps even the possibility of socialism. Though there are many cross-currents in European national politics, one of the formal political divisions is still that of capital and labour. In most, this is the main formal division; to some people, this division makes sense of everything else.

Even in Scandinavia the monuments to the early martyrs of these parties tend to be subdued. Only a wall plaque commemorates the founding martyr in Denmark, Louis Pio, editor of the first labour publication, and gaoled for five years. Fifty-nine years after his death, there was a commemoration of Norway's founding martyr, Marcus Thrane, who in 1849 formed Norway's first labour organisation and was later charged with sedition and sentenced to seven year's hard labour. His body was brought back from the United States and buried in Oslo's pantheon, the Grove of Honour in the Var Frelsers Cemetery, under a simple rustic stone bearing the inscription 'Fighter and martyr for the rights of the workers'. In Oslo's town hall, two murals are juxtaposed. One, donated by the Oslo trade unions, shows nineteenth-century slums, the arrest of Marcus Thrane, and a police baton charge: this represents the past. Another section of the mural shows well-fed children, happy athletes and contented old people resting in front of the municipal apartment houses of the welfare state. The other mural, donated by the Oslo Stock Exchange, shows the benefits of capitalism. This juxtaposition is seen as achieving balance.

Among the 31 pieces of sculpture and 45 symbolic motifs outside Oslo Town Hall are six bronze figures straining their muscles with social realism, representing those workers who constructed the building; some Norwegians find these repellent because they seem to represent the threat of organised labour. In Sweden, there are not the same inhibitions. In the foyer of the central Stockholm Folkets Hus, one of the three large murals glorifies organised labour, health services, welfare schemes and paid vacations and the other two show how benefits were earned through strikes, riots, the gaoling of labour leaders and even killings. Banners and red flags wave in depictions of famously heroic working-class demonstrations. Throughout the building are paintings and statues of symbolic workers, of labour leaders and of intellectuals who supported the labour movement. Listening to the old songs and looking at the red flags on May Day, one might imagine Stockholm in the grip of revolution.

Yet in that continuing reviling of Sweden that goes on in most of the other European liberal-democratic societies, the fact that its labour movement preserves working-class symbolism is usually suppressed, and not much serious consideration is given to the fact that for socialists Swedish social democracy may provide the only visible alternative to the Communist societies. To the right, Sweden's welfarism was seen to destroy incentive, even if, by conventional measurements, Sweden remained close to being the world's most prosperous capitalist nation. Statistics and sheer assertions were produced about Swedish crime rates, suicide rates, drug addiction, aimlessness, rebelliousness – as if these were not normal characteristics of modern industrial societies. To the left, Sweden's welfarism was seen to destroy socialism – yet Sweden was the only country where socialism, in the sense of

10. Communist Europe

Prophets of the revolution

Only three pieces of furniture in the reading room of the library in Chetham's Hospital, Manchester, have descriptive cards. One card notes a particularly tall grandfather clock; one draws attention to what may be the worlds's largest gate-legged table; the third indicates the reading desk Marx and Engels used for research in the library (which boasts it is the oldest public library in continuing use in Europe). The notice on the desk quotes from a letter Engels wrote to Marx: 'During the last few days I have again spent a good deal of time sitting at the four-sided desk in the alcove where we sat together twenty-four years ago. I am very fond of the place. The stained-glass window ensures that the weather is always fine here. Old Jones the librarian is still alive, but he is very old and no longer active. I have not seen him on this occasion.'

Each side of the large, black reading desk slopes up to a square centrepiece, on which there is usually a jug of flowers. There is fluorescent lighting on either side of the window, and now almost no one visits the library: its seventeenth-century panelling and cupboards are black with age; there is not a sound, apart from those coming from music practice in the school that shares the old manor house with the library. In the reading room, the stained glass has been replaced by clear glass, but the room is so enclosed in old, dark panelling that the weather can still seem always fine.

One can imagine that outside is the Manchester of the early 1840s when a young German, Frederick Engels, spent two years working in the English branch of his father's cotton business, and where his observations of Manchester – the city he saw as the 'masterworks' of industrial capitalism – were to lead him at the age of 24 to write *The Condition of the Working Class in England in*

1844, from Personal Observations and Authentic Sources, the first book to be published about the new working class created by industrialisation. Everywhere, said Engels, there was barbarous indifference, hard selfishness on one side, unspeakable misery on the other, everywhere social war, every person's house a fortress, everywhere marauders who plundered under the protection of the law.

The old, black desk, surrounded on the alcove's three sides by an old, black bench, evokes not only Engels's Manchester, but all that rustling of pages and scratching of pens that has gone into the composition of what came to be known as marxism. This emphasis on the word, and in particular the words of the founding texts of Marx and Engels, is the official basis for what can be described as revelation for a third of the world's people. To what extent they are read, in themselves, or believed in, is another matter. They do, however, provide the aura for whole education systems; they provide the principal proclaimed basis for scholarship; they are seen as providing the key to life's present meaning and action, and, in language apocalyptic and millennarian, for promising future paradise on earth: they are expected to have explained everything.

Even in capitalist countries they seem essential to much intellectual discussion. As with Christian texts, quotations can be found to support both sides in a great debate. Excerpts from the works of Marx provide a form of enquiry, alive with tension, that is now indispensable to an analysis of industrial societies and they offer a possibility of uniquely ruthless demystification and realism, with a compensatory promise of binding historical categories ('ancient', 'feudal', 'bourgeois'). They provide a sense of conflict that, like the Christian message, is both tragic and liberationary, with its promises of human perfectibility in a utopia without class or domination. In advanced capitalist societies they are used in generating discourse ranging from the most complex academic talmudism to the most violent simplifications. In developing societies they can be used for almost anything.

This emphasis on theoretical correctness, supported by the evidence of books and manuscripts, desks and reading lamps, is one of the two main threads in Moscow's Marx and Engels Museum – the other being the emphasis on strong action. After passing staircase busts of Marx and Engels with their votive flowers, one enters a room that shows early editions of the books seen as influential on the young Marx. Then books and manuscripts provide the trail to one of the two key rooms of the museum – The Room of *The Communist Manifesto*. A relief metal sculpture shows a worker breaking his chains: on the opposite wall are displayed, like rays of the sun, 150 different editions in various languages of the *Manifesto*. In one of the transition rooms it is the relics of scholarship that dominate the Marx memorabilia – his books, his paper knife, his reading chair and, above all, a model of the British Museum Reading Room. The second key room devotes itself to the celebration of *Capital* – translations of *Capital* cover three of its four walls.

In other rooms, action is celebrated; in particular, the revolutions of 1848 and 1871 and the founding of the International. In one room, Marx and Engels stand stolidly in marble amidst a display of banners, portraits and heroes and drawings of heroic events in the insurrections of 1848. Along the wall of another, there are celebrations of the Paris Commune and the executions in Père Lachaise; a map of Paris shows scenes of action; proclamatory posters are on show. Two walls of the same room are relics honouring Marx's International Working Men's Association at 18 Greek Street, Soho, London. A map then shows how the movement spread throughout the world from that address. A collection of rubber stamps in many languages – the stamps of the newly formed socialist groups – shows their organisational strength.

What remains of Marx's body is under the control of the capitalist system, in London's Highgate Cemetery. The cemetery used to be owned by a private company and it took until the 1950s for them to permit any special commemoration of Marx. In 1954, they allowed his body, along with the headstone of his grave, to be moved to a position where pilgrims could pay homage. It is now on the ceremonial agenda of all the tours of Britain run by Intourist, the Soviet tourist agency. Above a lawn where there are always flower offerings, a large block of granite bears in bold letters of gold the announcement, 'Workers of all lands unite'; above the granite stands a colossal bronze head of Marx. The sculptural style is of the traditional philosopher's head, found by the dozen in Rome's Capitoline Museum; underneath, however, in equally

large letters is the quotation: 'The philosophers have only interpreted the world in various ways. The point, however, is to change
it.'

When the company that owned the cemetery proposed to shut it
down, a voluntary group, the Friends of Highgate Cemetery,
emerged to keep it open (other eminent people are buried there:
Charles Dickens, George Eliot and John Galsworthy). The new
Marx grave is so prominent that random walking will reveal it, but
the site of the original grave, although marked by a special
commemorative tablet, is impossible to find without help. This
first, humble spot is not on the itineraries of the Intourist coach
parties.

Lenin as redeemer

Even walls, floor and ceiling of the 'Lenin Hall' of Prague's
V.I. Lenin Museum are themselves museum pieces. This is the
small room where, in 1912, Lenin chaired the sixth conference of
the Russian Social Democratic Party. The 12-day conference was
illegal and the whole setting of the room has the fugitive quality of
the early workers' movements – brown lino on the floors, four
simple desks with a couple of dozen cheap wooden chairs grouped
around them, a rough wooden cupboard at the back, a bust of
Marx and a table with a green-shaded lamp for the minutes
secretary. In the anteroom to the Lenin Hall, along with documents
on the 1912 conference there is, in relief, a heroicised presentation
of the conference to match the heroic mood of M. Sladky's
painting *V.I. Lenin Presides over the Sixth Conference of the
Russian Social Democratic Party*, in which Lenin leads by intellectual persuasion and nobility of character, and strong men
follow.

The 26 halls of the Prague museum glorify Lenin in copies of the
books and pamphlets he wrote, in the newspaper *Iskra* he edited,
in revolutionary posters and cartoons, old flags, and a recording of
his voice. They pay homage to Lenin 'as leader of genius of the
world proletariat, founder of a new type of revolutionary party,
creator of the first socialist state, and as an extremely modest and
self-sacrificing person not sparing any effort for the benefit of the
happy future of the whole of mankind'. The museum's presentation

veers between the old palatial style and the style of the modern documentary. The room in which Lenin chaired the meeting is at the rear, in a less pretentious part of a palace which belonged to the Counts Kinský until it was acquired by the Czech Social Democratic Party in 1907 and renamed, like other Socialist headquarters in Europe, 'The House of the People'. Its splendour is now used to reflect Lenin's greatness. For the first 13 halls, red carpet runs along marble floors, connecting one hall with the next; in the fourteenth hall, to the Great October Socialist Revolution, the red carpet expands to cover the whole floor and is matched by a red wall featuring a mural of armed workers: a statue shows Lenin marching into a socialist future with Stalin behind him carrying the necessary books and documents. The red carpet spreads wall to wall for several more halls, then retreats to produce a straight line of red running over marble through five more halls to a statue of Lenin in majesty, where, in triumph, the carpet again floods the marble floor.

In the V.I. Lenin Museum in Prague, and in the V.I. Lenin Museums in other Communist countries and throughout the Soviet Union, Lenin is celebrated as redeemer of humankind. Characteristically, part of the celebration is to recall the famous coups by which he changed the Russian socialist movement, and then the world. The conference in Prague was an audacious move: Lenin called a meeting of his own followers who elected a central committee which then claimed supreme power over the Russian Social Democratic Party, and the sole mandate to represent the Russian proletariat. Each of his acts of daring commitment and of violent differentiation of his faction is now legend – from his gaining control of *Iskra* at the second conference and then turning the paper's distribution into a conspiratorial organisational network, to the coup of the October Revolution itself, and the heroic risks that followed. Each bold deed is portrayed in famous paintings done in the heroic style: they are the marxist equivalent of paintings of the life of Christ and, in part, their message is the same: those who are humble, derided and oppressed can, through destiny and faith, triumph over the apparently mighty.

Lenin's particular heroic quality was not of the bourgeois kind, but the classical heroism of a Hercules; there was brutality and cunning as well as bravery and such an enjoyment of commitment and the thrill of the chase that he appropriated Napoleon's tag, *'On s'engage et puis on voit'* ('One gets involved and then one sees'). In the sheer high spirits with which the famous heroic paintings show Lenin addressing his comrades there is something of his willpower and his singleminded concentration on his own correctness in all situations, his unstinting determinism to establish uniqueness for his faction, his hatred of heresy (as he defines it) and his readiness for any sacrifice. But in a way this confidence comes through most compellingly in an enlarged snapshot in the V.I. Lenin Museum, Warsaw: Lenin is delighted by a smart move he has just made in a game of chess during his exile in Switzerland. But the exultation is for the move's correctness – everything else signals personal modesty.

As with the celebration of Marx in museums, Lenin Museums emphasise the sanctity of *the word.* In the Prague museum, among Lenin's articles and books, are huge blow-ups of key paragraphs from his writings, evidence of his correctness. In Berlin, his scholarship is emphasised: a plaque in the State Library in the Unter den Linden recalls how, during his stay in 1895, Lenin used the reading room of what was then the Royal Library; a Lenin Hall, with a coloured-glass mosaic, honours his visit. The small Lenin in Berlin Museum in the Old Arsenal Building has a reconstruction of the section of the library where Lenin worked. In the main Lenin Museum in Leningrad (established in a marble palace given by Catherine the Great to a favourite), some of the most important relics of Lenin's youth are manuscripts of his early writings. Also preserved are an oil lamp he used as a reading lamp, and the writing table and chair from the dacha where he lived in Finland; a sculptured group of workers reading a newspaper glorifies the party press and, in a special display, are all the reference works Lenin used in Zurich when he wrote *Imperialism, the Highest Stage of Capitalism.* There is a model of his study in the Smolny Institute in Leningrad and a painting shows him writing there. In the Smolny itself this study is kept as a small museum, open for inspection to favoured visitors.

In the Central Lenin Museum, Moscow, the emphasis on *the word* continues, and on the studious and scholarly. The first room shows a reconstruction of one of Lenin's early studies – a plain table, with candlesticks and inkpot; the second celebrates his editing of *Iskra* and the writing of *What Is To Be Done*? The third room has a photograph of the public library at the University of Geneva, and the armchair Lenin used there. A painting of Lenin in exile shows him as a scholar calmly writing. There are manuscripts of famous words he wrote in 1917 – on a single sheet of paper, now framed in a heavy red velvet, the scrawled speaker's notes for what were later to be revered as 'The April Theses', a scrap of paper that now seems to have forecast the October Revolution. One of the blue copy-books in which wrote *The State and Revolution* is displayed, along with the draft of a proclamation to the 'Citizens of Russia', telling them that the Provisional Government had been overthrown. The second last room has one of the most poignant of all Lenin souvenirs –the typewriter used for typing his last article.

The five-room apartment in the Kremlin where Lenin lived with his wife and his sister is also a museum. Again, there is over-whelming emphasis on simplicity and scholarship. The study has a plain wickerwork chair and green baize-topped desk on which are a green-shaded desk light, penholders, gluepot, penknife, scissors, paper knife and writing pad, along with records, plans, files and newspapers in revolving stands; there are nearly 2,000 books in the cabinets around the walls. It might be a scholar's study were it not for the small wooden stand on the desk that has on it the party programme, a party pamphlet and a railway timetable. Altogether Lenin had 10,000 books, in 20 languages: most are stacked in the hallways of this apartment. In each of the three bedrooms is a desk.

The larger Lenin Museums are arranged to illustrate the correctness, one by one, of Lenin's main theoretical lines. Thus the large opening hall at the Central V.I. Lenin Museum, Moscow, presents Lenin's early denunciations of the populists, the 'legal marxists' and the 'economists', and the establishment of the League of Struggle for the Liberation of the Working People; then *What Is To Be Done?* is glorified as is the 'foundation of a party of a new type', a socialist vanguard of full-time professionals, the only bearers of true working-class consciousness because under capital-ism the workers, left to themselves, would develop only a trade union mentality. Then Lenin's prescience is demonstrated, in manuscripts, photographs, furniture, memorabilia, maps, models and paintings. Specially chosen schoolchildren, when sworn in as

Pioneers (the Communist Party's youth organisation) celebrate the ceremony in a Lenin Museum. In Moscow, in red caps and scarves, holding flowers and red banners, they line up on the top floor and dedicate themselves to the ideals of Lenin; along the corridor, a whole exhibition is devoted to various Lenin representations – in painting and sculpture, in vases, tapestries, glass and ceramics.

The 'Passion' of Lenin

Leningrad has reminders of earlier uprisings. A square is named after the Decembrists' Uprising (1825), and in the former commandant's house in the Peter and Paul Fortress there is a reconstruction of the interrogation room where for six months suspects were questioned. Palace Square is a memorial to Bloody Sunday (1905) and Insurrection Square to the February Revolution. Beneath Insurrection Square, the hall of marble and bronze and crystal between the two platforms of the metro station displays bronze medallions with oak leaves which explain how Lenin made proletarian sense out of this bourgeois revolution. But Leningrad's sacred revolutionary ground is the Field of Mars, one of the largest squares in the city. There, between four large red flags, stands the Monument to the Heroes of the Revolution and the Civil War.

This monument, erected in 1919, was one of the first monuments to Great October Socialist Revolution – an event as important in Communist faith as the crucifixion is to Christians, in that they both seemed to open ways to human liberation and, in some ways, did so. Yet, apart from depictions of the storming of the Winter Palace, the October Revolution is celebrated more as an example of Lenin's genius than as a proletarian revolution. Leningrad has 253 monuments specifically commemorating Lenin, from the V.I. Lenin Museum itself to small plaques recording places where he addressed the workers. Some go back to pre-revolutionary days, but most commemorate actions of Lenin from the night he arrived at the Finland Station. The period of Christ's Passion begins on his entry into Jerusalem; the period of Lenin's Passion begins on his return to Petrograd, in April 1917, and the period of his majesty and judgement begins on 8 November when, a few hours after the arrest of the Provisional Government in the Winter Palace, Lenin presented the 'Decree on Peace' and, later, the 'Decree on Land', to the Second Congress of Soviets.

A statue of Lenin, the second erected, stands outside the Finland Station where, on 16 April, from the top of a tank, searchlights pinpointing him, he proclaimed to a mass of workers, soldiers and sailors in a forest of red-and-gold banners that the socialist revolution had now begun and would spread throughout the world. In statue form he stands on the stylisation of an armoured car, his right arm out, his left hand on the lapel of his overcoat, an image of robust faith. Plaques mark street intersections where the armoured car stopped for Lenin to make further proclamations about the beginning of a new world. It was not until after midnight that the car reached the Kshesinskaya Palace which the Bolsheviks had previously seized as their headquarters. There, under the frescoed ceilings and the crystal candelabra of this former dwelling of a prima ballerina and tsar's favourite, and next door, in the former mansion of a rich bourgeois, are now the 36 halls and 8,000 exhibits of the Museum of the Revolution.

Sections of the building itself are part of this 'museum': the balcony, from which he thrice addressed the masses on the night of his arrival, and which in the coming months became a favourite speaking place (the 'Bolshevik University'); the room where, on the night he arrived, three tables were laid out in his honour with tea, bread and margarine; the meeting hall where he often spoke, and where the touring parties now assemble. In the room where he worked there is a bust of him, and two famous banners. The muzak plays his favourite Mozart sonata.

It was in his brother-in-law's apartment, in what is now 52 Lenin Street, that, at about 10 o'clock on the morning after his arrival at the Finland Station, Lenin scribbled out the page of notes later known as 'The April Theses'. These analysed how the bourgeois democratic revolution could be turned into a socialist revolution. Lenin continued to live in this apartment for the next four months, and tourists now put on felt overshoes before entering what has become a V.I. Lenin Memorial Museum. A bedroom contains the two iron bedsteads on which Lenin and his wife slept, a suit of his clothes, his desk and, under glass, his favourite armchair and the dining-room table at which he and his comrades would decide who was right and who was wrong. In one room, a map shows the 24 places where, between April and July, he made speeches. (Paintings have been made of him delivering some of these speeches. The most famous, *Lenin Addressing the Putilov Factory Workers*, now in Moscow's Central V.I. Lenin Museum, was painted for the Paris World Fair of 1937.) To Soviet tourists the apartment is already familiar: it is one of the stock backgrounds in films about the life of Lenin.

Several rooms in the Leningrad Museum of the Revolution show the party tickets, posters and rubber stamps, with which Lenin's Bolsheviks demonstrated their new status as a legal organisation. But soon comes one of the most famous photographs of the revolution, that of peaceful demonstrators being shot down by Provisional Government forces. As an explanation of what happened in Leningrad during the street disturbances of 'the July days', it is blindingly misleading; nonetheless, its emotional appeal – a massacre of political innocents – sustains the assertion that the bourgeois government had by this time become a military dictatorship. Lenin's arrest was ordered. He went into hiding.

At the museum, Lenin's fugitive journey is celebrated in maps which show each resting-place. Each is now preserved as a museum or reconstructed in a museum; there is even a reconstruction of the locomotive engine in which he escaped into Finland disguised as a fireman. The most romantic hideout – and the most popular – is on an island beside a lake in part of what is now a holiday area the tourist literature calls the 'Soviet Switzerland'. It is close to Rasliv, a village near Leningrad, where Lenin, disguised as a hay-cutter, hid for three weeks in a clearing surrounded by forest. The hayfield is now a large parking area, serviced by souvenir shops. A walk leads along the lake, past a reconstruction of the hollowed-out hayrick in which Lenin lived and a granite stylisation of it, to a museum which pays homage with relief maps, models and photographs to the ingenuity and bravery of Lenin and those who helped him. Among the relics – a scythe, a hay rake, a saw, an axe, a pot – is some of the sand on which he first trod when stepping from the boat to the island.

This brief idyll at Rasliv is a favourite among official painters. In art museums as well as in Lenin Museums and Museums of the

Revolution, there are paintings of the sincerity and authenticity of simple outdoor living: Lenin boils a pot of potatoes suspended on forked sticks over a camp fire; Lenin crouches over his papers, spread on a tree stump, in a 'study' of willow shrubs (the famous 'green study', a particularly popular subject). At Rasliv, a statue of Lenin in this green study marks the turn-off to the museum. The same statue is repeated at the Rasliv museum. Outside, two sawn-off tree stumps mark 'the exact site' of the green study, which has become the ultimate image of the simple scholar – the man of goodwill studying so that he can help the people.

In the Rasliv museum, pages from one of Lenin's blue notebooks are a reminder that this period of hiding produced *The State and Revolution*, the most utopian of his works. Almost anarchist, it proclaims that after the destruction of the bourgeois state, the proletarian state would wither into a completely free and communal society; what was left of government would be nothing much more than a supply agency. ('So long as the state exists there is no freedom; when freedom exists there will be no state.') But also on the walls are monumental quotations from letters and articles he wrote in his hiding places. They express the most decisive of all Lenin's theoretical lines, the decision that shook the world: that it was time for an armed uprising.

In front of Leningrad's yellow-and-white Smolny Institute (once a convent school for daughters of the aristocracy), with its blue-and-white cupola, is the first Lenin statue to be erected. Cap in right hand, he is arguing the correctness of the decision to mount an armed insurrection. It was from the Smolny that the armed coup was organised and it was there, when he took over, that Lenin set up office. In the park opposite, a monument displays a map of the city on the night of the coup. It marks the strongpoints to be seized. Busts of Marx and Engels add their approval. Moored on the banks of the Neva is the cruiser *Aurora*, on which tourists photograph the gun that fired the blanks that legend sees as signalling the storming of the Winter Palace and therefore the beginning of the October Revolution. In fact, by then, the Petrograd coup was already over; all other strongpoints had been occupied before breakfast. But the fall of the Winter Palace is as necessary to the mythology of the Great October Socialist

Revolution as the fall of the Bastille was to the mythology of the French Revolution.

The centre point of the Leningrad Museum of the Revolution is a *son et lumière* spectacle of the attack on the palace. Beneath a bust of Lenin, and by a map on which counter-revolutionary strongpoints are shown in black, tourists receive a lecture on the topography of the revolution. They then move on to the tableau of the storming. The lights are turned off. A voice sets the scene, the shot rings out from the *Aurora*, machine guns clatter, there is other scattered fire. Then comes the great roar of the triumphant workers and soldiers as they seize the last bastion of reaction. A choir sings the 'Internationale'. The revolution is won.

Revolution as salvation

In a palatial hall in Bucharest, ornately ceilinged and with letters in gold along its walls, the centrepiece is a large, splendidly polished factory siren. A card certifying its authenticity explains that this is the siren which gave the signal for a strike in February 1933. It is one of the holy relics of Romania.

In each of the Communist capitals of Europe there are similar relics in the red-carpeted and sumptuously presented museums of revolution. These museums proclaim the legitimacy of present regimes by recalling the struggles of the revolutionary past in an evidentiary display of *objets* and effects: workers' rifles and revolutionary banners, socialist realist statues and murals, collages of illegal pamphlets, the soft click of changing slides, the murmur of taped voices, fashionably blurred photographic blow-ups, the eyeglasses of revolutionary leaders or the leg-irons that went around their feet. It is through these symbols that all the revolution museums begin the task – to the sceptical western tourist, and to some of their own people, a difficult one – of demonstrating that the Communist governments came to power by proletarian revolution and not by 'socialism from above' or Soviet support. From dioramas of revolutionary battles to handwritten drafts of revolutionary manifestos, from displays of revolutionary flags to displays of revolutionaries' typewriters, they glorify proletarian revolution as the great liberating force in history.

Each museum begins with a vestibule, usually marble with a red carpet, in which busts, statues and murals of Marx, Engels and Lenin are juxtaposed with local Communist leaders to establish apostolic succession. Genteely dressed leaders of early working-class organisations courteously pose for the cameras; in some museums election posters, flags and maps show Communist successes in bourgeois parliaments; more usually there are police mug-shots of party leaders and photostats of police records on party suspects. Party leaders are shown in prison translating marxist texts, playing chess and in discussion. There is usually an episode when the party loses its unity in factionalism before regaining it with doctrinal purity.

As well as similarities, each country has its own specialities in its revolution museum. In Belgrade, Ferdinand's assassination is hailed as a glorious blow for the subject nations against the Austrian and Hungarian oppressors. In the GDR, the martyrs of the 1848 revolution (the 'March dead') are honoured along with martyrs of the 'November Revolution' of 1918 and the Spartacist revolt of 1919. In Prague, beneath the ornate ceiling of the Munich Room in the bank-palace turned Klement Gottwald Museum, Hitler's liquidation of Czechoslovakia is blamed on bourgeois liberals and social democrats. In Sofia, the Museum of the Revolutionary Movement has photographs of the town of Samekov, one of the first municipalities in Europe to elect a socialist council.

Although some reverence is paid to Lenin and although the October Revolution is always presented as the great dividing-line, revolution museums outside the Soviet Union give more importance to the masses – or at least to the activists – than does the Soviet Union with its cult of Lenin. In Budapest, the Museum of the Workers' Movement has tableaux of the dingy rooms and the atrocious working conditions that lead to the formation of the Hungarian Social Democratic Party; the emergent party and trade unions are given life in group photographs, the desks of early working-class leaders and the rubber stamps of worker organisations. In Sofia, the action begins with artists' illustrations of the secret meeting that founded the Bulgarian Social Democratic Party on a mountain in the Balkan Range. The party's growth is shown in its pamphlets, the inkwell of one of its editors, blown-up photographs of protest meetings and robust May Day celebrations. There are photographs of young party members in athletic singlets beside gymnastic equipment, the music score for 'The Working-class March'. The Romanian Communist Party's birth is commemorated by a reconstruction of the small meeting room where the founding 'congress' took place: glasses and a jug of water sit on the table, and portraits of Marx and Engels adorn the wall behind it. The birth is made real by the spectacles of a leading party theorist.

In its museums, Hungary has an advantage because – for the 133 days of the 1919 Hungarian Soviet Republic – it was the first nation after the Soviet Union to declare a dictatorship of the proletariat. With the army's collapse in 1918 and signs of the end of the old social order, there are proclamation posters and large blow-ups of crowd scenes: in October, the bourgeois democratic revolution is declared, with a programme of peace, democracy and national independence. Well-designed 'modernistic' posters become increasingly revolutionary. Then, in photographs of the crowded street scenes on 21 March 1919, the Hungarian Soviet Republic is proclaimed. Photographs show meetings of councils of workers, peasants and soldiers; posters announce the nationalisation of large estates, major companies, mines and tenement houses; photographs show children enjoying free education and free holidays; there are copies of plans for lowering rents and extending social insurance; there are displays of Hungarian Red Army uniforms. Then other uniforms appear – those of the intervention (Czech and Romanian) and of the counter-revolution There are dioramas of small battles and maps with moving battle-lines: the battle-lines waver – the Hungarian Red Army disintegrates; the Revolutionary Governing Council resigns; the Romanians occupy Budapest. Then: hangings, the uniforms of paramilitary groups, a clandestine printing press, prison cells.

Certain twentieth-century symbols of revolt and repression are now so obvious that one can get the general gist of a revolution museum without understanding the language of the explanatory texts. The objects themselves 'describe' what happened. A collection of rubber stamps in a display case in a late-nineteenth- or early-twentieth-century setting suggests that trade unions or other working-class organisations were forming: with the rubber stamps will be posters, banners, group photographs, journals on cheap newsprint. A small printing press suggests illegality: it may be accompanied by a model of a meeting hall concealed in a basement. Blow-ups of pictures of popular demonstrations are followed by blow-ups of processions carrying coffins. Group photographs are followed by photographs of prison cells, chess sets, police mug-shots. Drawings of men in top hats are followed by drawings of factory slaves.

It is with the display cases of German helmets, concentration-camp jackets, manacles, truncheons and other symbols of Nazi oppression that the beginning of a transformation to a revolutionary situation occurs – in the home-made bombs, home-made rifles and forage caps of a people's resistance. In visual terms, this transformation is most credibly presented in Yugoslavia, where the resistance was strongest and the Soviet army least important. In the revolution museum in Belgrade, when Yugoslavia capitulates to the Nazis it is the Communist Party that is shown leading the call to resistance: the grandeur and misery of a Yugoslavia dismembered by the Axis partners are shown in a concentration-camp uniform, a pair of leg-irons, photographs of Nazi shootings and hangings and counterpointing representations of the gallantry and success of Tito's partisans. In a poignantly imaginative panel are a number of enlargements of different elements in the famous photograph, perhaps the most heroic candid-camera shot in existence (taken surreptitiously at a public execution) of a young patriot, the noose around his neck, shouting defiance at the Fascists in the moment before he dies. The exhibition explains how 'the army of liberation' was also an 'army of revolution'. When Socialism comes to Yugoslavia, the photographs change from black-and-white harshness to the softness and warm hope of sepia.

The transformation can also seem credible in Bulgaria, with its history of seeing Russia as its liberator from the Turks. In the Sofia museum, a hall is devoted to the partisan groups, with details on each zone, leading, at the end of the hall, to a statue of a partisan, fist raised in salute, with paintings of dramatic incidents behind him. Then, shown as the culmination of Bulgarian history to that date is the 'September Revolution', begun in 1944 while the Soviet armies waited on the frontier to see what would happen. There are blown-up photographs of strikes and demonstrations in Sofia on 6 and 7 September and the liberation of political prisoners as the partisans come down from the mountains; there is special treatment of the 'great strike of Plovdiv' on 7 and 8 September. The Soviet Army crosses the frontier and, on 8 September, the 'Fatherland Front' (a Communist-led coalition of Communists, left agrarians and left social-democrats) takes over key buildings in Sofia: blow-ups show clenched fists, a map shows action in other centres. Then tricolours and red flags come out to welcome the liberators. A caption announces: 'The victory of the socialist revolution caused boundless joy among the people.'

In the Klement Gottwald Museum, Prague, the transformation to a Socialist revolution begins with the announcement that resistance to the Nazis was a national and democratic revolution headed by the Czech Communist Party. But in documents and photographs, the February 1948 constitutional coup (the 'February victory of the working people and the definitive defeat of the bourgeois reaction') is presented as the moment of transformation of a national democratic revolution into a Socialist revolution: a blow-up of a photograph of Gottwald addressing a meeting in the Old Town Square on the day of the coup and a recording of his speech provide evidence for this assertion.

The Museum of the Workers' Movement in Budapest acknowledges that there was an uprising against the Hungarian Communist government in 1956. It describes it as a counter-revolution and exhibits photographs of people dying from the actions of counter-revolutionaries and of the destruction of property, the knocking down of symbols and the burning of books. Wrecked street-signs on Lenin Boulevard are presented as particular evidence of counter-revolutionary depravity. With the counter-revolution crushed, the museum continues to commemorate the Socialist revolution, in displays of television sets and other symbols of the consumer society.

The revolution museums in the Soviet Union present the early trials of civil war, foreign intervention and famine with patriotic reality. Illuminated maps show the redness drain out of most of Russia, and then flood back in, giving life and victory. Display cases of captured White Russian weapons demonstrate that they came from the capitalist nations. There are reminders of atrocities – a glove made from human skin, a tree branch with welts worn into it by the hangman's rope and inscribed with notches for each person killed. Photographs record the bravery and sacrifice of the war's heroes, paintings and dioramas immortalise famous military actions, while home-made weapons, ration cards, and photographs of popular demonstrations recall civilian resistance. The birth of the Red Army is celebrated, and there are notes about how the army uniform resulted from a competition in which keeping a folk element was seen as essential, so that the cap design was based on that of an ancient Russian warrior hat.

This draws on the Russian patriotism that sees the nation as capable of overwhelming any invader. What is missing for the foreign tourist, though – and, no doubt, for many Soviet citizens – is any recognition of the millions of deaths from purges, starvation, pestilence and negligence attendant on the disasters and persecutions of the Stalin era. The best one can find is a monument by association, in the museum of the tsarist prison in the Trubetskoi bastion of Leningrad's Peter and Paul Fortress. The tour of this museum is of a kind familiar to a tourist of Europe's symbolic prisons, incorporating displays of prison uniforms, manacles, straitjackets and the cells themselves with their fixed iron bedsteads and tables, their windows looking out on to a wall, and, on their doors, mug-shots of famous prisoners. But in its 45 years as an interrogation centre, it had only about 1,500 prisoners; Stalin's labour camps had millions.

Part five

The Europe of nationalities

11. Images of nationality

Nations

Nationality can be one of the principal colourings of the tourist vision. Turning ancient objects into 'monuments' began largely to occur while the nation-states were forming and concepts of nationality were being created. Whether recognising it or not, as tourist–pilgrims we pay our respects to nationality; most obviously, in tourism's most stereotyped cultural forms – the souvenir, the national dish, the national drink, the picturesque quarter, the quaint folk ceremony, the phrase book, national dress. But even relatively universal forms can seem national. In England, architectural styles from romanesque to regency were derived from other cultures, yet they can be presented as distinctively English, with distinctively English histories. Likewise, although 'gothic' was a French invention, nineteenth-century Germans took it for their own and German nationality plunged romantically into medieval chivalry and even medieval fairy-tales; a castle on the Rhine became an image of Germany, with effects still evident in the travel poster industry. The structures in stone or metal, or glass, and all the creations in paint which served to justify power – whether the power of church or of nobles or of people, whether this power was seen as conservative, liberal, social-democratic or Communist – can also be seen in terms of nationality. For this reason, most of what has so far been described in this book, can be seen as an expression of nationality.

In most of the capital cities of Europe and in many provincial cities, there are the statues, in their frock coats or their togas or their military uniforms, of the great nineteenth-century nationalists. Their arms are usually raised, in gestures of liberation over what is now motor traffic. Whether they are citizen nationalists of the

Jacobin kind, or romantic cultural nationalists, a remarkable number are artists, scholars, writers, educators, or other intellectuals. But if one were to imagine a tourism of nationalism, it might more appropriately begin earlier, in the first printing presses and the books they produced in the vernacular languages; then in the special styles of the new state churches; in the documents of the secretaries, officials and clerks of the small but growing 'bureaucracies' of the centralising monarchs and their growing obsession with war; and in the national feeling in the works of Cervantes, Shakespeare, Camoës and others. There are other directions in which to look: at the beginnings of the secularisation of Europe; at the expanded belief in schooling; and at the dissolution of traditional society; and the need 'to belong', in some new way. In some cases (England, France, Spain, Russia, most notably), nationalism was used as a unifying policy by an established central government; at the time of the 1789 revolution, only half the people in France spoke French. In others (Germany and Italy, most notably), it provided the ideological justification for unification of peoples who were already claimed to be of common nationality. In the case of the old nation-states, their new nationalism (which usually then became imperialism) was directly related to the old rulers and the new business class. There was, however, another nationalism – usually of a romantic, cultural nationalist kind – in the struggle to establish new nation-states in lands controlled by those who were seen as an alien power. The class basis of this 'new' nationalism was much more diverse, comprising merchants and functionaries and, more generally, the educated classes (perhaps members of the lower clergy or the discontented gentry). In Poland, the main nationalist strength came from the nobility. In the Balkans, to intellectuals, clergy and merchants, there could be added support from rebellious peasants and from traditional bandits.

However, in all cases, the modern nation-state, when it formed, needed to give 'the people' a dramatised sense that they were part of the state, with a share in its future. And as nation-states also became industrial states, built around the need to accumulate capital and to organise labour, new means of communication were needed to pass on new ways of behaving and to mobilise new forms of support. Out of all this came new ways of constructing images of what the world was like, and what mattered in it – new ways of how to behave and how to be human.

Sport, for instance, became one of the great symbolic expressions of nationalism. By the time of the First World War, participation in international sporting contests had become measures of national achievement, sporting winners had become national heroes and the games people themselves watched or played had become testaments of nationality. In 1914, soldiers went off to the slaughter with the rhetoric of sporting metaphors, as well as the sound of church bells, ringing in their ears. Sport had become a determinant of 'national character'.

Thus, to Norwegians, skiing is not merely skiing. As celebrated in the Ski Museum at the famous Holmenkollen jump in Oslo, it is an expression of Norwegian history and Norwegian character – to such an extent that when the museum was established in 1923, it was built in the shape of a stave church. Outside the present museum is a replica of a rock carving from near the Arctic Circle, reckoned to be 4,000 years old (demonstrating the antiquity of the Norwegian character) and showing a Stone Age man skiing; inside the museum, ski fragments taken from bogs (one fragment is estimated to be more than 2,000 years old) maintain the thread of historical continuity; evidence is presented that the Vikings were good skiers. In relics of Arctic and Antarctic expeditions – sleighs, kayaks, a faded red tent, a stuffed dog – there are recollections of Norwegian bravery; constitutional cosiness is recalled in the display of skis owned by members of the royal family. Above all, the museum confirms the image of the Norwegians as a hardy people of the mountains.

In Bern's Swiss Alpine Museum, mountaineering as sport is put forward as a contribution to world civilisation. The museum shows early mountain maps, which are beautiful but have no detail; then appear, maps as large as battle paintings, which scientifically detail every wrinkle; paintings rejoice in early expeditions as voyages of scientific discovery. There are portraits of famous climbers and guides, and displays of equipment and clothing: modern displays of new technology make mountaineering seem as serious as space travel. Only a few sequestered models of little huts and folk artifacts and a handful of watercolours admit that in the Alps people can have fun.

In Bayonne, the Museé de la Pelote defines the Basques by their national sport. Bats and balls with famous autographs are shown, while photographs of great teams and players as well as paintings project the distinctive national spirit of the game – young men in white clothes with red sashes and berets (the Basque colours) display the joyful thrust of the true Basque spirit.

In Madrid's Museo Tauro, the true Spanish spirit is celebrated in the gold-spangled costumes of great matadors and the stuffed heads of great bulls, with an emphasis on style, and on life as a theatre for the brave.

In London's Memorial Gallery at Lord's Cricket Ground, the English national character is celebrated partly in whimsical curiosities – a sparrow killed by a cricket ball, a silver toast-rack with cricket emblems, W. G. Grace's snuff box. But in the paintings of playing-fields throughout the empire, from Lahore to Georgetown, there are reminders of cricket's imperial dominion over palm and pine, and in eighteenth- and early-nineteenth-century paintings there are reminders both of gentlemanly civility and of true English pluck. A collection of *Punch* jokes shows the use of cricket in social stereotyping; a nearby collection of political cartoons from the mid-eighteenth to the mid-nineteenth centuries shows cricket's importance in the symbolism of what are seen as the unique virtues of the English political system.

Nationality through landscape

A dirty-brown spire flecked with dingy gold rises with tawdry ornateness 60 metres above the traffic lights in Princes Street, Edinburgh, facing the sturdy Scottish baronial façade of the North British Hotel across the sunken platforms of the Waverley Railway Station. Among the monument's dark mass of arches and spires, only the figure in grey marble at its centre, wrapped in a shepherd's plaid, a staghound at his feet, is immediately intelligible to the sightseer. This central statue is of Sir Walter Scott, whose novels told all Europe about Scotland (the kingdom England had absorbed into Great Britain) and set off historical-romance writing in other countries. Around him, most of them unnoticeable in the grime, are 64 statuettes of characters he invented and characters from Scottish history. Nearby, the memorial to the poet

Robert Burns commemorates a more democratic Scotland, and the Martyrs Monument in the Kirkyard of Greyfriars, where the presbyterians' covenant was signed, commemorates a tough, legalistic, Calvinist Scotland. But it was Scott's romantic Scotland that best suited the English, the European romantics, and nineteenth-century tourists.

At a time, ironically, when the Highland dwellers were being brutally cleared out of their mountain glens, it was the exotic Scotland of the Highlands that provided a suitably romantic image of Scotland to marry with English nationalism. This exoticism could seem of a piece with Macpherson's *Ossian*, with traveller's descriptions of tours through the Scottish wilds and with the emerging collections of Scottish folk-songs and poems; after George IV's state visit in 1822 (partly stage-managed by Scott), the English royal family learned how to put on tartans and, for a fixed part of the year, act as if they were true Scots. Queen Victoria's Albert developed a liking for the kilt and plaid. At Balmoral, her Scottish country estate, Victoria installed tartan carpets. Now this Scotland of the Highlands is part of the universal tourist experience. It has almost 1,000 pipe bands and 'research' has 'authenticated' more than 1,000 tartans. In one Highlands holiday centre, a computer helps tourists find a clan for themselves. As sightseers wear their 'Nessie' (Loch Ness Monster) T-shirts at the vinyl-covered tables of Inverness's Wimpy Bar, ferocious armed clansmen make the famous Highland charge on the wall paintings around them.

This romantic Scotland could not have existed without its mountains. As with the Swiss, mountains were essential to the creation of a 'Scottish character'. When mountains came into fashion with the romantic movement and the beginning of the tourist industry at the end of the eighteenth century, the new romantic imagination saw them as essential to bodily and spiritual health. This also accommodated the new nationalist imagination, often the same thing: mountain folk and mountain rocks could symbolise the spirit of a people, or a 'race'. The mountains of Scotland were the home of a tough, mountain 'breed'.

When in 1978 the National Gallery of Scotland arranged a special exhibition ('The Discovery of Scotland: the Appreciation of Scottish Scenery through Two Centuries of Painting'), two versions of a landscape by Paul Sandby indicated how landscapes can become 'national'. The first, by Sandby himself, was the kind of 'view' that the market demanded in the mid-eighteenth century: an obviously straightforward, 'realistic' account, accurate in detail. But an engraving of the scene made 30 years later improved on nature: the mountains were made higher and more rugged, and two stage props – fir trees and a man in a kilt – were added to cover some of the barrenness. That was the kind of 'Scotland' people had come to demand.

Before painters transformed Scotland into an international symbol of the romantic imagination, its moors and mountains were regarded as empty, barren, boring, sullen and crude. Similarly, in Switzerland, before tourists began asking for a 'Mont Blanc' or a 'Jungfrau' and before alpine peaks had become emblematic of that 'true Swiss freedom' which justified the turning of the Swiss cantons into a nation-state, the Alps were the badlands of ice and snow, white deserts fit only for gnomes. As part of those disorders in society that produced the romantic movement, writers and artists began to use mountains as symbols of the 'natural' and the 'sublime' – and so faults became virtues. To Scott 'the very nakedness of the land' had 'something bold and stern and solitary about it'. In Geneva, the painter Alexandre Calame produced symbols of the fashionably 'sublime' for foreign art purchasers, and the Swiss were to discover their nationalism in metaphors of what then seemed the cleansing freedom of the Alps – a metaphor now essential to the winter tourist trade.

Norway's self-definition was also helped by mountains. An international market for Norwegian mountain landscapes was opened by Johan Christian Dahl, the pioneer of 'Nordic nature'. He did most of his work in Dresden, where he was a professor at the academy, but he made five summer trips home to Norway to sketch mountains for later use in canvasses which, by projecting great drama from storm clouds and light, portrayed a Norway of natural majesty and grandeur – a view of Norway also presented in Peder Balke's seascapes. The next generation looked to the academy at Düsseldorf rather than to Dresden. There, it found a more romantic Norway, one that matched the new mood in painting, with the mysteries of hills and water or of dark forests and, in the case of the deranged painter Lars Hertevig, with the mysteries of a madman's landscape menaced by the use of white. Those middle-class Norwegians who were anxious to establish Norwegians as a unique 'race', continued to define themselves as a mountain people. (The Danes and the Swedes were deficient in mountains!)

Despite Sweden's lack of mountains, it absorbed Dahl's invention of 'Nordic nature' through the Düsseldorf-inspired eyes of the Swedish Marcus Larsson. Larsson's huge compositions – such as *Waterfall in Smoland*, in the Stockholm National Museum – helped define a Sweden different from that suggested by folk dancing on the green or scenes of calm water. For him, nature was an immense primitive force: the thrust of a flooded river prostrates trees and threatens rocks; the sky is ripped apart by storm; the ground trembles.

In European picture galleries, one can see how nations acquired new meaning partly through new styles in landscape painting. 'Meaning' does not exist in a vacuum. The very styles of painting could become part of the national style – ironically, since the styles of painting themselves were international. In the Hungarian National Gallery's many nineteenth-century studies of historical disasters, sombre faces emerge from lustrous greens and blacks as armed men cut down the naked body of a hanged man, or a woman mourns the corpse beneath a blood-stained sheet. Then, with landscape painting, especially in the work of Géza Mészöly, comes the beginning of an optimism implied in that new interest in light in what was to become known as 'impressionism'. A change in painting technique, with a more serene treatment of light suggests a possibly less restless Hungary: but it is a very qualified optimism, depending on hazy-grey tones across swampy marshlands or the misty shores of Lake Baloton; it reaches its most confident in a soft light spreading through a cloudy sky.

In Leningrad's Russian Museum, new painterly interests in natural grandeur and then in colour and light give to traditionally melancholy landscapes hints of a more hopeful Russia: Ivan Shiskin finds in forests a romantic majesty, and Alexander Kiseliov's Caucasus has a grandeur that matched western European fashions. A painterly interest in colour vibrancy projects a lyrical Russia; Fiodor Vasilev's *Scene on the Volga* is a radiant litany of praise to the tranquil security of a summer morning; his *Bog in a*

Forest shows a golden shimmer across a pale-blue sky. Then come Isaak Levitan's struggles towards the light: his early landscapes have a golden melancholy; then he seeks the serenity in light. But, as with Mészöly, the hope he projects with this light is qualified: in his Volga studies, a gentle light comes through rain; in his autumnal studies, there are the last shinings of light before the cold sets in. It is still a melancholy Russia.

National anthems, one of the simplest and strongest of all national symbols, often rely on appeals to landscapes as national emblems. According to its anthem, Austria is not only a home of great sons, but a nation blessed by its sense of beauty, a land of mountains, a land of fields, a land of streams; the Czech lands are of wondrous beauty with streams rushing through their meadows while, amid the rocks, the fragrant pine groves sigh; Denmark is a lovely land whose charming beech woods grow near the Baltic strand; in Ireland, the soldier's song echoes on valley green and towering crag; in Finland, the patriot's song is compared to the buds that burst their sheaths with spring; God has been lavish with Monaco in its ever-clear sky and ever-blossoming shores; Norway looms rugged and storm-scarred o'er the ocean; Portugal is a happy land kissed by the ocean that murmurs with love; in Romania, fine orchards bear fruit under the peaceful sky; with its sun, its skies, its flowery valleys, its Alp-crowned north, Sweden is the fairest of lands on earth; in Yugoslavia, the tempest might rage, the rocks be riven, the oaks uplifted, the whole earth tremble – but Yugoslavs will stand steadfast and constant like one of their own granite mountains.

Nationality through the peasantry

As the old peasant life began to drain away at the end of the nineteenth century, relics of it became not only significant collectors' items but also important symbols of nationalism. For conservatives in established nations, the peasants could be presented as breathing the true spirit that held a regime together: for those trying to establish the uniqueness of 'new nations' against imperial occupiers, the peculiar customs of the peasantry could be made to seem 'proof' of the unique culture of the nation, and of its long history. A peasant painting in Russia could be shown to breathe the true spirit of Mother Russia; a peasant painting in Russian-occupied Poland could be shown to breathe the true spirit of an independent Poland. Both paintings might be done in much the same style. Detailed presentation of peasant dress and handcrafts and of the interiors of peasants' cottages were part of the general stock-in-trade of popular nineteenth-century genre paintings.

When the Slovenian middle classes were cultivating their nationalism in the nineteenth century after five centuries of Habsburg rule, it was in the peasant that they could find what was 'truly Slovenian'. In the Ljubljana National Gallery, Jurij Subic's *Before the Hunt* shows the true Slovene standing firm in the sunlight at the door of his simple cottage, in blue blouse, the eyes in his wise, wrinkled face inspecting his gun; in Jožef Petkovšek's *At Home*, the essence of the Slovene is to be found in a simple family grouped with the stolidity of wood around a plain wooden table. At times, the concern with accurate observation can overwhelm even pathos. In the Belgrade Museum, Uroš Predić's *The Refugees from Herzegovina* is intended to be a patriotic set-piece showing victims of oppression fleeing along a rocky mountain pass. However, his concern with each item of dress and ornament and accoutrement is so great that the effect is of enough peasant handcrafts to stock a small folk museum.

Sometimes, a nationalist painter lived in a foreign city, drawing strength from an academy and returning home for an occasional summer to make a number of working sketches. As with landscape painting, the approach to art of that particular academy might then help determine how the painter portrayed 'national character' in peasant paintings. In the Oslo Gallery, all the peasant figures are presented as austerely devout, living in harmony in their simple lives. Whereas Adolph Tidemund saw this simplicity through one brand of German romanticism – that of the academy at Düsseldorf, where he lived – painters who trained in Munich found a softer and more colourful simplicity. The latter were followed by a new generation, who drew inspiration not from German romanticism but from 1880s Parisian naturalism; presentation of the Norwegian character again changed in emphasis to suit a new painting style.

One can walk past the nineteenth-century paintings in the Art

Museum of the Socialist Republic of Romania and see the birth of famous Eastern European stereotypes of peasant life, especially in the painting of Nicolae Grigorescu and Ion Andrescu. Here are landscapes with a now familiar concentration on the rough country-road and the picturesque ox cart or hay wagon, the ploughing scenes, the women working in the fields, the market scenes. In particular, especially in Grigorescu's peasant portraits, one can see some of the finest developments of a famous peasant cliché – the woman in kerchief. His most famous painting, *Peasant Girl of Musecel*, is a national monument: with white kerchief, clear, smooth skin, calm eyes, full, friendly lips, she is both reassuring and trusting. This section of the museum abounds in wise women in kerchiefs, presented as typically Romanian. But in Sofia there are similar women – presented as typically Bulgarian. Again, in the Russian Museum, Leningrad, and the Tretyakov Art Gallery, Moscow, although there is a greater concentration – most famously in Ivan Kramskoy's *Mina Moiseyev* – on the good-humoured, all-pervading wisdom of bearded male peasants, there are plenty of women in kerchiefs. This time they are typically Russian.

Painters used the peasantry to make paintings. The chauvinists of the Great Powers used them to justify their continued rule. Self-appointed patriots in the occupied lands used them to justify the overthrow of that rule. The peasants themselves did not see the paintings. Now their descendants can buy postcards of them in the shops of the art museums.

At the time peasant life was being turned by painters into patriotic symbols, peasant dwellings were being assembled in 'folk' museums, as another manifestation of 'national character' to complement the simultaneous creation of ethnographic museums. Towards the end of the nineteenth century, more than 100 wooden farm buildings from various parts of Norway were dismantled and put together in an open-air museum on the outskirts of Oslo. (During summer, tourists in the 'folk restaurant' at the museum can now decide whether to order peasant food or international cuisine, and can buy pottery of traditional designs from an old pottery reassembled on the site.) In Denmark not only was an open-air museum assembled, peasant buildings were also re-erected inside the ethnographic section of the National Museum, where the tourist can now walk over old reconstructed peasant floors that creak with reality.

Folklorists also observed the peasants, in ways that could serve both romantics and nationalists (or romantic nationalists). In Finland, a million words of folk epic were recorded and became the basis for a whole school of Finnish verse and paintings. Serbian peasant ballads, German fairy-stories and Scottish folk-songs were written down and became part both of the European romantic imagination, and individual theories of Serbian, German and Scottish national identity. The Czech polka and galop along with the Polish mazurka, swept the ballrooms of Europe; Russian, Polish, Czech, Norwegian and Finnish folk-tunes provided the basis for famous works of nineteenth-century music.

In the Bern Art Museum, an oil painting recording the festival of mountain people at Unspunnen in the Bernese Oberland in 1808 shows one of the most ambitious early attempts to preserve and glorify peasant culture and, through it, to project the virtues of the nation. On a meadow, with the Jungfrau in the distance, mountain peasants from all over Switzerland contest in wrestling, shooting with crossbows and guns, dancing, singing, yodelling, alp-horn playing. The idea for a festival had come from a mayor of Bern who wanted to attract foreign tourists to the Alps, thereby demonstrating to Swiss townsfolk the worth of the mountain rustics and, by this national folk festival, to strengthen a feeling of national unity. Such motives still remain in Switzerland. When the Society for Swiss National Costumes held a festival at Unspunnen, in 1955, to celebrate the one-hundred-and-fiftieth anniversary of the first Unspunnen festival, it was not only celebrating the success of the Swiss tourist industry, it was also celebrating the modern identification of the Swiss with memories of mountain peasant culture.

Swiss folk-songs first appeared with text and musical annotation in Bern in the early nineteenth century; from 1826, dances and music.making were also recorded; the alp-horn has now become a national symbol, cowbell music an art form and yodelling clubs one of the most frequently organised forms of Swiss sociability.

Nationality from the golden past

As the idea of a 'nation' developed in both the new nation-states that were to be formed and the old nation-states whose imaginations were being refurbished, the nineteenth century produced – in history books, museums, paintings, literature and statuary – a national past that could be seen as 'golden' and could help give new meaning to the present.

Thus, archaeological finds from the 'Age of the Vikings' produced quivers of national fervour and an obsession with dragon designs in Norway; Old Norse literature became part of the western world's scholarship industries, and Norway drew honour from this. Oslo's Viking Ships Museum is a cruciform building the size of a cathedral. Each of the three ships' black sweeps of wood, has its own hall of simple, rounded, white walls and stone floor, with a gallery above for devotions. What is celebrated are not Vikings as gangster–plunderers and military conquerors, but as spreaders of a trading civilisation that stretched eastwards and southwards along merchant posts on the rivers of Russia as far as the Caspian and the Black Sea and from there into the eastern Mediterranean, and stretched westwards to settlements in France, England, Ireland, Iceland, Greenland and probably, at least in passing, to North America.

The archaeological finds from which scholars created a Golden Age for Norway emphasise that the Vikings were farmers and traders in a complex, peaceful society. In the Viking Ships Museum, finds from burial graves include finely carved sleighs, weaving looms, farm tools, and a splendidly decorated cart that presents the Vikings as a horse and chariot people. The Historical Museum emphasises the Vikings as belonging to a sophisticated Iron Age society; exhibits of iron ingots, smelters, and smithy tools almost suggest an early industrial society. The Vikings were not the only Golden Age for Norwegian nationalism. One of the statues in front of the Oslo University depicts a scholar in a frock coat, with a document in hand as if about to defend a scholarly point. This is F. A. Munch, a professor of history who helped 'create' Norway by giving scholarly credibility to the idea of the country as a great centre of medieval civilisation: a sense of continuity was demonstrated in the new museums in displays of national tapestries and wood carvings; the stave church became as much a symbol of the old Norway as the Viking ship. And folklorists drew on the golden past of the folk imagination in glorifying the trolls, mythical mountain-beings who became complex enough in character for Ibsen to use them in *Peer Gynt* and for Edvard Grieg to call his house, now one of the tourist attractions of Bergen, Trolls' Hill. The trolls, hairy and stupid, some good-natured, some malevolent, now leer from souvenir shops in the tourist centres.

In Romania, art historians collected medieval paintings and carvings and Romanian painters represented the great battles of Vlad the Impaler and Michael the Brave as symbols of a Romanian Golden Age. In Belgrade's National Museum, monumental canvasses in colours both soft and bright create the Golden Age of the Serbian emperor Dušan, whose empire threatened Byzantine power.

Bulgarian historians found two Golden Ages in Bulgaria's past, and venerated the monasteries as treasure houses of state documents and craft masterpieces. They decided that the signing of the peace treaty in 681 (the year after the Byzantine emperor's defeat by the 'proto-Bulgarians' and their allies) marked the beginning of Bulgaria: in 1981, the Bulgarian government celebrated the thirteen-hundredth anniversary of the Bulgarian nation in ceremonies throught the world.

The Zagreb Railway Station is listed in the tourist guide as one of Zagreb's 'outstanding sights', not least because it is a typical Habsburg empire railway station. Opposite, though, is a different kind of symbol: an equestrian statue of Tomislav – first of the rulers of what might seem the beginning of an independent Croatia – shakes his sceptre at the station's neoclassical portico. Whether Tomislav was really a king is disputed, and it is more than 1,000 years since he asserted his power. In the nineteenth century, however, the middle-class 'creation' of Croatia as a nation required a founder: Tomislav suited that purpose. That the state he founded (if that was what he did) lasted less than 200 years before falling to the Hungarians, added point to his memory.

At the end of the nineteenth century in Hungary it seemed, at least to the ruling class, that the country should have an official foundation date. The year 896 was chosen and patriotic manifestations were encouraged in a nation which had lost independence in the sixteenth century and had itself become overlord of four national minorities. Historians provided exciting versions of how, in the year 896, 400,000 Magyar tribesmen reached the Carpathian plain and established a unique civilisation. Budapest's Millennary Monument (begun in 1886) has, on a high column at its centre, the Archangel Gabriel raising his wings in praise of Hungary: at the foot of the column, conquering Magyar chiefs on horseback survey the broad, long Avenue of the People's Republic, as if pausing before galloping along it to seize the intersection with Lenin Boulevard.

One of the greatest spectres from the past to haunt the European national imagination was the eclipse of Poland's Golden Age in the dismemberings which still provide maps in school history books. Poland's nineteenth-century exiles had some of the persuasive force of prophets of civilisation. Unlike 'submerged nations' such as Croatia or Norway, Poland had been a great power in modern history. After the Poles defeated the Teutonic Knights in the fifteenth century at Grunwald, the Polish state had stretched from the Baltic almost to the Black Sea: for a time, Poland seemed to have the dominance that later Russia was to achieve. In Krakow, the Grunwald Monument just beyond the old Barbican has the crowned Polish conqueror still riding victoriously, five-and-a-half centuries later, six metres above the figure of the fallen Teuton in elaborate armour. Jan Matejko's *The Battle of Grunwald*, in Warsaw's National Museum, is one of the nineteenth-century's largest battle canvasses and, some critics say, the best. Taking three years to paint, extraordinary in both violent action and character interest, *The Battle of Grunwald* is a vision of mortal combat between the power of aggression and the lust for freedom, between Teutonic might and ill-clad Polish patriots led by their duke-commander, a St Michael of virtue and bravery. Matejko lived in Krakow, where the Austrian authorities were relatively liberal, and his grand reconstructions of Poland's past provided not only symbols which still have meaning, but also, for him, a successful career and medals from international exhibitions.

Matejko's celebrations of the renaissance in Poland project the clear, serene richness of a Golden Age, when Krakow's Wawel Castle could seem a centre of civilisation. Wawel is still a national symbol, with the dimly lit, intimate congestion of its small, crowded cathedral and the arcaded courtyard of its renaissance palace where there is a display of gifts to Polish kings from Turkish sultans, Persian shahs and Tartar khans. It remains the object of a pilgrimage undertaken by almost all Poles. In the Krakow market square, Adam Mickiewicz stands in statue as poet–prophet, cloaked and proud. In 1968 when audiences applauded criticisms of tsarist Russia in a play by Mickiewicz, the Soviets had the play banned. The ban produced demonstrations in which more than 1,000 students were arrested.

This Polish use of monuments reached its most heroic in the reconstruction of the Royal Castle in Warsaw as a national symbol. Under the tsars, the castle had become a 'political grave', despoiled as a matter of policy, and therefore symbolically important. It was in the castle that, in the 1830 uprising, the Polish parliament passed a decree deposing the tsar; in the 1861 uprising, the funeral of five Poles killed in front of the castle was used as a huge patriotic occasion. Aware of the castle's symbolic importance, the Nazis bombed and then shelled it in 1939, and later, following the 1944 uprising, blew it up. After the war fragments were dug out of the rubbish, numbered and stored along with the furnishings, paintings, sculptures, doors and fireplaces which had been hidden from the Nazis. A complete documentation of the castle made in the 1920s (in case of future sacking) had survived in leaden containers kept in a garrison outside Warsaw. In January 1971, a decision was made to build a replica of the castle, using the inventory as a base and incorporating the 6,000 individual items that had been preserved, including one intact piece of wall. It was the biggest single reconstruction ever undertaken in Europe. The rebuilding of 380 rooms and halls, with fragments of the original castle embedded in them, was finished by 1979: the Poles then speculated about whether the Soviets would allow them to open the castle. It was seen as a Polish victory when the gates were admitting visitors once more.

12. The great liberation movement

Europeans as 'cattle'

For western Europeans, laughing at other people's nationalism has been a justifying language for their own nationalism, as if they were the only ones to get nationalism right. This kind of high-handedness is especially reserved for 'the Balkans' (the European territories still controlled by the Ottoman empire in the nineteenth century) and for Turkey itself (which is seen as 'oriental).

The historical predicament of this part of Europe is poignantly remembered in many of its monuments, whether of defeat or victory. But many of these monuments are also reminders that only the accidents of geography and the luck of battle protected western Europe from the attacks by the Turks that socially and economically so frustrated Europeans of the south-east, to their long disadvantage.

The greatest of all the tourist displays in this area is in Istanbul. It is Topkapi Sorayi, formerly a palace town of 5,000 people, now an ambivalent monument, meaning what tourists make of it. For most of its existence, Topkapi Sorayi was the administrative centre of the Ottoman empire and the residence of the emperor. As tourists pass by the cash desk through the middle gate, the atmosphere can at once seem 'oriental'. Here, says the guide, are the stones where decapitated heads used to be displayed and the fountain where the executioner would cleanse his hands. To the right of the gate stretches what might seem, with its ten chimneys, to be a large early factory; it turns out to be the kitchens. These are now a museum containing a world renowned collection of Chinese porcelain. They run along one side of a vast courtyard where several thousand soldiers and many officials wearing distinctively graded court dress used to assemble four times a week. Tourists pass from the domed hall of the divan, the imperial council, restored in the sixteenth-century style with low couches covered with carpets running along walls decorated with tiles from the best Ottoman period, to the public records office, whose rococo style has been conserved; then to the office of the grand vizier, now a museum of baldachin tents, and the treasury, with its eight domes, now a museum of armour. Beyond the next gate, the Gate of Felicity, is the throne room, with its marble columns and delicate yellow and green tiles, where the divan's decisions were submitted to the emperor. In this courtyard is a treasure museum so extravagant in clichés of wealth that it could satisfy the props department of an old-style Hollywood spectacular: 'emeralds as big as a small fist', 'bejewelled turbans', 'richly embroidered robes'. Two gold candelabras are set with 6,000 diamonds, and one of the four thrones is set with 25,000 pearls.

The next courtyard was a privileged relaxation place of gardens, pavilions, kiosks, stately pleasure domes and marble terraces with princely views of the waters of the Marmara and the Golden Horn. But tourists queue to be titillated by the harem, a labyrinthine settlement of 300 rooms, almost all cramped, set on six different levels, and connected by staircases, courts, lanes and narrow corridors. The tour offers flashes of sybaritism (the three marble-paved rooms of the Sultan's bath and the arcaded courtyard, shut off by a large net, where favoured odalisques had their dormitories), and there is miniature splendour in occasional chambers, superbly tiled and painted. But the main mood is one of constraint, signified by narrow passages and dark, tiny rooms.

The emphasis is on cruelty, hierarchy and ostentation and can comfort the European tourist with cliché images of oriental opulence and tyranny. Such images, however, conceal the fact that compared with a Christian Europe dominated by hereditary right and divisiveness, the Ottoman empire, at the time when the great palace was established, was rationally unified and coherent, and careers in its administration were open to talent. In the Ottoman's most powerful period, when scarcely one grand vizier in nine was Turkish by birth, the imperial administration training schools of which the palace was the centre would have been unimaginable in Christian Europe; this also applies to the Ottoman's professionalised imperial army and civil service.

Topkapi can also be a reminder of a stubborn Ottoman ambition to control the known world: at much the same time as modern western Europeans were beginning their imperial victories, the Turks were moving into central and southern Europe. The peoples there were thought of as 'cattle' who were to be maintained and protected if they worked obediently. Once Topkapi was established after the Turks had captured Constantinople, it seemed the natural centre for their God-endorsed domination of Europe, Africa and Asia.

The capture of Constantinople is celebrated in Istanbul's Military Museum as the Turks' greatest symbolic victory. Dioramas and tableaux show the planning and execution of this famous siege, ending in a triumphal group with Mehmet the Conqueror in armour, surrounded by his flamboyantly dressed officials, riding into the fallen city. The centre of the display is part of the chain the Christians used as a defence boom across the Golden Horn, and sightseers on half-day excursions along the European shore of the Bosphorous, past modern Istanbul's apartment houses and occasional old wooden mansions, can inspect the battlemented walls of Rumeli Husar. This huge fort, with its three large towers and six smaller towers was constructed in an incredible three months, on Mehmet's instructions, so that with the smaller fort on the other side, he could squeeze the Bosphorous narrows and prevent help coming to Constantinople from the Black Sea. Rumeli Husar was restored by the Turks in 1953 to celebrate the five-hundredth anniversary of their capture of Constantinople. In the Istanbul Museum the next greatest occasion is the battle of Mohács (1526), when the Turks defeated the Hungarians and gained territory from which a generation later they were able to move on to the walls of Vienna. The entrance hall of the Military Museum is dominated by life-size dummies of the sultan and his staff on their way to Vienna.

On the Christian side, the first great date is 64 years before Constantinople fell – 1389, the year of the battle on the Serbian field of Kosovo. This battle is commemorated at least as far to the west as Vienna and Prague. Melancholy tales of this defeat enchanted nineteenth-century Europe with their exquisite sadness, and scholars collected and translated folk ballads. Tombs and monuments to both Christians and Turks sprinkled the battle field and in summer coach parties drive from one monument to the next; the place of Kosovo in the Serbian imagination, however, is better discovered in Belgrade's Military Museum. Scenes of Serbia's golden period of empire precede the section devoted to it. In the fourteenth century, Serbia is an expanding power of 'international importance', rich in mining and farming, a nation with its own religion and its own culture, that reaches its peak in the reign of Dǔsan – 'Emperor and Autocrat of the Serbs and Greeks, the Bulgarians and Albanians' – who set his vision on winning Constantinople, the natural seat for his empire, from the Byzantines. The next exhibit shows the order of battle at Kosovo, with representations of those who fought and relics of the weapons they used: on one side, is the Christian alliance of Serbs, Albanians, Croats, Bulgarians and Hungarians; on the other, the Turks. The Turks won their famous victory. In fact, its symbolic significance is greater than its reality, but later, one by one, the Balkan states were to fall: Bulgaria was conquered after the capture of its capital, Turnovo, in 1393; Serbia was finished off with the capture of the fortifications of Smederovo in 1459; Bosnia went in 1463; Albania in 1478; Hercegovina in 1487. Only Montenegro survived, as a beleaguered territory of wild country whose barren limestone hills, rocks and caves provided natural fortresses from which a few Christian herdsmen, ruled by monks, fought guerilla actions against the Turks.

Monuments to these mournful losses were to become monuments to national pride. The National Museum in Budapest mourns the defeat at Mohács with the wedding-dresses of King Louis II of Hungary and his wife: like most of his army, Louis was killed at Mohács. Hungary was finished; the Austrians absorbed the western part; the Turks took over Buda and Pest and absorbed the rest. Pest declined to a village; Buda became a military outpost in a desolate landscape; the royal palace was turned into a barracks; palaces, monasteries and churches were quarried for stone for Turkish fortifications. In the Hungarian National Gallery sombre paintings recall Ottoman rule. A recurrent theme is of a man and a woman in hopeless flight from a blazing city while Turkish cavalry pursue them; another dominant image is of a Hungarian over-whelmed by Turks who are about to kill him.

In Bucharest, the nineteenth-century nationalist painter Theodor

Aman appealed to Romanian pride by painting Turkish massacres; Nicolaos Gyzis, one of the most famous Greek sentimental artists of the nineteenth century, produced a painting of Turks recruiting Greek boys which is still a postcard favourite in the National Gallery in Athens. The Sofia gallery has paintings of Bulgarians martyred by the Turks. The Belgrade Military Museum has representations of the forms of death the Turks imposed on the *hajduks*, bandits now seen in Serbia as patriots: one panel shows a type of impaling which drove a stake up a man's back without tearing vital organs, thus postponing his dying for as long as a day, his nervous system turned into an instrument of torture provoking exemplary screams. In all these representations, the cruelties are accurately presented; in a rational world, though, they would be set against Christian paintings of the same periods depicting equal cruelty. There are no paintings of those Christians who wanted their children recruited by the Turks for the sake of their careers, or of the Christian officials, or of merchants who made fortunes out of the Turkish empire, or of the peasants who in good times were better-off than peasants in some Christian countries. Memories such as these do not make monuments to a national pride partly based on struggle against the Turks.

Liberation

Obsession with Islam was the moving spirit of Europe's longest-lasting liberation movement. In Budapest, in front of the Museum of War History on Castle Hill, a statue of a Franciscan friar rushing forward with a face of hate, calls men to battle. This is Johannes Capistranus, an Italian who became a mob orator and prophet of the Turkish threat. A few streets away is a statue of a knight in armour who rests victoriously on his drawn sword. He is János Hunyadi, a daring campaigner against the Turks who was proclaimed saviour of Europe after a victory so famous that the Pope ordered church bells, henceforth and for ever, to sound at midday throughout Christendom. But the Hungarians remember their liberation with some wryness. The Vienna Gate on Castle Hill celebrates the two-hundred-and-fiftieth anniversary of the Christian army's victory at Buda – but the reality of the Habsburg liberation of Hungary was so devastating that what was left of the country was treated by the Habsburgs as a conquered territory.

In Bucharest, between a statue of the founder of the Philharmonic Society and a statue of the founder of the first Romanian language high school, there is a bronze statue of an armoured warrior on prancing horse, lifting his double-headed battle-axe on high. It represents Michael the Brave, who briefly unified the feudal principalities of Romania and was a noted fighter against the Turks. Bucharest's Central Army Museum has special displays of the fortification systems and campaigns of Michael and other prince–patriots – Vlad the Impaler, Stephen the Great and Ion the Terrible. In the last ten years or so, new monuments have gone up to two Romanian prince–patriots, and there has been a lively literary rehabilitation of Vlad the Impaler, previously sensation-alised in the nineteenth century as a sadistic tyrant of refined cruelty: a book came out in 1979 praising Vlad as wise and brave, intent on eradicating evil, guarding the frontier and promoting national unity. Thus, the famous anti-Ottoman Romanian princes are used to suit the purposes of modern Romania.

The defeat of the Turks besieging Vienna in 1683 is celebrated less enthusiastically there than in Warsaw, where it is presented as a great Polish victory – the most efficient Christian commander being Jan III Sobieski, King of Poland. In Vienna itself, com-memoration of the Christian victory is largely confined to an obelisk opposite the university. The bus stop at Kahlenberg Heights, near which the Ottoman force panicked and disintegrated under attack, has a ceramic relief celebrating victory; the tourist guides list Kahlenberg not for the saving of Christian Europe, but for its restaurant ('Unforgettable! The most exciting view over Vienna and the Blue Danube') which offers daily music from a Hammond organ. As victor over the Turks, the Austrians prefer their own man, Prince Eugene, whose statue now rises on his prancing charger, above a Vienna parking lot – although what he gained between 1697 and 1717 was soon lost.

Then, in the nineteenth century, came the liberations of Serbia, Greece, Romania and Bulgaria, and the building within these reconstructed nations of a new sense of nationality.

In Serbia, the *gusle* is a souvenir of liberation for sale in miniature to tourists. This simple, one-stringed fiddle used by Serbian minstrels for background noise to nostalgic tales of Serbia's heroic past, is seen as a symbol of national spirit because the ballads it accompanied kept national traditions alive. Following the Belgrade Military Museum's honouring of the *gusle* and the *hajduks*, come the flags, improvised uniforms and maps that recall what is now seen as the First Serbian Uprising (1804–13), when Kara George – a pig-trader who thought he would get a better deal from the Turks by a show of force – used bands of peasants to rout Turkish armies and seize Turkish citadels. Eventually the Turks replied with an overwhelming force that recaptured Belgrade. At Niš, as a terrible warning, they piled up a 'Tower of Skulls' of defeated Serbs (now an obligatory stopping-point on guided tours). Though immortalised in verse by Lamartine as an example of Serb nationalism, there is not much evidence in Kara George's uprising of any contemporary form of Serbian nationalism.

In Belgrade's main square, the reliefs beneath the statue of Michael Obrenović riding above the traffic on his war horse, show incidents from the Second Serbian Uprising, which began in 1815 in Obrenovićs' village and ended in 1817 with Serbia proclaimed a small autonomous principality. At Kalagmedan Fortress, a plaque recalls that here, in 1867, the Turkish governor announced that all Turkish garrisons in Serbia would be abandoned; by that time there *was* some nationalism in the new Serbia. Perhaps that is why, as the story of the Serbian uprising unfolds in the Military Museum, there is increasing splendour in uniforms. As the maps show Serbian independence and territory growing, the uniforms in the glass cases develop all the frills of nineteenth-century soldiers; as the decades pass, epaulettes grow from shoulders, red ribands swell across breasts, orders and medals light up jackets, proclaiming that Serbia became a nation. The rival families of Kara George and Obrenović became rival 'dynasties' struggling for power; between them, they provided twelve rulers of Serbia, four of whom were deposed and three assassinated.

In Athens, the National Historical Museum (formerly the house of the Greek parliament) and the Benaki Museum (once a millionaire's mansion) display their mementoes of the rise of modern Greece out of Turkish control. Almost all the exhibits are to do with fighting. There are ornamental daggers, silver-decorated pistols, famous bullets that caused the deaths of martyrs. In one painting, Christ on high, supported by angels, directs a skirmish to favour Greeks against Turks. Even the tobacco pouches and snuffboxes are those of warrior–patriots and the pectoral crosses are those of warrior–priests. The one Bible on display was bayoneted by Turks. However, the realities are better found in mementoes of four other kinds of struggle.

There are reminders of one of these struggles in the Historical Museum's glass showcases that display memorable detritus of the Philiki Etairia (or, 'Friendly Society') – one of the more successful international secret societies that came after the French Revolution. Seals and documents, ceremonial crosses and tapers recall its beginning, when wealthy Greek merchants swore oaths in Odessa in 1814, and its spread among the Greek merchants who dominated trade in so many towns in Europe and sea routes in the Mediterranean. It was the Etrairia that co-ordinated the uprisings against the Turks in 1821 and began the Greek War of Independence.

A painting by Vryzakis in the Greek National Gallery shows the uprising's official beginning – Bishop Germanis, dressed in gold vestments, his hands raised, blesses the flag of revolution on 25 March, now the Greek National Day. This shows another aspect of the revolutionary struggle – some revolutionaries were clergy. But some of the greatest opponents of revolution were also clergy. The most exalted of these is the Patriarch Grigorios V, who in 1789 had written in praise of the Ottoman emperor as the protector of Christianity. He subsequently became the revolution's most famous martyr when the Turks executed him in Constantinople in revenge for the uprising. An oil painting in the Historical Museum shows Grigorios, a noose around his neck, standing as a business-like figure in black among gaudily dressed Turks who are occupied with something else; patiently he waits to do his duty. A room is devoted to his relics.

Outside the old parliament building in Athens, near the main tourist centre, is a symbol of a third aspect of the uprising: a statue, dressed as a god of war, of Kolokotronis, a chieftain of the *kléphtes*. Like the *hajduks*, inspirers of folk epics, the *kléphtes* were to do much of the fighting – and to introduce the tradition of military intervention in Greek government. The statue of Kolokotronis may symbolise more than was intended.

The most significant symbol of the fourth aspect of Greek liberation is the white-marble image of Byron about to be embraced by Hellas. In the Athens museum Byron's helmet is laid out, as is his portable writing desk and the camp bed he died on. A street in the Plaka is named after him. *Lord Byron at Missolonghi* is one of the great patriotic canvasses by Vryzakis. Byron is significant not for himself, but as a symbol of western European support for Greece as the birthplace of civilisation – of Delacroix, Shelley and others, of the fund-raising committees, the newspaper campaigns, the public meetings and then of the great power diplomacy that finally led the European nations to intervene, and gain independence for the Greeks despite the Greeks' own failures and despite the uneasiness of European governments about unsettling Turkish rule in eastern Europe.

The great victory of European intervention, the 'Battle' of Navarino, was really an accident in which 70 or so Turkish ships were unintentionally sunk; to the Greeks, however, Navarino can still be presented as a sublime patriotic occasion.

In the National Gallery, Sofia, a painting, *The Hanging of Vassil Levsky*, shows what happened to the first internal revolutionary movement against the Turks in Bulgaria. In the snow, Levsky boldly confronts noose and hangman. Moving around the countryside as a dedicated conspirator, he had founded 500 revolutionary committees but was betrayed by an informer in 1873. The Turks hanged him on the then outskirts of Sofia. An obelisk with a relief portrait at its base, set in a garden between four brackets of lamps, now marks where he died.

The great year of Bulgarian martyrs came after the murderous fiasco of the April Uprising of 1876 in which the plans for an uprising were revealed by informers to the Turks. The event is celebrated all over Bulgaria, but the centre of this cult is in the mountain holiday town of Koprivshtitsa. This was where the revolutionaries, when they learned that their plan had been betrayed, rose prematurely, in desperation. Near a reconstructed old-style inn are the Bridge of the First Rifle Shot and the Monument to the First Rifle Shot, marking the spot where the first

Turk was killed. In the 20 April Square nearby, in the Mausoleum of the Fallen, are the bones of 'true patriots and apostles of freedom'.

The Bulgarian April Uprising failed in a legendary manner, helping to build the ideal of a Bulgarian nation, and it at once 'shocked world opinion': atrocity stories appeared in the newspapers of western Europe; Gladstone campaigned in the British parliament, and Hugo in the French; Garibaldi, Darwin, Tolstoy and dozens of other celebrities wrote and spoke on Bulgaria's behalf. A year after the uprising's failure, when the Russo-Turkish War began, the Bulgarian Central Committee formed volunteer detachments to fight on the Russian side, and after the Russians' victory, part of Bulgaria gained a restricted autonomy. Bulgarian gratitude to the Russians as liberators is ingrained in Bulgarian history. The Alexander Nevsky Church in Sofia with its gold and green domes was built in a joint project by Russians and Bulgarians to commemorate their fallen. In the next square, in the Monument to the Liberators (unveiled in 1907), Tsar Alexander II rides in bronze above the goddess of victory and bronze reliefs of stirring battles. A hundred or so memorials in Bulgaria commemorate Russian actions in the fighting of 1877–78, and just as monuments to Bulgarian national revolutionaries can seem monuments to social revolution, these memorials to Russian actions in 1877 can seem natural precursors to monuments to Soviet actions in 1944.

In the end, after the First World War, with all their foreign possessions gone, it remained for the Turks themselves to discard the Ottoman empire and become a Turkish nation. Their own nationalism had had a theatrical première in Macedonia in 1908, with the uprising of the Committee of Union and Progress (the Young Turks – the last of the Mazzinian 'Youth' movements that had begun in the 1830s with Young Italy, Young Poland, Young Switzerland, Young Germany and Young France).

A brown, double-fronted house next to the Turkish consulate in Thessaloniki marks the birthplace of Mustapha Kemal, one of the Young Turks. It is open to sightseers approved by the consular staff. However, it is not as Young Turk but as national liberator, and not as Mustapha Kemal but as Kemal Ataturk that Kemal is honoured in memorials in every city, town, suburb and village in Turkey. (In the clock museum in Topkapi Sorayi the clocks are all stopped at 9.05, the moment of his death.) In the Military Museum, Istanbul, Kemal stands above the staircase in a stylised representation of the hero leading his people; then, in a museum that begins its exhibits with a display of the court dress of the officials of the Ottoman empire, there are the final scenes in which Kemal abolishes the sultanate and proclaims a Republic of Turkey in 1923. In Taksim Square, in the Monument to the Republic, under a canopy of delicate pink and green, Ataturk stands as liberator.

Istanbul (like London or Vienna) can now seem a monument to collapsed power. Except for the bright brass of the shoe cleaners' stands, Taksim Square is grimy and featureless, dominated at ground level by a bus station and, as the eyes rise, by the big 'S' in the Hotel Sheraton. It leads into what used to be La Grande Rue de Pera, the most fashionable avenue of the Ottoman empire, where the palace-embassies of the great powers sheltered in stately gardens beside the mansions of the richest pashas. Now, it has become Istikial Caddesi, the Avenue of Independence; behind their high wall and wrought-iron gates, some of the old embassies, reduced to consulates, maintain a little of the old style and the Pera Palas Hotel has survived, with its dark, gleaming woods, glossy marble, burnished copper and lavishly wasted space – one of the last hotels of the 'Orient'. But the street has filled up with shops and eating places and come down in the world: its pavements have been eroded, its façades moulder; it is replaced for smartness by a much wider Istanbul boulevard dominated by the Sheraton, the Hilton and the airline offices.

In the days when Europe still seemed the centre of the world, and the Ottoman empire an important part of it, Turkish policy was spoken of as being the work of the 'Sublime Porte' – as people also spoke of policy coming from 'Whitehall' or the 'Quai d'Orsay'. The Sublime Porte itself was a gateway to the palace and offices of the Grand Vizier – receiving its final form in 1843, in Turkish rococo. Where is the Sublime Porte now? The map directions lead to the beginnings of a broken-backed, narrow street devoted to the accumulation of second- third- and fourth-hand motor parts. What is left of the Sublime Porte is a shabby gateway, for the better part defaced and eroded, although some gold-on-green calligraphy remains on top and a wooden canopy survives. It is opposite some fruit stalls. Empty fruit cases are stacked along its sides.

13. Salvationary nationalism

The 'liberators'

Of the 16 European nations that freed themselves from foreign controllers, all but Czechoslovakia, Finland and Norway had some history of 'fighting for their freedom', and monuments to their nationality are partly monuments to fighting heroes. Six of these nations (Spain, Portugal, Greece, Serbia, Romania and Bulgaria) were freed from Islamic conquest. Of the other seven which had 'fought for freedom', Switzerland and the Netherlands had been founded sufficiently long enough ago for the nationalist impulses of the nineteenth century to mark merely an elaboration of existing myth-making. For four of the remaining five (Italy, Hungary, Poland and Ireland, but not Belgium), the late eighteenth and nineteenth centuries were the periods when the liberation heroes they created proved to be some of nineteenth-century Europe's – and the world's – most celebrated political figures. They symbolised not only nationality, but also the human freedom that was seen, in the rhetoric of liberal nationalism, as nationalism's principal justifying aim. Humankind would be saved through national self-expression. In the 1980s, we can see what 'use' is still made of them.

In the case of Belgium, the creation of heroes was to come to nothing and what were monuments to nationalism became monuments to the failure of nationalism. One of these can be found in what used to be the Place St Michael, built in neoclassical style in Brussels in the late eighteenth century when 'Belgium' was still in the Austrian Netherlands; it was renamed the Place des Martyres after the 1830 uprising. At the centre of this shabby square with its stiff, faded houses is a statue of a woman with a lion, allegorising the *patrie* and honouring those who died in 1830. The bodies of the martyrs are buried in a sunken arcaded courtyard beneath the statue; another statue honours the author of the words of the Belgium national anthem ('From out the tomb of bondage and slavery has Belgium at last risen free/And has recovered her bravery, her name, her flag, her liberty,' etc.). An idealised version of the 1830 revolution is told in the Royal Military Museum, Brussels, in a hall with walls decorated with swords arranged in rising-sun pattern, portraits of patriots, gleaming breastplates and drums. ('Liberty! Homeland! Victory! The hour of deliverance has arrived!') But the shabby triumphs of the Place des Martyres and the drums and gleaming breastplates in the Royal Military Museum assert a Belgian 'nationalism' that died not long after the hour of its birth, killed by the Dutch-speaking Belgians of Flanders when they contested the power of the French-speaking Belgians who had made the revolution. Belgium was to be held together not by nationalism, but by a lack of alternatives, and by its railway system. Monuments to the heroes of 1830 are reminders of the failure of the French-speaking Belgians to create the Belgium they had intended.

In Italy, every city celebrates nineteenth-century national heroes and martyrs. In the Via Calibritto, one of the smartest shopping streets in Naples, long red carpets run along the pavements up to a piazza, also surrounded by fashionable shops: this is the Piazza dei Martiri; in its centre, a winged victory rises above lions and palms of triumph to recall the gallantry of the dead of the 1799, 1820, 1848 and 1860 revolts against the Bourbons. In Venice, revolts against the Habsburgs are commemorated in a low relief of Mazzini, the revolutionary, near Vaporetto Station 7, and in a statue of Daniele Manin, the moderate, caught in Napoleonic pose with the sash of liberty across his breast, and at his feet a winged lion modelled on the Carpaccio lion in the Doge's Palace. In Florence, in the Piazza Mentana, now a parking lot, the statue of a gallant soldier, left arm bearing both tattered tricolour and wounded comrade, uses his right hand to fire his pistol at the oppressive foe. In Siena, the old Palazzo Publico has a huge room, now the Hall of the Risorgimento, with a ceiling painting of a personified Italy flanked by Liberty and Independence and six large frescoes brightly glorifying Victor Emmanuel. In Rome, the Central Museum of the Risorgimento celebrates independence and unity with secular relics, from Mazzini's death mask to a wine bottle opened by Garibaldi, and streets are named after battles of the wars of independence. The Victor Emmanuel Monument brings every known classical device to the aid of the idea of the nation: quadrigas, columns, low reliefs, standing statuary, fountains, colonnades, altars and winged victories celebrate action and thought, patriotism and labour, war and revolution, philosophy and politics.

Who cares? Not the tourists: they don't go to Italy to look at nationalist monuments. The Italians? There is scarcely any evidence of interest. The monuments become monuments to bombast and failure. Two of the figures celebrated in statues and columns, frescoes and museums, corsos and piazzas throughout Italy – Mazzini and Garibaldi – became two of the most famous world figures of the nineteenth century, symbolising how a revolution in human betterment might be gained through national freedom. But this was a revolution that, in Italy itself, did not happen. The 'national unity' imposed on Italy was used to suppress that kind of revolution.

In the square facing the parliament building in Budapest, a horseman in 1930s baroque proclaims (in Latin): 'The wounds of the noble Hungarian nation burst open.' These are the opening words of Prince Ferenc Rácóczi's declaration when, in 1703, he raised his red-and-white banners (one of which is in the National Museum) against the Habsburgs and promised freedom from serfdom to all peasants who came to arms to defend Hungary against this oppressor. In Blood Meadow Park, Budapest, a stone memorial commemorates the seven Hungarian Jacobin leaders beheaded there in May 1795; the axe used to execute them now hangs in the National Museum above the stool where they rested their heads. The National Museum also has the armchairs, upholstered in red velvet and arranged in a semicircle, of Hungary's first responsible government, which sat in them for a few months in 1848. On Castle Hill, near where the tourist coaches park, a goddess holds the crown of victory over a victorious warrior in frogged jacket who stands in operative victor's pose, left leg delicately bent, sabre drawn, standard held high; the statue recalls the great months of 1849 when Kossuth's 'Honvéd' army seemed about to win. And it is in Kossuth Square, in front of the Kossuth

Memorial erected by the government in 1952, that the flag of the Hungarian People's Republic is ceremoniously raised on national days. Like Garibaldi and Mazzini, Kossuth became a world figure. In exile in the United States, he made 600 nationalist speeches to cheering audiences. (That he spoke as a Hungarian nationalist whose nationalism was not that of Hungary's Croat, Romanian, Slovak and Serb minorities is another matter.) And, like Garibaldi and Mazzini, he was also seen as a social revolutionary. For peasants in 1848–49 it was their emancipation from serfdom, espoused by Kossuth, not their Hungarian-ness, that mattered. Given this, the regime of Hungary can make more 'use' of Kossuth than the Italians can of Mazzini and Garibaldi. The 1952 Kossuth Memorial shows Kossuth not as nationalist, but as revolutionary leader of peasants, workers and students.

The monuments of Polish nationalism reflect the struggle for Poland's 'soul' as one of the great intellectual melodramas of the nineteenth century. Polish émigré intellectuals in Paris were to represent the heroic ideal of failed nationalist aspiration. In Warsaw and in Krakow, statues of Adam Mickiewicz, his cloak and hair flowing, are still rallying points for scepticism about the Russian style. Mickiewicz's epic poem, 'Pan Tadeusz', gave genius to the myths of nationhood and offered Poland a Christ-figure who was ready to suffer for the salvation of the world and redeem the nations of sin so that they would be worthy of freedom. Seen as one of Europe's greatest nationalist fighters, Tadeusz Kosciusko, stands guard on horseback at the entrance to Wawel Castle, citadel of Polish nationalism: every year at the memorial plaque in the Krakow Town Square that marks the spot where, on 24 March 1794, Kosciusko raised the standards against Russia and took his oath to the Polish nation, men in ceremonial dress stand guard with scythes, symbolising Kosciusko's support from the peasants. In the Warsaw National Museum's 1979 exhibition, 'The Road to Independence', the triumphs of Kosciusko were idealised, though at the time they were followed by paintings of disasters. In one huge canvas, Polonia, like Prometheus, is chained to a rock where the dead are strewn around her, and a black Russian eagle spreads its wings. In the centre, Kosciusko, great hero of yesteryear, stands with drawn sword, reminder of more heroic times. Polish nationalism continues to 'use' the monuments of its past: perhaps they have wider meaning now than when they were erected.

Unlike Kosciusko, other nineteenth-century gentlemen insurrectionaries couldn't gain support from the peasants in Poland. In Ireland, on the other hand, nationalism had a popular base from the start.

One reason can be found in St Peter's at Drogheda, near Dublin. Here, behind a coin-in-the-slot machine that lights up electric 'candles', is displayed a severed head that, when the candles are not lit, appears the head of a live man – bald, with a deep suntan and sparkling white teeth. It is the head of St Oliver Plunkett, revered for his martyrdom in Ireland's cause during the seventeenth century. As Archbishop of Armagh, he was framed by the British, taken to London, hanged, drawn and quartered, and his fate acts as a reminder of the subjection of a people who were religiously suppressed and economically depressed to the point of starvation, with their own gentry acting as agents for foreign conquerers. It was in Ireland that the first mass nationalist movement of the nineteenth century began, largely due to the rhetoric of famous politician–orators who turned politics into an art form. In O'Connell Street, Dublin's largest and most heroically generous group of statues commemorates Daniel O'Connell, the greatest of the political orators. O'Connell was the first to give public form and credence to the catholic Irishness of peasant and priest, in contrast with the ascendant protestant Irishness of the gentry. His monument rises in three tiers: at the top, O'Connell, creator of one of the world's first modern political party machines, faces the rooftops with orator's confidence; beneath him, figures represent the movement with which he is virtually synonymous – the Catholic Association, formed in 1823 to promote political rights for catholics with the parish as organisation bases and priests as party agents; in the bottom tier, four female figures represent Patriotism, Fidelity, Eloquence and Courage.

O'Connell was among the most successful articulators of popular emotion in Europe. 'You are not only a man of one nation; you are a man of all Christendom,' said Lamartine.

Kilmainham Gaol, Ireland's 'Bastille', is a shrine to the Irish Republican Army, for whom it can commemorate all the grandeurs and sorrows of Irish revolt. Abandoned after the civil war, it was restored as a museum by volunteers and now its old, flaking stone, rusting iron and narrow corridors where martyrs' names are brightly lettered above their cells, recall Ireland's long history of struggle. In the grey prison-yards walled in with bleak stone, plaques recall the places where rebels were executed by hanging or shooting. Among the tourists, innocently reading inscriptions and listening to the guides, there can still be present day Irish nationalist revolutionaries, visiting their shrine. Nationalism remains embedded in the Irish imagination, creating a cultural tradition of revolution in a society which is deeply conservative.

Towards the end of the eighteenth century, the Swiss myth of William Tell had begun to gather new meanings and to spread into the nationalism of other countries. With the plays *Guillaume Tell* (1744) by a Frenchman and *Wilhelm Tell* (1777) by a German Swiss, Tell became a fighter not only for hearth and home but for the rights of humanity. At the time of the French Revolution he was seen, like Brutus, to be one of the revolution's precursors; as new movements of national liberation grew, he has seen as a precursor of nationalism as well. Schiller wrote his *Wilhelm Tell* (1804) as a drama of national struggle and freedom; Rossini's opera *Guillaume Tell* (1829), was seen, in an Italy dominated by Habsburgs and Bourbons, as a declaration of Independence.

As the hardy mountaineer who defied the foreign oppressor and led a simple, hard-working people in their struggle for a life that was free and equal, Tell became an international symbol of the national spirit, a hero of freedom along with Washington, Bolivar, San Martin, Mazzini, Garibaldi, Kossuth, Kosciusko. He was the most satisfactory of them all, entirely malleable for mythographers, iconographers and engravers, since he did not exist. Now he means very little to the world at large. To tourists, he is probably not much more than quaint. To the Swiss themselves, however, he can still be a useful, and contested symbol.

The domestic tourism of language creation

Language itself was the most important of all of the components of nationality taken as liberation and self-expression. Developing a nation was not only a matter for orators and freedom-fighters. It could also be a matter for orthographers, grammarians, translators, schoolmasters, writers and others who helped create a written language where previously there had been none. This has created a kind of domestic tourism, with meanings within a nation that the visiting sightseer might not observe.

A museum in Belgrade that reminds Serbians of much about the creation of modern Serbia is on the upper floor of an old Turkish-style house that was part of Belgrade's first high school, opened in 1808 by Dositiej Obradović, later Serbia's first Minister for Education. This building is a reminder that not only had Serbia been physically neglected by the Turks, it had also been culturally desolated, and as its independence grew it was largely to Serbs like Obradović, from the Serbian middle class of south Hungary, that the new government had to look – not only for many of its officials, but for people who could indicate what it might mean to be a Serb. Without a Serbian school system, a modern Serbia could not have existed.

The museum in Obradović's high school displays relics of greater significance than even the first Serbian schoolbooks: the memorabilia of Vuk Karadužić show the acts of creating the modern Serbian language – the first grammars of popular Serbian speech, recorded by Karadužić to give importance to the language of the people, and relics of his creation of a modern Serbian alphabet. The church and conservatives had wanted to maintain the clumsily elaborate Old Slavonic; Karadužić used Cyrillic letters to invent an alphabet based on strictly phonetic principles, giving Serbs what they now claim to be the world's most simple and effective alphabet. In the museum are books using the new alphabet at first banned by the Serbian authorities, and the Serbian dictionary that completed this invention of a new literary language.

In Romania, the Greek language was one of the enemies of the new nationalism: Greek had been the Romanian upper-class language; now they were to learn to talk and write like Romanians. The History Museum, Bucharest, shows this process; by the first half of the nineteenth century books give evidence that education in Greek had been replaced by education in Romanian – school textbooks, the opening speech of the first course in Romanian national history, the first newspapers printed in Romanian. The flourish of statues in front of Bucharest University continues the story: a marble statue in frogged uniform and robe, a book in its hands, depicts Gheorghe Lazar, who opened the first Romanian language high school in 1818, and later the first institute of higher education for the Romanian language; in a marble statue in frock coat, an early Romanian journalist, one of the men of letters who continued Lazar's work, leans slightly forward, one arm and one leg slightly tilted, as if requesting a dance; another marble statue shows a statesman in frock coat, very upright, hands resting firmly on a pedestal, as if about to begin a lecture – another nation-creator.

In Athens, among the classical revival statuary in front of the university's marble colonnades, a patriot in flowing robes raises manacled wrists to the sky – the statue is of Rhigas Pheraios, one of the most satisfactorily romantic of Europe's revolutionary poets, and a symbol of the recreation of Greece through cultural revival. Author of superb songs, prophet of the unifying force of culture and education, Rhigas was trapped by the Austrian police in Trieste in 1797, handed over to the Turks, and executed. Nearby, in the same gardens, is another statue of a scholar lost in stylised patterns of thought; his briefcase, his reading chair and some of his manuscripts are in the National Historical Musuem. The statue and the relics celebrate Adamantios Koraïs, a Smyrnan of the Enlightenment who settled in Paris from where he tried to spread the notion – new to most Greeks, who looked to Constantinople for their history – that they had a connection with classical Greece so strong that their written language should be concocted not from the demotic, the contemporary spoken language, but based on ancient Greek. This new artificial language, Katharévousa, was intended both to be a 'middle way' between classical Greek and the vernacular, and to increase the importance of the nation by relating its language to the classical past. It was, however, to cause an intractable social and political conflict, with Katharévousa supported by conservatives and the demotic language by liberals and populists: in 1901, a government fell over the issue of a vernacular translation of the New Testament. The language issue remained an ingrained part of political life. When the colonels were in power, they took the school texts out of demotic Greek and restored Katharévousa.

At the end of Wenceslas Square, now the main shopping centre in Prague, in the quiet side square dominated by the Church of Our Lady of the Snows, where once the Hussites rallied the poor against the rich, there is a statue of Josef Jungmann, the philologist who strengthened the status of the Czech language by giving it a framework scholarly enough for it to be taught in schools; across the river, at the edge of a park on Kampa Island, a bust commemorates Father Dobrovsky, author of the first comprehensive Czech grammar. On Castle Hill, Budapest, a statue commemorates Ferenc Kazinczy, a Jacobin member of the Enlightenment, who was a leader in the movement for Hungarian language reform; in the early ninteenth century, when newspapers and journals written in Hungarian began to appear, Hungarian became the language of the schools and replaced Latin as the language of administration. In a little park in Vörösmarty Square, Budapest, now centre of the smart district, with pedestrian malls, airline offices, boutiques, restaurants and souvenir shops, Mihály Vörösmarty, the early-nineteenth-century poet, sits amidst Hungarians from different classes who are depicted singing his 'Appeal', written as a national song. By writing sadly of lost greatness, Vörösmarty helped create a sense of a Hungarian past; the square is now noted for an old-style tea room called the Vörösmarty Pastry Shop. In the garden of Budapest's National Museum, János Arany sits in storyteller's pose, beside characters from his long, historical narrative poems.

In the Ljubljana market place a statue was erected to the priest–scholar Valentin Vodnik who founded the first Slovenian newspaper in 1797. Seen as the leader of the 'Slovenian awakening', Vodnik devoted his life to demonstrating that Slovenes had a language and a history; in the high period of nationalism when Napoleon made Ljubljana capital of the 'Illyrian Provinces', a high school was founded and Vodnik became a teacher; by then, another priest–scholar had produced a Slovene grammar. With the return of the Austrians after Napoleon, German again became dominant. Nevertheless, the belief in a Slovenian written language continued to grow, receiving in the work of the poet France Prešeren the vindication of genius of European stature (even if Prešeren's European reputation came from his German rather than his Slovenian writings). Now Prešeren's statue, green among the mellow browns, stands in the busiest square of the old section of Ljubljana, opposite the church of the Jesuits who had earlier so opposed a Slovenian written language; the muse of verse gladly holds the olive branch over his head. The busts of national heroes that decorate the Slovenian club of emigrants to the new world are busts of writers and grammarians.

Outside Sofia's National Library are joint statues of SS Cyril and Methodius, the Thessaloniki brothers who, in the ninth century, developed a Slavonic alphabet and whose persecuted disciples settled in Bulgaria, making it the centre of written Slav culture: Sofia University is named after their disciple, Clement, whose statue is in a park opposite. It was Clement who perfected their alphabet into the present Cyrillic alphabet, named after Cyril, which then spread to Russia and other Slav lands. At the time of 'national revival' in the nineteenth century when the question arose of defining a new Bulgarian nation, the fact that Bulgaria had, 1,000 years before, been a centre of Slav culture helped sustain faith: with liberation from the Turks, one of the first cultural institutes founded in Bulgaria was the National Library, and its custodians began collecting Old Bulgarian manuscripts. To a foreigner, the joint statues of Cyril and Methodius, and of Clement with his arms raised, might seem merely some leftovers from religious orthodoxy. To Bulgarians, though – whose nation-state is the most neglected in the western European imagination – these can be assertions of Bulgaria's claim to be the heartland of Slavonic culture. With this ambition, and the ambition to be seen as precursors of both the renaissance and the reformation, they have made the feast day of Cyril and Methodius a national holiday, 'The Day of Culture, Public Education and Slavonic Writing'.

The domestic tourism of 'national awakenings'

In Bulgaria, the word 'renaissance' – one of the coveted words in the language of modernising Europe – is used to describe the 'cultural revival' or 'national awakening' of Bulgaria in the nineteenth century. In each of what were to become the new nation-states, there was a 'renaissance' or a 'revival' or an 'awakening', in which true Bulgarian-ness, or Finnish-ness, or

Romanian-ness or whatever, was defined. This, too, was usually seen in liberal, progressive terms of self-expression. It has also created its domestic tourism. Just as significant now to the National Library in Sofia as its collection of Old Bulgarian manuscripts, is its collection of books, periodicals, documents, photographs and portraits – a million units in all – of the 'Bulgarian renaissance'.

'Revival' is a theme of one of Bulgaria's tourist attractions, the now heavily conserved and carefully reconstructed Old Plovdiv, part of Bulgaria's second largest city. To the tourist, Plovdiv can seem merely quaint, colourful, authentic, and so forth; but the people who reconstructed Old Plovdiv have provided an interpretation by which one can see in these houses the development of self-esteem among Plovdiv's new Bulgarian merchants. From being a mainly Turkish town, Plovdiv, because of new needs in the Ottoman empire, became a business centre in which Bulgarians took up land along the hillsides and built houses that displayed their new status (if behind high walls so as not to provoke the Turks). It was with merchants such as these, as well as the new contractors and a few owners of small factories, that ideas of autonomy and even of nationalism were in the air.

In Old Plovdiv, as interpreted by the guides, the process can be seen to begin in the late eighteenth century: though houses are still rambling and modest, they have some pretension, with ambitiously carved wooden ceilings and painted walls. Then façades become more decorated; oriels and bay windows push out. Then comes something new, the 'symmetrical house' of the next generation of rich merchants: it is much larger, its façade symmetrically designed, often with specifically Plovidivian curves and gracefully designed bulges, with porticoes and columns and ornate external paintwork. Inside, the ceilings become even more ornately carved; the walls are painted in elaborate patterns, à la frange niches appear in every room with their own landscape paintings; the traditional backless couches of the Ottoman world remain around most of the walls, but expensive furniture from many parts of Europe also appears; and there is a grandiose use of space for display.

The Bulgarian owners of these houses, although they might send their own children abroad to be educated, often to Russia, needed a system of secular education in Bulgaria itself to help sustain them. Many children went to Greek schools, but the chauvinist Hellenism of the Greeks could affront nascent Bulgarianism. The founding book in the Bulgarianising of education, *Slav-Bulgarian History*, written in 1762 by the monk Paissiy, had given people a factual basis for believing they were Bulgarian, a matter to which they previously may not have given much connected thought. There is a statue of Paissiy in Sofia, shown as barefooted monk, right arm upraised, left arm sweeping across the body and holding up a book on which are the words 'Bulgarians, you should know your own people and your own language!' Petur Beron, a weaver's son who had qualified as doctor of medicine had produced another of the works essential to accepted nationality: he wrote a basic manual for schools in the spoken language. In the Rila Monastery, a plaque on an outside wall commemorates Neofit Rilsky, a monk who was the first teacher in the first Bulgarian language school, founded in 1835 by a wealthy merchant who had repented his Hellenism; the monastery museum houses relics of Rilsky – photographs, letters, textbooks, translations. Within a decade, 20 schools of this type were teaching children to be Bulgarian; by the 1850s, most towns and larger villages had such schools. At the same time, the Bulgarian church was a force for 'revival', in its struggle to be independent of Greek control. When the Turks recognised an independent Bulgarian exarchate in 1870, many Bulgarians inferred the existence of a Bulgarian nation. A statue of the first patriarch of the independent Bulgarian church now stands in Sofia, cross in hand, slightly smaller than life, beside the tram track in a five-way traffic junction.

The sense of Bulgarian 'renaissance' reached its personification in the figure of Ivan Vasov, a merchant's son and a revolutionary under the Turks, who became Bulgaria's first professional writer. Proclaimed on his seventieth birthday by the National Assembly as the 'national poet', he wrote *Under the Yoke*, a novel that gave great legendary force to the April Rising against the Turks in 1876 – both to Bulgarians and, in translations, to foreigners. The house where he died in Sofia has become a museum–memorial where, as well as the usual memorabilia, there is a bottle containing his brain and another bottle containing his heart. Along with his statue and his tomb (opened in 1907), the National Theatre is also a memorial to Vasov. As with a National Library, the building of a National

Theatre and a National Opera House, and the establishment of a National Gallery and a Philharmonic Orchestra were important elements in nation-building.

The construction of such buildings was important to national 'awakenings' throughout Europe. The National Theatre, Zagreb, with its gold, white and red, its painted ceilings and chandeliers, was built in the Viennese style. Nevertheless, it was a symbol of the new nationalism – signifying the right, forbidden by the Hungarian masters until 1848, of Croatians to perform plays and operas in their own language. Admission tickets to the National Theatre still carry a nationalist message: on one side, there is a colour reproduction of a famous Croatian painting showing all the main artists and intellectuals of the mid-nineteenth-century movement which took as its name the 'Illyrian Revival', and aimed to unite the Croatians and Serbians. (The Hungarians had banned public use of the word 'Illyria'.) Near the National Theatre is Meštrović's statue of Bishop Strossmayer, sitting outside the south Slav (Yugoslav) Academy of Science and Art. He founded the Academy in 1867 to publish editions of early Croatian poets and antiquarian studies of the southern Slavs; in 1874, he also founded a Croatian University.

Similarly, in adjoining Slovenia no battles were fought against the occupying Austrians, but 'penny collections' financed the building in Ljubljana of a National Slovene House (now the National Gallery) in a nineteenth-century attempt to affirm a sense of a separate culture with the buildings to house it. As part of the same building programme, the Provincial Theatre (now the National Theatre) and a concert hall for the Slovenian Philharmonic Society were built, and a Provincial Museum (now the National Museum) erected to house collections of artifacts that could show aspects of what it might mean to be Slovenian.

Equally, in the Czech lands, struggle with the Habsburgs was a matter of national 'awakening', not of national insurrection – an 'awakening' not even in politics, but in philology, opera, newspapers, poetry and museums. A great deal of this can be reconstructed within a few hundred metres of the neo-renaissance National Museum, Prague. The museum was seen as the central thread in reconstructing a culture by observing the peasants – the ways they spoke, the songs they sang, the proverbs they used, their ceremonies and feasts. For a couple of hundred years the peasants had been almost the only practitioners of ways of being Czech. Within the museum is a collection of the nineteenth-century Czech national painting school which created a distinctive Czech landscape, a glorious Czech past and a special Czech folk virtue; in front of the museum is an early-twentieth-century statue of 'Good King Wenceslas', a failed Bohemian prince who had provided for nineteenth-century Czech-definers a hero-figure of a past Golden Age and, in 1968, in the 'Prague Spring', a rallying point for demonstrators. Around the corner, the neo-renaissance Smetana Theatre recalls in its name the new national music of the Czechs. In a street running out of Jungmann Square, a plaque marks the house of František Palacký, the historian who devoted five volumes to the creation of a credible history for the Czechs, dividing their past into convenient periods of light and darkness. (The street is named after him.) By the river, the neo-renaissance National Theatre recalls the self-definitions of drama. At the foot of the Prague hills, in the old summer palace of the Counts Kinský, collections in the Ethnographic Museum recall the importance of the Czech Ethnographic Exposition of 1895; and in the Museum of National Literature (formerly a building in the old Strahov Monastery) there are assertions of how the 'Hussite tradition' was established in the nineteenth century as a reminder of a Golden Age of national struggle.

In Helsinki's National Museum, there is a painting, *Attack*, which became a national favourite with prints of it hanging on many humble Finnish walls. Done in Berlin in 1899 by the patriot painter Eetu Isto, it depicts the maiden Finlandia in white tunic and blue cloak, on a rock beside the Baltic sea; she is attempting to repulse the two-headed Russian eagle: one eagle head attacks her face; the other, shown chewing a book labelled *Lex*, attacks the laws. It represents a romanticisation of the growing Finnish nationalism of the 1899–1905 conflict with Russia at a time when Finns, or their leaders, wanted to be *Finns*. Helsinki is littered with monuments to this nineteenth-century romantic nationalism which helped create a national 'awakening' and a modern Finland. In front of the Bank of Finland in that elegant part of Helsinki built as a new capital in the neo-classical image of St Petersburg, is a statue of the journalist–professor–statesman J.V. Snellman, seated, hands on thighs. The statue is aptly placed in front of a bank: Snellman is known as 'awakener of the Finnish spirit' because of his successful campaign for Finnish as an official language of administration and law, and also because he won his campaign for Finland to have its own currency. In the Esplanade, at the edge of Helsinki's 'Petersburg' section (used in making the film *Reds*) is another statue. J.L. Runeberg, right hand on heart, is depicted near a maiden who holds up the words he wrote for 'Our Land', the Finnish national anthem, and first sung by a group of students (rebelliously), in May 1848, in what was Helsinki's contribution to the year of revolution. Runeberg was creator (if in Swedish) of the archetypal Finn as a noble-minded, simple-living, hard-working farmer – an image he manufactured so successfully that it might still be drawn on by Finns in crisis. The third statue, in Lönnrot Street, shows the poet Elias Lönnrot – intelligent, kindly, whimsical, getting it all down with pencil and paper; beside him in the sculpture group are two of his best-known characters. Lönnrot put folk poetry together into a collection, the *Kalevala* (1835) that became the national epic, demonstrating the distinctiveness of the Finns. The painter Akseli Gallen-Kallela used *Kalevala*'s themes in his museum frescoes; Sibelius, himself commemorated in a structure of pipes in Helsinki's Sibelius Park, went through a *Kalevala* period. As one of the early twentieth century's most famous modernist railway stations, the Helsinki Station, designed by Eero Saarinen, also became a symbol of national esteem.

In front of the Royal Flemish Theatre in Gent, between the Lakenhalle's grandiose belfry, part of the architectural pride of Flanders, and St Baafskathedraal, where an admission fee gains access to Van Eyck's *Adoration of the Lamb*, two allegorical figures preside over a statue to J.F. Willems, a nineteenth-century philologist. Willems is seen as father of the Flemish movement which struggled for a century-and-a-half to create within the Belgium state a separate Flemish nation: five million people in an area 200 kilometres by 70 kilometres who, because they spoke Dutch, saw themselves as belonging to western Europe's sixth-largest language group. Willems represents the Flemish autonomous movement; he and other Flemish intellectuals 'created' (that is to say, articulated) Flemishness as an autonomous nationality. They gave form to the sense of Flemishness by writing its history; they provided 'dates' and 'periods'. In doing this, they performed an act of cultural violence against the overlordship of the French-speaking upper and middle classes who had imagined, after their revolt against the Netherlands, that the 'Belgium' founded in 1831, was a new, French-speaking nation. In Brugge, in the centre of the Markt, a bronze statue honours Jan Breidel and Pieter de Coninck, leaders of the temporarily successful 1302 revolt against the French; but the erection of the statue in 1887 marked a different and longer-lasting success from that of Breidel and de Coninck. The statue itself was a symbol of the revolt of Belgian Dutch-speakers against the dominance of the French language. When an Antwerp romantic novelist wrote an historical novel in Dutch and a Brugge poet wrote verse in Dutch, they, too, were erecting 'monuments'; Flemish songs were popularised; Rubens, whose statue in Antwerp (1840) already commemorated him as a 'Belgian', became instead a Flemish culture hero; a Flemish Opera, a Flemish Academy of Music and a Flemish Theatre were established; Van Eyck and other early Flemish masters, little heard of in 1831 when Belgium was 'invented', were seen as symbols of how Flemish civilisation helped bring all Europe its cultural revival.

As a European backwoods, Wales, unlike Flanders, could not present itself as having once been a centre of European civilisation. But as a 'nation' within a nation, like Flanders, it defined itself through a cultural awakening. As the Folk Museum at St Fagan's shows, the Welsh found a past in dreamy ideas of the druids and in the celticness that prevailed before the conquests, and, in particular, in the idea of the early bards: they celebrated their newly defined Welshness with their voices, in chapel, quarry and colliery choirs, and in Eisteddfodau competition (revived at the end of the eighteenth century). By the mid-nineteenth century Cymru (Wales), was seen as a distinct entity with its own language and culture; in 1885, the Society for Utilising the Welsh Language was formed. Within a few years, it had won the right for Welsh to be a teaching language.

Part six

Imperial Europe

14. Conquest of the world

Imperialism was the nationalism of the great powers, and the enemy of the nationalism of all lesser powers. With the assumption that white people had been divinely chosen to hold dominion over all other peoples, the remaining question was merely: Which race of people could successfully assert that God had chosen it for his purposes? In the two world wars, Europeans turned this imperialism inwards, on to themselves.

Along with the other relics of power that tourists walk among are monuments to the wreckage of Europe's greatest ambition – to rule the world. It is for its imperialism rather than its nationalism that Europe remains distrusted. The characteristic monuments of imperialism are of emperors, viceroys, missionaries, field marshals and 'discoverers' – monuments to conquerors. The characteristic monuments of nineteenth-century nationalism are of writers and artists, educators, and grammarians, rebels – monuments to liberators. Most nineteenth-century nationalist movements were liberal, self-expressive, optimistic, enlightened, secular. Nineteenth-century imperial imaginations were not limited, but pre-emptive and total: they fed upon gigantic phatasmagoria sprung from an endless and many-sided gargantuan struggle of service and sacrifice, in which the heroic objective was to save the world; moreover, they were based on grandiose assumptions that God had chosen only one race (Anglo-Saxon, Slav, Teuton, Latin – depending on the point of view) to impose order on humankind.

Fascism, (Nazism, in particular) was a form of nineteenth-century imperialism – not only in the uniforms, the glittering orders, the struttings and the choreographed ceremonies, but also in the confidence of its imperialist racism. Fascist movements were not 'nationalist' in any ordinary historical sense. Most nationalist movements were middle-class programmes for secular progress.

Nazism was, among other matters, a huge programme based on imperialism and racism, for the destruction of nationalism. Nazism transformed into 'natives' many of the peoples of Europe itself. The confidence with which European racism had divided the rest of the world into the master race of the whites and the sub-human races of the 'coloureds' now turned in on itself: if Africans had seemed sub-human, so could Slavs.

Every social order in Europe has had its victims. The best one can do is to evaluate them in terms of greater or lesser evils. This last part of the book is concerned with those aspects of the European experience which can be most concerned with a body-count of victims: the imperialism that transformed the world and then killed such a significant proportion of Europeans themselves that the memorialising of their deaths has been one of the most sorrowful themes in European tourism.

European monopoly of the world

The tourist in Lisbon is directed to three particularly significant modern monuments, each of which can be seen from the site of the others. One is the huge cement representation of Christ, illuminated at night, on the left bank of the Tagus; the second, a symbol of modern growth, is boasted to be the longest suspension bridge in Europe; the third is the Monument to the Discoveries, a vast, bleak structure shaped in part like a ship's prow, which celebrates the sea-faring missions that opened the whole world to Europe's ambition. In fact, Portugal gained such enormous prospects of potency that the Pope divided the globe between it and Spain.

But the idea of 'discovery' is a European and not just a Portuguese idea. The Europeans both replaced China as self-acclaimed centre of the world and expanded the horizons of 'the world' wider than previously imagined. Until the rise of the Japanese, Europeans were to maintain this new type of power as their monopoly, although fighting about it among themselves for several centuries. The word 'discovery' suggested that Asia, America, central and southern Africa assumed importance only when European 'discoverers' set eyes on them. Thus, despite its

Portuguese emphasis, the Monument to the Discoveries honours all Europe.

In the vestibule of the Portuguese Maritime Museum, Prince Henry – 'The Navigator' – is celebrated with a statue and an outline, in a stained-glass window, of his genealogical tree. Between statue and window is a map showing the great Portuguese explorations – the slow pushings, cape by cape, down the west coast of Africa to establish warehouses and forts for trade in ivory, slaves and gold; then the great voyage to India of Vasco da Gama's four ships and the voyages to Canton, and the spice islands. In the Maritime Museum's main hall, Prince Henry is represented in a tapestry with the sea captains, map-makers, astronomers, instrument-makers and ship-builders who met with him in his long, obsessive retreat in the small court he established at Sagres, on the tip of south-west Portugal. Intent on applying reason to the practical problems of spreading the Christian faith and Portuguese trade, and of outflanking the Moslems by sea, he and his court symbolise European enterprise and expertise. In symbolism it is matched by a model, in a small glass case, of the lateen caravel – the three-masted ship with triangular ('lateen') sails, designed to travel longer distances with smaller crews, and so facilitate European 'discovery'. In other display cases are accompanying technological advances: compasses, charts, manuals, astrolabes, primitive quadrants. Then the museum presents another technological advance: the cannon. Models show how the Portuguese introduced broadside gunfire and, in mementoes of great battles, how they used this new technique to revolutionise naval strategy. Instead of using ships mainly for boarding, and guns merely for killing, the Portuguese used broadside gunfire to sink ships, rather than to kill men. By developing this technique, a minor European power was able to sail into the Indian Ocean and, within a few years, suppress competition from the commercially more efficient Arab traders by blowing up their ships. The battle of Diu, fought off the west coast of India in 1509, only a decade after da Gama's voyage, is one of history's most significant naval battles: a great, Venice-backed armada of Indian, Egyptian and Arabian ships lost against the interloping Portuguese, who used their new broadside technique and the greater range and accuracy of their cannonfire not only to defeat the armada, but to sink most of it. The museum shows how in the next year they captured Goa then, four years later, seized the Arabian fort at Hormu, one of Asia's greatest markets, and established another base. For 100 years, with their Indian Ocean navy, their stone forts, warehouses, dockyards and barracks, the Portuguese dominated a trading area of 25 million square kilometres.

This period of sudden riches is marvellously commemorated in Lisbon's Belém Tower and in the Jerónimos Monastery. The latter was begun not long after da Gama's return and houses his sepulchral monument in its church. The monastery and the tower are both in white stone in a style whose motifs and decorations, as well as being obviously Christian, reflect a love of the sea and a period of confidence that formed its own architectural style. And its own epic poetry: opposite da Gama's monument, an effigy crowned in laurel rests above the tomb of Luiz de Camoës, Portugal's national poet, who made an epic out of the 'discoveries'. In both the church and the monastery cloisters, ships' ropes are recurrently stylised in stone columns and arches; and the Belém Tower fortress seems held together by carved-stone rope and carved nautical knots. There are other motifs of the sea, in corals, shells, fish, and reminders of the areas the Portuguese dominated: a palm tree in stone, a carved rhinoceros, stone elephants supporting a tomb. In their confidence, the superb and intricate decorations of the monastery do not mar its elegance: while the Belém casemate is thick and sturdy, beside it is a delicately designed cloister; its robustly battlemented parapet makes an elegant terrace. Though the tower itself is equally robust, it also offers balconies with lacelike stone, splendid chambers with generous fireplaces and expansive windows, and an airy loggia with stone filigree.

Now green fern grows in niches in the monastery walls and tourists jostle on the narrow stairs of the Belém Tower. Beside the tower, a few palms rise above the snackbar and souvenir stalls, recalling the old expansion; across the river, the new realities of trade are recalled by the storage tanks put up by Esso.

In the harbour at Barcelona, against a background of cranes and large ships, there is a tiny wooden vessel, less than 30 metres long, painted mainly in black, with some red and green. It is a copy of Columbus's *Santa Maria*. In a minute or two, sightseers can walk around an area where the 40 or so sailors lived during their crossing of the Atlantic. This, rather than the monuments of Portugal, can seem the true Monument to the Discoveries. But Portugal was the true innovator of a new relationship with the world, even though the cult of Christopher Columbus gives Spain the fame. Nevertheless, despite his enormous error in thinking it was the outskirts of Asia he had reached and not the outskirts of America, Columbus became one of the most important hero-figures in the European imagination. Prince Henry, with his expertness and his team work, was much more distinctively European, as was the way the government of Portugal, one of the first nation-states, developed a long programme for supporting exploration, experiment, trade and conquest. The Columbus story is merely a tale of doggedness and boldness. The Portuguese experts were right in rejecting his ill-prepared proposal for reaching Asia: it was based on false assumptions. But it is Columbus who is seen as characteristic of European enterprise.

As with Lenin, painters have invented episodes of his 'Passion' to symbolise Columbus the visionary. They can be found among nineteenth-century academic 'history paintings' in European and United States museums. These paintings are set around certain famous episodes in the Columbus cycle. In the first episode, he is the prophet ignored or derided by the wise men of the age – as a sage mocked by the committee of enquiry at Salamanca – or alternatively as the individual of iron initiative who declared, 'You can do anything when you know how.' Then there is the moment when his genius is recognised by the friars at La Rabida, whose superior writes a recommendation to the queen. Paintings of the heroic departure are followed by paintings of Columbus as captain of the *Santa Maria*, a solitary seer whose special vision illuminates the lonely, spiritual journey. Then comes the episode of triumph – in huge canvasses by nineteenth-century French romantics – of his greatest day, when he is received at court and presents to Ferdinand and Isabella gold, exotic artifacts, parrots and Indians. The penultimate scene shows the 'martyrdom' of the far-seeing seer: his arrival home in chains after his third voyage. The last episode marks the lonely death of a great man who has been neglected, ill-used and misjudged.

In the Paseo de Colón, in Barcelona, behind the replica of the

Santa Maria, triumphant lions and allegorical figures in the cast-iron Columbus monument symbolise the Christian and civilising mission of Spain. Behind the monument are the beautifully preserved interconnected naves of the Royal Arsenals. One of Spain's greatest shipyards, it added military and technical skill to the high confidence of a sure Christian faith, and to the crusading delight in plunder and glory. Helped by European diseases spreading among populations which had no resistance to them, this high confidence within a few decades inspired the destruction of most of the previously well-established societies in the larger part of a whole continent. But the people who run the Museo de America, Madrid, do not seem to have given this any thought.

The museum opens in a large hall with vaulted ceiling and green marble floor, with the gold of pre-Columbian objects shining from display cases in the next hall: a map, lit by pressing buttons, shows the great Spanish crossings of the Atlantic, and their purposes; there is a model of the *Santa Maria*, a painting of Columbus and a copy of the report he presented to Ferdinand and Isabella. In the halls that follow, one has statuary stripped from the pyramids of Mexico and another has Amerindian ceramics – but then, after a corridor of Inca ceramics and a ragbag collection from an exhibition in 1862, there is nothing more about the original Americans. The rest of the Museo de America displays oddments of what happened later. Displaying traditional obsession with authentic relics and 'fine things', the museum records developments in the artifacts of America; there is no reference to the destruction of the native societies that ensued as the Spaniards created gold and silver mines, sheep and cattle ranches, tobacco plantations, and sugar plantations – all worked by African slaves.

Cults of the sea

Amsterdam's maritime museum (the Nederlands Scheepvarte Museum) is in a vast old trading-house built on 18,000 piles in the mid-seventeenth century – exactly the right period, since with the decline of Portugal and the faltering of Spain, the Netherlands had become the next great imperial power, and with its 'empire of the seas', the world's greatest trading nation. The model in the museum most significant of this change is the *fluyt*, the most innovatory ship of the seventeenth century. Cheaply built, it was a kind of seagoing barge, with plenty of room for cargo, and required only a small crew. The Dutch developed this ship in the 1590s and it helped give them domination of bulk cargo-carrying in the Baltic, the Mediterranean and West Africa, then some of the local American trade and, as soon as they overwhelmed the Portuguese, local trade in the Indian Ocean.

The Rijksmuseum's colonial history rooms of the Dutch history section figure the self-satisfied faces of the kind of men who built the elegant houses along Amsterdam's Keizergracht that provide the greatest reminders of the Netherlands' Golden Age. Their portraits look down on glass cases containing exotic objects in gold, silver and porcelain, souvenirs of the extraordinary speed with which the Dutch replaced the Portuguese in Asia, where they captured the Portuguese forts and trading-posts and, on the ruins of the Javanese town of Jakarta, set up their own town of Batavia. This latter became the centre of their spices monopoly and of the trading-fleets they sent to China, India and Japan for textiles, coffee, tea and porcelain.

In the Amsterdam Historical Museum is a painting called *The Spirit of Amsterdam Receives the Tribute of the World*, in which Amsterdam, a young woman, displays her left breast as she leans her right hand on a globe of the world; behind her, Mercury, as god of commerce, supervises the multiracial traders of the world as they lay their merchandise at Amsterdam's feet.

In art museums throughout Europe, Dutch seascapes reflect the serenity of those who had become at home in the sea – ships' timbers, sails, water and Dutchmen all seem part of the same substance. For a season, the Dutch seemed to own the oceans. Among the colonial history paintings in the Rijksmuseum are pictures of Dutch trading-posts in the East. The Dutch *factorijen* had replaced the Portugese *feitorias*; these trading 'factories', with their fortified harbours and garrisons, display the strength and the geometrical order of those who seemed the final masters. But there were to be no final masters. A Dutch governor-general in Batavia said in 1614, 'We cannot carry on trade without war, nor war without trade.' The globe was now disputed by European powers, and the Pope could no longer resolve the conflict by dividing the world: the Dutch fought their commercial rivals in the East Indies, the West Indies, North America, Southern Africa, Brazil. Around the walls of one room in the Rijksmuseum are paintings of battles they fought at sea: little ships are seen letting off clouds of smoke. As one follows the chronological trail among these clouds of smoke and flashes of fire, the Dutch lose to the British – and it is in Britain that reminders of the European cult of the sea acquire their greatest gusto.

On the banks of the Thames at Greenwich, in splendid buildings seen as London's finest architectural group, the National Maritime Museum uses the failure of the Spanish Armada as the starting-point in its confidently expansive chronicle of the rise of Britannia to 'rule the waves' (in the words of the eighteenth-century song). Contemporary models of ships, paintings of men and battles, along with maps, navigation instruments, uniforms and weapons tell how the British defeated the Dutch, and moved into the long haul of British successes in the wars of the eighteenth century that led to the cult of Horatio Nelson. As a hero 'son of the sea', Nelson and his successes gave extra sheen to British imperialism. Portraits at Greenwich show Nelson as a young second-lieutenant boarding a prize ship in 1777, then as the heroic victor of the battles of St Vincent, the Nile and Copenhagen; in one famous portrait, his mistress poses as seductive innocent and in another, his own mischievous adventurer's face rises out of the solemn uniform of a rear admiral as if he had dressed in it for a joke. In his apotheosis, Nelson rises to heaven supported by clouds and appropriately beautiful women. In Trafalgar Square, in one of the nineteenth-century's most famous colossal monuments, Nelson stands on his Corinthian column, 50 metres above the buses. In the *Victory* museum at Portsmouth, they show the dozens of forms of contemporary kitsch in which his fame was celebrated – medallions, wine glasses, snuff boxes, shaving mugs, and several dozen other products of the early nineteenth-century souvenir trade.

Nelson's light-heartedness can seem foreign against the solid comfort aspired to by nineteenth-century Britannia. But there was organisation behind the 'Nelson touch'. In one section of the National Maritime Museum, contemporary models of royal dock-yards show some of the organisation that combined with the Nelson magic to support British power. In Plymouth, at a dockyard established by William III, the Royal Navy now runs official tours. Across the bay, the Royal William Victualling Yard is still used by the navy, but is also claimed by industrial archaeologists as a precious monument to nineteenth-century vision. Set over two-and-half hectares, the Royal William Victualling Yard provides a study in the confidence of neoclassical design. A classical archway and two colonnaded arcades lead into a symmetrically balanced avenue. A square of green grass is surrounded by highly stylised buildings of silvery stone. Beside a pool, a neoclassical palace with a fine clock confronts a small stone-walled harbour. It was assembled in the 1830s with steam engines and slaughterhouses as a place to make chocolate, cure meat, grind flour, bake biscuits and brew beer. Now it is a monument of nostalgia not only to lost sea power, but also to a lost confidence in architectural design.

In the Place du Petit Sablon, Brussels, among the semicircle of statues of famous Low Country sixteenth-century humanists, that of Gerhardus Mercator, the Flemish geographer, holds in its hand a model of the sphere he succeeded in projecting on to a flat sheet of parchment as a map. All the maritime museums of Europe show the maps and almanacs and quadrants and chronometers and other instruments the Europeans used to order the world.

Of all these reminders of precision, the most precise is the strip of brass in the old Royal Observatory at Greenwich, near the Maritime Museum. Above it are the words:

The Prime Meridian of the World
East   West

The observatory was established in the seventeenth century to settle the question of longitude, to bring the world more predictably under the control of European ships. The observatory museum shows the kinds of instruments by which the heavens were searched for answers and the kinds of maps and mathematical tables that turned these observations into practice. The Maritime Museum houses mementoes of the meticulously orderly James Cook, one of the greatest navigational practitioners: his charts, sketches done by his artists, the work he did on scurvy and anti-scorbutics, the portable tent he would set up for astronomical observations, his styles in sextant, quadrant, compass and chronometer – symbols of his skill and reasonableness. Then the painting by John Zoffany shows the chance killing by Hawaiians of this model of eighteenth-century rationality.

The painting symbolises both the systematic enquiry that went into European command of the oceans and the slaughters that followed it. While British monuments and museums can celebrate both the sense of power and the sense of reason that impelled European expansion, they don't seem to capture 'the love of the sea'.

The Maritime Museum, Oslo, is more successful in doing this – and appropriately so. Obsession with the sea made the Norwegians, despite their small population, the world's third-largest maritime power by 1914. The museum presents the great clichés (familiar to all readers of sea stories) of tamed oceans: the crew's fo'c'sle, the ship's galley, the ship's bridge with its sense of lonely command, and the first-class passengers' quarters, affirming, in smoke room, dining-room and cabins, the confidence of fine linen and leather and polished wood.

Land conquest

The Russian Museum in Leningrad has a huge nineteenth-century canvas commemorating one of the heroes of the tsarist conquest of a large part of Asia. It is painted by Vasily Surikov and, with an all-inclusive brevity, is called *Yermak's Conquest of Siberia*. On one side of the painting are the sixteenth-century Cossack adventurer and his troops with their guns; on the other side are the Tartars with their bows and arrows. By the end of the sixteenth century, the Russians had conquered western Siberia; in the seventeenth century, they reached the Pacific Ocean; by the end of the eighteenth century, Russia had expanded into central Asia and Alaska and half its empire's population were conquered peoples, many Moslems or pagans; in the nineteenth century, this greatest of all colonial land expansions was to continue – by war, diplomatic bullying, and guerilla penetrations and seizures, in mountains and forests, steppes and deserts. 'The frontier' had deep meanings in tsarist Russia, as it did in the United States. Imperial expansion was Russia's manifest destiny. In 1864, the tsarist Minister for Foreign Affairs explained to the great powers that, as with the British in India and the European settlers in North America, when Russia's civilising mission brought it into contact with one barbarous tribe, it would be forced to subdue these natives – and so come into contact with the tribe beyond. Thus, argued the minister, the boundaries of civilisation were inevitably extended; Russia had no aggressive designs, only a duty to uphold order and civilisation.

All that the souvenir museums now directly celebrate of this uniquely successful European land expansion is the occupation of the Arctic. In Leningrad, the Arctic Museum is in an old church where frescoes of exploration have replaced most of the religious symbols, although guides will still point to the remaining religious decoration as if it were more important than Arctic objects. There are relics, of thirteenth-century Novgorod merchants' trading goods retrieved from the ice, a model of a seventeenth-century wooden fortress, eighteenth-century navigation plans, and then, from 1877 onwards, relics of what is labelled 'the period of Arctic expeditions under capitalism' – ropes, cans, a discarded camera, a wristwatch, a knife, a razor. The project gains greater authority in 1920 with a painting of Lenin meeting the Arctic scientists: there follow dioramas of base camps; there is an Arctic tent, an Arctic plane, air-force goggles, morse-code sets, Soviet medals. In an upper gallery are the pelts of animals – ermine, Arctic fox, sable – the search for which sent Russian fur-traders across Siberia and into Alaska, as it also sent French and British fur-traders scouring the north and the west of America for animal pelts to sell to Europe. Some idea of the scope of tsarist subjugation of Asian lands comes in another Leningrad museum, the Ethnographical Museum of the Peoples of the USSR, built mainly out of collections made in the late nineteenth and early twentieth centuries, of artifacts from conquered cultures. Their vastness and diversity ranges from Siberian folk costumes made from fish skin to beer mugs from Livonia.

The Royal Museum of Central Africa near Brussels has assembled leftovers showing something of the development of European consciousness of Africa – the maps which got the Europeans there, the crucifixes which gave them faith, animals and humans who gave curiosity to the 'dark continent'. The museum's Memorial Room is a leftover of astounding imperial arrogance. A larger-than-life statue of Leopold II, one of the most lurid names in anti-imperialist demonology, dominates a room celebrating the triumphs of colonialism with the guns and flags of expeditions and the chests carried by native bearers, the plumed hats of the conquerors, models of their railway lines and the honoured names of those who laid down their lives controlling the natives. However, in another room one case of exhibits shows African-made statues and paintings of Belgians: they have turned-up moustaches, pop eyes, plastered hair and weak chins.

The museum also honours the 'explorers', in particular with mementoes of Stanley and Livingstone – including a contemporary children's game, 'Stanley's March Across the Dark Continent' ('new, instructive, amusing') and leaves gathered from the tree beneath which Livingstone's heart was buried. The 'explorers' are also honoured in Paris, in a large memorial to Commandant Marchant, leader of a French African expedition; the sculpture group shows a European tending a native while the other native bearers quietly carry their burdens. Across the road from the memorial, on the outside of what used to be the French Colonial Exhibition building, is one of the world's largest stone reliefs. At its centre, 'natives' represent Abundance (a Buddha-like native), Peace (a somnolent native) and Liberty (a dancing native). They are surrounded by a busy world of rubber-tapping, tea-picking, fish-netting, rice-growing, timber-cutting – and other tasks that God had given.

The heart of the explorers' cult is Kensington Gore, London. Here, standing in niches in the brick wall of the Royal Geographical Society, are statues of Shackleton (a knight in white Antarctic armour) and of Livingstone (a gentleman ready for an afternoon stroll on a rather warm day). Inside the building are 600,000 map sheets, 100,000 books and commemorations and relics of the British explorers of Africa, Australia, the Antarctic and Asia. There is a whole section of the tree under which Livingstone's heart was buried.

Though it was from the Royal Geographical Society that many of the British land explorations of the nineteenth century were subsidised – or at least honoured – there is an even fuller commemoration of empire across the road, in the Albert Memorial. Each of its four supports is a large sculpture group representing one of the four continents. Two of them point east: 'Asia' consists of an Indian princess on a kneeling elephant accompanied by a Chinese with a porcelain vase, and two Arabs, one of whom has brought his saddle; 'Africa' is a queen of Ancient Egypt on a camel accompanied by Arabs and blacks.

In some lands, the Europeans installed colonial versions of their society within other civilisations, and living as alien overlords supervising mines or plantations or trading-posts, partly disintegrated those societies. In lands where the indigenous civilisation lacked resistance, the Europeans seized the 'wilderness' (so defined because it wasn't being used for European-style purposes), pushed the natives aside as if they were troublesome animals, and turned the land into farms. They transfigured landscapes, produced new cities and towns and created new societies. In Europe itself by the end of the nineteenth century, imperialism as a secular faith accommodated both the aristocrats who administered the empires' armies and navies, and the bourgeois who made fortunes from imperial financing and trading. In the new democratic mode, membership of a dominant 'race' – Slav, Anglo-Saxon, Teutonic, Latin – could also confer dignity on even the humblest citizen. All could imagine they shared the task, given by God, to save humanity by making it European. Colonial conquerors became secular saints, with statues to their honour. The people sang the new imperial hymns and celebrated the cleansing cults of blood. The war of 1914–18 allowed them to put their songs into action.

15. The imperialists' war

The 'Great War' of 1914–18

The Austrian Museum of Military History gives over a long gallery to the military glory of the reign of Franz Josef. This long gallery suggests an approaching triumph with its two processional rows of regimental flags, its bugles and paintings of battles and ceremonial pomp, its showy uniforms and swords. But instead of triumph is a long, black car, its hood down, its spare tyre beside the brake on the running board, its back seat as capacious as a landau, a flag on its left-hand side, a carriage lamp at its back. It is the car in which Franz Ferdinand was assassinated on 28 June 1914. Also in this room, laid out in a glass clase like an honoured corpse, is the most famous of all the gorgeous uniforms of Austrian pretension – the helmet with green plumes, the blue jacket with red and gold facings, the black trousers with a red stripe and the golden sword tassles of the uniform Franz Ferdinand wore that day. There is a rip along the left-hand sleeve of the jacket and over the heart; the dried blood has faded, but it still puckers the cloth. In the glass case opposite, precise to the last minute, is the printed timetable for the day's ceremonies at Sarajevo, the order of the small procession of cars and the seating list, souvenir menu and printed music programme for the dinner to have been held that night.

The monuments to the 'Great War' gave a new meaning to the idea of tourist pilgrimage. It was a war that mobilised 65 million, killed 18 million – civilians as well as soldiers – wounded 22 million, disabled 7 million and turned millions more into civilian refugees or military prisoners. It was fought in the crusading, salvationary and apocalyptic style of the contemporary creed of imperialism. It was nineteenth-century imperialism's logical conclusion.

Yet in some museums treatment is almost frivolous. Most of the Austrian museum is devoted to presenting Austria as a military power of great world consequence, demonstrated in the brilliant colours of its military uniforms and flags, and in the sheen of its cannon and armour. One of the four longest galleries in the moorish-byzantine-revival building that houses the museum is taken up with presenting in paintings, flags, figureheads, uniforms and models, Austrian *sea power* ('little-known and wrongly ignored'). After the museum's display on Franz Ferdinand's assassination, all that follows about the Great War is a collection of war artists' paintings and a row of peepshow machines with handles which tourists can turn to produce a series of photographs of Austro-Hungarian grandeur and débâcle.

In almost pathologically bad taste, the Army Museum, Paris, presents the Great War as if it were nothing new. To match its general presentation of war as a fashion parade of pretty flags, bright clothes and decorated weapons, the museum's emphasis in the 1914–18 display is on the uniforms of the allies – as if what were most remarkable about so many millions of dead were the clothes in which they died.

For their own reasons, the Soviet and German museums record almost nothing of the warfare on the Eastern Front. Yet even in just one of its complex battles of manoeuvre, hundreds of thousands could be captured or killed; the Russians alone had almost two million dead.

Like the Austrians, the Military Museum in Istanbul also shrinks from the war's disasters. There is some celebration of the defence of the Dardanelles – the last victory of the Ottoman empire – but almost nothing about the fronts on which the Turks, at the end, collapsed and saw the collapse of all their conquests.

In the marble palace inside the Victor Emmanual Monument in Rome, the circular gallery given over to the Italian role in the First World War presents it with a stylish understatement that seems inappropriate to its horrors. There is an emphasis on war propaganda posters whose bright colours take the eyes from the otherwise dominating presence of marble. The Italian retreat from Caporetto, in which nearly 600,000 were lost, is underplayed; so, too, is the great Italian recovery at the Piave when 29 Italian divisions halted 50 Austrian and German divisions – although one poster shows an Italian soldier, single-handed, repelling the helmeted snakes of Austria and Germany. The Army Museum in

Athens finds it difficult to acknowledge that the Allied Forces which set up a base in Thessaloniki had forced themselves into Greece and maintained their uneasy position at one stage by arranging a small march on Athens, and, at another, by compelling the king to abdicate.

However, the Military Museum, Belgrade, breathes passion. In letters as high as those accorded elsewhere in the museum to the words of Tito and Lenin is the famous die-to-the-last-man order. This was given to those soldiers chosen to cover the retreat when, having three times driven the Austrians back into Austria in 1914, the Serbian army was itself forced out of Serbia when challenged by combined Austrian, German, and Bulgarian troops. The order told the defenders of Belgrade that their names had been taken off the army rolls: 'Your unit is sacrificed for the honour of Belgrade and of our country. Don't worry about your lives; you don't exist any more.' A photograph in the museum shows the heroic Serbian retreat through the snow of the Albanian mountains into Corfu, where the Serbs rested and then went on to Thessaloniki to join the Allies. In Serbia, the First World War is still seen as a patriotic war in which more than a million of Serbia's five million people lost their lives – the most melancholy loss of any country.

In Poland, the war is the occasion of liberation. In the Army Museum, Warsaw, the display of uniforms of the Polish Legion is a reminder that the Poles, under Pilsudski, used the war to finish their struggle against Russia – and then rebelled against taking an oath of allegiance to the Germans. There are also uniforms from the other Polish armies which, under Haller, fought alongside the French on the Western Front to finish the struggle against Germans and Austrians. In Koprivshtitsa in Bulgaria in the garden of the house of the young poet Dimcho Debelyanov, killed on the Southern Front in 1916, stands his mother's pensive statue, nationally famous as the Monument of the Waiting Mother – a symbol of the disasters war had brought to Bulgaria. In Romania, the Great War memorials are inscribed with the dates '1916–18' – in 1916 Romania made a disastrous intervention on the Allied side; war was declared in late summer and lost in early winter, but towards the end, Romania came in again. In Bucharest in the Central Army Museum, is a representation of a dispirited machine-gun group, displaying Romanian gallantry.

The trenches

It is the Imperial War Museum, London, that reaches into the central part of the horror of the war. In its opening display the museum presents some of the proclamations issued while Britain, Germany, France and Austria-Hungary were moving towards war. Not only mobilisation notices, but notices about altered rail timetables, work on Sundays, bans on public demonstrations and on the use of carrier pigeons, rallying calls for the preservation of national honour, orders for the requisitioning of horses, appeals to remain calm and not to hoard small change. These were the kinds of orders traditionally put up on walls to make life ready for war. No one knew the awesomeness of the coming calamities. The distinctive tragedy of the war, apart from the immensity of its slaughter, was that, beginning with the efficient functioning of the mobilisation rail timetables, it was a demonstration of the European talents for rationality and organisation. If there is one word that summarises the horror that the use of this talent produced it is the *trenches*, and the Imperial War Museum has a special gallery anatomising the trench life.

With a background tape-recording of shells whizzing and exploding, soldiers' songs and marching feet, it shows the patterns by which millions lived and died in a war in which a battle might last not just an afternoon, nor for two or three days, but for many months and, caught in a state of mutual siege, cause hundreds of thousands of deaths. In these conditions, new ways of living were quickly improvised, turned into drill programmes and training manuals, and thus into a new normality with its own rules. The gallery recalls the layouts of the trenches – forward trenches, support trenches, communications trenches – and how men were reticulated between them with so many days in the Front Line, so many in the support line, so many in billets as reserves and so many in rest camp. It recalls the drill for moving men with their trench stores up into the Front Line, and of relieving them, each with 48 hours' rations in case something went wrong. It recalls the drills for routine Front Line duty: before dawn, one hour's stand-to; during the day, sentry duty and maintenance work (filling sandbags, digging drains); before sunset, one hour's stand-to. At night, the real work began: the arduous supplying of water, ammunition and provisions to the Front Line for the next day's eating and killing, the repairing and strengthening of the trench systems, the stringing up of barbed wire, and the essentials of scouting and patrolling.

The debris in these exhibit cases – toothbrushes, army biscuits, razors, cans of corned beef – are reminders that it was human beings who carried out these drill programmes, and there are bombs and bayonets and bullets, knuckledusters, clubs and knives as reminders of killing. But the main emphasis is on the organisation and the rationality of trench life as a social system – the networks of observation posts, the telephone wires and signal lamps, the unit signs that were developed so that, in this great mess of mud and men, soldiers could imagine they knew who they were by their signboards and shoulder patches. Rationalised, routinised, standardised, and with the main production systems of the world supporting them, the trenches could seem a murderous parody of industrialism.

In the timetables displayed on the railway stations of northern France there are still extra trains each year around 11 November to carry people commemorating Armistice Day. Ceremonials commemorating the fallen of the First World War became for many the most meaningful Christian ceremony. Visits to battlefields were necessary pilgrimages and they are still acceptable in tourist programmes, although most of those who mourned the dead are now also dead. Of all these sacred sites, the monuments of Verdun catch the most extreme meanings. At Verdun even the pretence of rationality failed. The slaughter was so hideous that even a trench system could not survive. Near Verdun in the memorial museum, erected on the site of the railway station of one of the nine villages that were obliterated and never replaced, is a 300-square-metre reconstruction of the 'battlefield' of 1916. It shows how earth was turned into a load of muck, and the reminders of human existence were scrap metal. In valleys, ridges and ravines, no signs of human culture survived. Enlarged photographs in the museum show what look like mountains of mud; from aerial shots the ground seems pustulous, infected, blistered, rotten – unrecognisable as earth. Humans existed in shell craters, hollows, blasted dug-outs; concepts of Front Line and support areas disappeared, and concepts of command were destroyed. Generals traced lines on maps and issued orders, and in matters as systematic as, say, an artillery barrage, the orders were carried out (before one offensive the Germans shot off 200,000 canisters of poison gas); for the infantry, however, ideas such as 'division' and 'regiment' simply dissolved in the mud. Men came out of their holes and crevices to kill each other individually; two-thirds of the dead were left to rot.

Driving to the museum you pass a statue of a dead lion – a superb evocation of the idea that even courage failed. This monument marks the Germans' furthest advance, to a redoubt that was quickly seized, then quickly lost. At the next rise if you look around at wooded hills and a valley of green fields, you are looking at the few kilometres where, in 10 months, nearly 700,000 died. There are many pilgrim spots, many memorials, many cemeteries – to cover the whole battlefield takes three separate coach tours over 13 hours. The prime attractions, though, are the forts over which so much blood and pride was spilt. Some are now reduced to mere rock formations surrounded by rusted barbed-wire pickets; others show casements smashed like broken teeth but are sound underneath and the stone of their tunnels rings to the shoes of guided tours. Also popular is the hilltop ossuary, an edifice built in brutal crematorium style; here, from pieces of men found in the fields, the bones of 100,000 dead – names and nationality unknown – were piled. At the back of this factory-sized charnel house, small windows have been let into the wall to show the crypt and its rubbish of old bones. At one window, thighbones and skulls are piled high, to make a better display for viewing.

Others make their pilgrimage to Verdun not by visiting the memorials but by walking through the woods, down slopes of quiet hills that still carry the outlines of bomb craters, to the bottom of some ravine, to stand and look at a clump of blasted iron. In the town, tourists inspect the memorials. One monument shows French soldiers forming a human wall of comradeship against the enemy. In another, France is personified as a medieval knight; resting on a sword, he dominates a steep flight of steps built into the old ramparts. There is another view of reality. Near the railway station, Rodin's statue shows a winged Victory as neither calm nor triumphant, but demented by rage and horror. Her legs are tangled in a dead soldier and she shrieks for survival.

Defending civilisation

The symbol of the war's end is the Armistice Carriage, the spanking-new dining-car given to Marshal Foch by the Wagons-Lits Company for use as an office. It was here that he conferred with German armistice envoys at the secret meetings in the forest of Compiègne. When the time came to preserve the war in memory, the site and its dining-car was turned into a 'sacred glade' – so sacred that in 1940 Hitler had the whole area blown up and ploughed over, leaving only the statue of Foch among the brambles to contemplate the fruits of defeat. Now there are replicas of the railway tracks and, placed in a museum, a replica of the dining-car. Tourists pass around the carriage looking at the gleam of the highly polished wood and the cheerful shimmer of brass. The fine wood of the main table shines from the lights under little lampshades fitted into brass candlesticks; it is as if rich people of good taste are expected for dinner. In one museum alcove there are trophies (machine guns, sabres, breastplates); in the other alcove are two semicircles of stereoscopic peep shows which demonstrate how France won the war.

To explain the First World War, when the slaughter was over, and to ennoble its memory, Europe's imagination returned to some of its deepest themes. In all countries, heroes' cemeteries turned away from individualistic assertions of a florid bourgeois style towards extremely simple and harmonious neoclassical designs. Often the cemeteries were laid out so that the grass and trees became part of the display, giving greater sincerity and authenticity. The sculptors looked to the elegance and strength of the male body as a symbol of force and purity. In its disregard for rank and its seeking for a binding humanity, the simplicity of the cemeteries expressed early Christian communality. Overall, the cult of the fallen used the Christian justifications without which high enterprise in Europe does not seem possible: the fallen heroes were martyrs who had suffered and died that others might be saved.

Each nation gave special honour to an anonymous battlefield corpse. The Unknown Warrior's tomb was among the most sacred places of pilgrimage in the cult of the fallen. In Westminster Abbey, London, an unknown warrior is buried in soil brought back from France and placed under a slab of black Belgian marble. In Rome, an unknown warrior is buried beneath a figured laurel wreath under the Altar of the Fatherland. In Berlin, a body was placed in the New Guard House on the Unter den Linden, under an oak wreath. (The body has now been moved to a military cemetery and, in a renamed Monument to the Victims of Fascism and Militarism, replaced by two bodies from Hitler's war – an unknown soldier and an unknown resistance fighter.) In Athens, an unknown warrior is interred beneath a marble wall outside the neoclassical parliament house, and on the wall, on either side of a misty outline of death, are the names of other Greek wars. In Paris, the unknown warrior is buried under the vaulted arch, as high as a cathedral, of Napoleon's Arc de Triomphe. In Warsaw, the tomb of the unknown warrior was built under part of the arcade of the General Staff building; though the Germans blew up the building, a fragment survived and now faces the vast stone base of the Victory Square. In Oslo, there is no unknown warrior, since Norway did not fight in the First World War; in the Norwegian parliament house, however, in a place of honour a book of copper records the names of Norwegian ships sunk during the war, and the names of those who died in them. In Brussels, the unknown warrior is buried at the foot of the Colonne de Congrès, between two lions and beneath an eternal flame. In Vienna, he lies beneath an effigy in red marble of an ornamental archway built to commemorate the victory over Napoleon at Leipzig. In Belgrade, the unknown warrior is buried on a hill which is a popular picnic resort in summer: a ceremonial way leads to a temple of black marble where eight women, sculpted to represent the eight regions of Yugoslavia, gravely mourn one million dead.

In these national ceremonies there were special meanings in the places chosen for the burying of the unnamed. If the unnamed body was buried in a new shrine, this proclaimed that the soldiers had died for progress. The meaning of the tomb in Belgrade was that soldiers had died to achieve unity for southern Slavs; in the Warsaw tomb, to set Poland free. There was nevertheless a more subversive potential meaning in these monuments to the common dead: what if the sacrifice of the Unknown Warrior was not that of a salvationary martyr, but of a massacred innocent?

16. Europeans as fascists

Triumphs

'Roman remains' are an essential part of the routings of European tourism, offering fixed views of the Roman world, pieced together out of the brick and stone the Romans left behind them. Thus, Herculaneum celebrates Roman refinement and luxury in the idea of the *villa*. In a field of ruins in Budapest, some hollow bricks and the remains of the cashier's booth recall the *baths*, symbol of a skill in central heating and a sense of cleanliness that makes the Romans seem North American. At Arles, enclosed in a huge black iron cage, is a symbol of the Romans as master organisers of spectator sports – the grey-stone *amphitheatre*, built to seat 25,000 and now used as a bullfighting arena. Over a square in Segovia, an *aqueduct* marches in graceful double arches, regular and reasoned, rounded and strong, force in each granite stone, an image of the Roman genius in logistics. From Newcastle, England, the Number 36 bus runs daily every summer to the ruins of a *Roman wall*, whose ditch, turrets and forts are reminders of vigilance against barbarians. Amidst the traffic in Thessaloniki's Navorino Square, what is left of the Arch of Galerius proclaims that his victories have brought peace and protection to humanity – and reminds the tourist of the characteristic Roman idea of the *triumphal arch*. The equally characteristic idea of the *column*, surmounted by a statue of the emperor, is recalled most ironically in Istanbul, where a few blackened stones, bound together by iron hoops and looking like a cigar butt, are all that remain of the Column of Constantine.

The *pax romana* is celebrated in the Ara Pacis (Altar of Peace). In Rome, the Ara Pacis Augustae, dedicated by Augustus in 9 BC on his return to Rome after reconquering Spain and Gaul, was covered in rubble until sixteenth-century excavations revealed some panels of the frieze. They were sold, and sawn up for easier removal. When Mussolini decided the Ara Pacis should be restored, more fragments were uncovered, some earlier discoveries were retrieved, others were copied. Now, the rebuilt Ara Pacis stands preserved in a building with huge glass walls and a flat top that looks like a display case in a giants' souvenir shop. On display are pieced-together fragments, both real and replica, along with guesswork sketches of what is missing, and some blanks. Friezes, supported by acanthus leaves and swans, show Augustus, his family and their officials in procession towards the dedication of a peace that was to be the longest-lasting in Europe's history. Just across the Via di Ripetta from the display case, the idea of the empire is preserved in the round, ruined lump of the Tumulus Caesarum – the mausoleum of Augustus and the Julia-Claudia family. One of the Roman world's most sacred places, it became a medieval warlord's fortress, then an amphitheatre, then a concert hall. Mussolini had it restored to the gravity of undisturbed ruin, a reminder of the family who gave us the titles 'prince', 'emperor', 'kaiser' and 'tsar'.

As with its symbols of simplicity, Europe has usually erected its monuments of order, power and triumph in classical forms which demonstrate a serene combination of proportion and strength. But how 'classical' were the Romans? It is possible both to admire the construction of leftovers in marble, brick or granite, and to recognise that the Romans did not display the same serene qualities in their behaviour as they showed in their architecture. Though their architecture had internal balance, the Romans themselves – despite their customary discipline – could also run amok: panic and slaughter were not unusual reactions to the unexpected. The Roman empire was a military state based on bombast, superstition and terror, with torture, mutilation and execution essential to its external power and even to the settlement of internal disputes. A Roman amphitheatre commemorates not order and reason, but a society which could begin a day's entertainment by watching fellow-humans being killed and eaten by beasts; which could watch the slaughter of up to 5,000 animals to make one spectacle; which at lunchtime could watch a series of 'combats' where an armed man would fight and kill an unarmed man, then, himself disarmed, be killed by a third, who in turn would be killed, and so on, down the line – over a season of 100 days, these same Romans could watch 5,000 pairs of gladiators duel to the death. When the Nazis adopted a neoclassical style they had a right to do so; they were among the heirs of Rome.

The two main dreams of a united Europe are those of 'Christendom', and those of 'Rome'. 'Christendom' – the dream of a common culture which, insofar as it existed, depended partly on organised fear – is now alive only among the Communist nations, if it is alive at all. More recurrent is the dream of conquest, of a new 'Rome', with a new Roman peace, possibly drawing its symbols from old boasts in stone – in particular, ruined Roman columns and the remains of triumphal arches that we admire for their style. Among the fragments in the Roman Forum, the Arch of Titus celebrates the suppression of the Jews and the sacking of Jerusalem; the Triple Arch of Septimus Severus carries enslaved barbarians at its base; the Arch of Constantine, which survived as part of the fortification of a family of medieval warlords and is now a background to ice-cream stalls, brags of triumphs and captives. The Column of Marcus Aurelius beside a fountain in the Piazza Colonna was built ungracefully wide so that all his military conquests could be fitted into the bas-reliefs that spiral to its top; Trajan's Column, to modern megalomaniacs the archetype of the Roman column, is preserved almost intact in the imperial forums. Mussolini had a replica made for his grandiose Museo della Civita Romana on the outskirts of Rome, and there, stretching out to the floor, are two rows of plaster casts of the story of Trajan's triumphs and boastings, cut up into sections like the dried skin of a giant snake.

Modern technology gave enlarged power to the fascist regimes which began to form in Europe in the 1920s and there was novelty in the way they used that distinctively modern institution, the political party. Nevertheless, in their ordered cruelty and in their self-justifying through myth, ceremony and monuments, Europe's fascist movements expressed the entrenched European values of the 'Roman'.

The normality of fascism

One way of understanding the normality of fascism is to visit the Army Museum, Madrid. The museum is just as bold and vivacious as the Army Museum, Paris, in celebrating the gaiety of armies and battles. In both museums, sheer excitement in the richness of flags and uniforms, and in the dazzle of armour, weapons and medals, suppresses the more sombre meanings of war. However, where the French keep at least a sense of period, the Spanish throw the whole lot in together – longbows near tommy guns; a 1970s uniform near a 1930s uniform; a dummy of an air pilot next to a dummy of a sixteenth-century halberdier. The main consideration seems to be the best combination of colour and glitter. One room has only armour, and another only weapons – the gleaming metal could be placed in more effective patterns that way. It doesn't matter which particular event is celebrated: all fighting is fun and glory.

This common theme of pomp and glitter, colour and excitement in the Madrid museum gives an immediate visual unity to all the halls, including the hall devoted to the Spanish Civil War (1936–39): it all seems the same kind of fighting. A huge canvas at one end of this hall shows Franco standing on a hill, directing a battle: standards and flags flow around the room, linking this painting with paintings of his generals. Franco and the others are in modern uniforms, but they celebrate victory in the style of older generals in fancier clothes, and they are surrounded by the same kinds of flags. The mementoes in the glass cases may have a certain modern drabness, and the wooden chair in which Franco sat at Burgos may not have been a throne – but all the battle canvasses are in traditional style: one shows innocents being slaughtered by the enemy, another the destruction caused by barbarians, another the miraculous appearance of the Madonna and Child to intervene in a great battle. The war is spoken of not as a civil war but as the 'War of National Liberation' – 'like other great crusades'.

In Rome's Palazzo di Venezia, behind a dark, brown and shabby exterior, is a large marble hall, with frescoes attributed to Mantegna, from which double doors lead to a balcony. Sightseers often go there not to see the frescoes or the tapestries and spears, but because the hall was Mussolini's study, and it was from the balcony that he made some of the most famous crowd speeches ever to be filmed for cinema newsreels. The palace was built for a renaissance cardinal, at a time when palaces were being erected for successful Italian adventurers no less ruthless or ambitious than Mussolini. The palace itself was constructed partly from stone plundered from the Colosseum: Mussolini's use of it was only one among many. At the Foro Italico which Mussolini ordered to be erected beside the Tiber, the mosaics are now partly torn away, leaving the square patchy with mud in wet weather; marble slabs are smothered with the blacks, yellows and reds of spraycan graffiti, suggesting a capriciously divided voice of the people. Nevertheless, the grandiose obelisk with the message 'Mussolini dux', and the avenue flanked with marble reminders of greatness would be at once intelligible to an Augustus or Napoleon, as would the palaces, avenues and colonnades of Mussolini's vast Esposizione Universale di Roma, six kilometres from the centre of Rome, planned for a 1942 exhibition to the world of the triumphs of fascism.

Even among what remains of Hitler's earthly Valhalla at Obersalzburg after its bombing in April 1945, it is possible to see continuing European traditions. The Platterhof (People's Palace) has been rebuilt to the original design and, with a Skyline Room added, it became a United States Rest and Recreation Centre called the Hotel General Walker. In the summer, tourists can take the bus up to Hitler's 'Eagle's Nest', now converted into a homely alpine inn of a reassuring Bavarian ordinariness. They can stroll past trees and lumps of masonry, the remains of Hitler's Berghof, and look out over the plains and hills and clouds, and recall dreams of mountains that helped define Europe.

These were the externals of fascism. In contemplating fascism's 'normality', one should go beyond these to the various horror museums of fascist cruelty: even here, one can contemplate how *ordinary*, as Europeans, the fascists were – even in their butchering and torturing. In fact, an objective effect of the piety of a tourist visit to one of these museums may be to distract attention from this ordinariness of the fascists.

An example is the Crypt of the Deported at one end of the Île de la Cité, Paris. Perhaps Europe's finest architectural monument to the sufferings of the imprisoned, it has abstracted the idea of confinement, suffering and death in a way that both represents and purifies. There is a deep descent between high, white walls beneath a portcullis of black blades into a high-walled courtyard recalling a gaol exercise-yard. Inside the crypt, on either side of the entrance, in unrelieved black and white, are cells – recognisable but abstracted. From the centre runs a long corridor of death. The low, outside wall is inscribed, 'To the 200,000 French martyrs who died in the deportation camps.' But the memorial would be appropriate to honour all persecuted Europeans under all regimes. It was only its scale and modernity that specially marked the Nazi terror.

The approach to the Plözensee Prison, Berlin, is by a narrow, brick-paved backstreet running alongside high walls of red brick with barbed wire on top. The prison's execution chamber, a small brick building set in a prison courtyard, looks like a factory outhouse; despite the wall of honour outside, and the memorial stone urn containing earth from Nazi concentration camps, it still seems, with its cement floor and cement-rendered walls, a conventional execution chamber. Only one item seems unusual – the iron beam running across the end of the room, with the eight iron hooks from which the Nazis hanged social democrats, trade union leaders, priests and communists. On one night in 1943, almost 200 people were hanged on these hooks in groups of eight. But even this has its historic parallels – in old engravings of the fate of the leaders of failed popular uprisings.

Similarly with more formal executions. The Danish Resistance Museum, Copenhagen, has three wooden execution posts in a glass case. They are the poles to which Danes were tied and shot at Ryvangen, the Gestapo execution ground north of Copenhagen. In Oslo, as tourists move down the ramp of the Norwegian Resistance Museum in Akerhus Castle, the faces of three young men look up from photographs engraved on three strips of metal: there are bullet holes beneath the faces. These were the first three Norwegians executed by the Nazis in a courtyard in the castle that was to become the city's main execution ground. In Belgrade, by the road at Jajinci, a monument with a low relief depicting people in the act of dying stands at the entrance to a small ceremonial way which winds up a slope and onto a level field. At the far end of this field, wooden posts rise from the ground: here, German trucks would arrive in the morning from the Banjica Camp, carrying men, women and children, who would be tied to the posts, and shot. Altogether, 70,000 Yugoslavs were shot on the execution ground. Across the flat field, long mounds of earth signify the comradeship of mass death. Yet the firing squad, as Goya's execution painting demonstrates, has been an essential part of the European imagination since the beginning of the nineteenth century. All that was remarkable about the Nazi executioners was the numbers shot and the fact that all over Europe the same schedules were operating at the same times.

In Poland, the Council for the Preservation of Monuments to Resistance and Martyrdom has produced a guide with more than 500 pages in which are listed 2,500 of the 20,000 recorded places marked by acts of Nazi brutality; on the inset maps, only sites of at least 50 killings are marked. Perhaps as many as 13 million children were killed during the war. Some died in bombings and battles; many died in Nazi-occupied countries through torture or slave labour, or by execution. They were killed separately or in groups (some in front of their parents); in camps, streets, fields or woods; by shooting, burning, gassing, injections of phenol or by being beaten to death or having their skulls shattered against cobblestones.

In a large child health centre in a Warsaw suburb, the Poles have built a monument to all children (two million of them Polish) killed in the war; the white walls are panelled with light woods and decorated with murals and ceramics. Yet these horrors and all the others of the Nazis seem foreshadowed in the room in the Prado given over to Goya's little sketches of the first famous celebration in art of the modern 'atrocity', in which dismembered bodies are sketched with the dispassionate care of a botanist's observation and acts of violation are recorded with the realism of a dream. None of the passing atrocities of the fascists were worse than these. Only the widespread nature of the Nazi horrors and the planning of them was new.

Of the many monuments recalling Nazi reprisals, among the most celebrated are the monuments to the destroyed village of Lidice, a settlement mainly of miners and foundry-workers, a bus journey out of Prague. This settlement was chosen by the Nazis to be obliterated after the shooting of Reinhard Heydrich in September

1941. The destruction of Lidice was the main theatrical event in a terror campaign of reprisals that resulted in 18,000 Czechs being killed. On the side of the gentle slope on which Lidice once stood, there is now a cement rotunda, bearing in its arcades, pleas for peace marked out in gold leaf. In the museum are the names, carved in marble, of men from the village – all of whom were lined up beside a farmhouse and shot; along one wall, their faces look out from photographs hung above enlarged photographs of their corpses. There are also photographs of the buildings of the village that was burned, pounded into rubble and ploughed into the earth. Again, to the historically minded, there is nothing new: Lidice is part of that Bohemia in which, for 30 years during the religious wars, every village was subject to barbarities. For that matter, an exemplary ploughing into the earth of a destroyed settlement was a device of colonialism, taken from the Romans and practised by some of the African administrations.

Even the interrogation room is only partly an exception. The Gestapo Security Police Command District of Warsaw was set up in a large building in Szucha Avenue and the avenue itself was shut off at either end. Systematic 'interrogations' took place in this building – beatings, bone-breakings, mutilation. In the basement, now reached by passing through a secular chapel, there is a reconstruction of an interrogation room. In one corner stands a hat-stand for the interrogator's cap and jacket; in the centre are the interrogator's chair and desk, with its desk lamp; there is also a plain table with typewriter and, alongside it, the backless bench (also used as a whipping-block) where the prisoner sat. A cane is laid across the bench. On a wall is Hitler's portrait. The room seems one of the unique symbols of twentieth-century wolfishness – but only if it is taken to recall the 'confessions' of the Stalin terror as well as Nazi interrogations. It can also symbolise, if to a lesser extent, the beatings of natives in colonial outposts and even what was for a while one of the clichés of Hollywood, 'the third degree'. In the sense that the room recalls only Nazi brutishness, it has a false effect: there are no similar monuments to victims of other twentieth-century terrors. But even if a collective monument to all the victims of twentieth-century interrogation were put together it would not establish twentieth-century uniqueness: there were the torture chambers of the dungeons and the confessions forced by the Inquisition, seeking a universal faith and a universal order.

Heroes and victims

Of the European monuments to the dead, only the Soviet and Yugoslav memorials are credible as celebrations of significant martyrdom – of sacrifices that led to victory.

The Soviet monuments outside the USSR's own boundaries are in the triumphal style of the Roman empire, sometimes even made from the marble of Hitler's palaces and with statues cast from the melted-down cannon of the defeated enemy. Within the USSR, however, they celebrate in the revolutionary or Christian tradition, the sacrifices of martyrs whose sufferings were related to victory. In the Piskarev Memorial Garden, Leningrad, a path between two pavilions leads to an eternal flame; beyond, granite slabs and a rose garden now cover the common graves of some of those who died in the siege of the city; plaques show the hammer and sickle, symbol of faith, and the oak leaf, symbol of invincibility, and at the rear, a statue of a woman seven metres high and representing the motherland, holds a wreath towards the million dead of a Leningrad Hitler had intended to raze to the marshes and swamps on which it was founded by Peter the Great. Set against the Kremlin Wall of Moscow's Alexandrovsky Gardens is the Tomb of the Unknown Warrior, carved in black labradorite and surrounded by a square of red granite; along the wall, nine slabs of red porphyry conceal caskets of war sanctified earth from the Soviet Union's 'hero cities'; an eternal flame, lit from the one on Leningrad's Field of Mars, mourns the 20 million Soviet dead.

Outside the Soviet Union and Yugoslavia there were no really indigenous victories: the Nazis were defeated by the Soviets and the United States. But there were acts of gallantry, and when the museums record these they do it most credibly when they celebrate the courage of those who failed.

It is not surprising that this can be done so successfully in martyred Poland, with its six million dead and its long understanding of failure. To take one example: at the edge of the complex of apartment houses built on the desolation of the destroyed Warsaw ghetto is a shattered gateway, some fragments of a wall, a tree from which hang medallions commemorating victims, and a huge mound of earth. Beneath the mound is a museum which contains a reconstructed fragment of the Pawiak Gaol, used by the Gestapo for more than four years as a staging camp and blown up by the Nazis in August 1944. Altogether, 100,000 people spent time in this gaol before they were passed on to the concentration camps, or were hanged as exemplars in the streets, or killed by the execution squads that operated in the forests surrounding Warsaw and in the rubble of the ghetto. The central part of the museum is a reconstruction of one of the basement corridors of the gaol, ill-lit under its rounded ceiling, but without the dirt, the lice, the damp, and the shouting and the beatings. Several cells have been reconstructed, showing the space in which the Gestapo crowded two or three times as many people as the cells were built to hold. The display has a small lump of bread recalling the starvation rations; there are torture weapons, and reminders of how, twice a day, shipments of prisoners were sent for interrogation to Gestapo headquarters in Szucha Avenue. A map of Warsaw shows, in red dots, the places of public execution and, in green dots, places of execution in the forests. Against a brick wall, like playbills announcing a performance are proclamations of the names of those to be executed on a certain day. Amongst these exhibits of horror, however, are also mementoes of the resilience of human beings: messages smuggled out of the gaol, underground. In a dark room, bare but for the shadows of fragments of prison bars, taped voices read some of those messages: a woman tells her husband, calmly and accurately, of her torture; a man describes to his wife, in a detached style, details of the horror of the cells; a father describes prison food to his children; a mother warns her child to be careful when crossing the road.

Similarly, although Jewish people are usually portrayed as victims, there are also representations of gallantry. In the museum–shrine that was once the 'annexe' of the Amsterdam house where Anne Frank and her family hid for two years with the Van Daan family and the dentist Dussel, there are five small, bare rooms looking out over a courtyard and a garden. These have been left as they were after the German Security Police, accompanied by Dutch Nazis, passed through the bookcase that camouflaged the doorway and captured their inmates. Tourists file past the stove, the sink, the small map on which the Allied advance through

France was marked in pins, the pictures Anne Frank had cut from magazines and pasted on the walls, the pencil marks recording the heights of the children.

In an obliquely described 'Museum of Art in the Concentration Camp', set up in the Jewish quarter of Prague, is a testament to the gallantry of the Jews of Tereziń, Czechoslovakia. Built as a fortress town, Tereziń was, at the time of the Nazi occupation, a settlement of about 3,500 people; in 1941, the Nazis put a wall around it, turned the fortress into a Gestapo gaol, and the town into a ghetto. Although their propaganda presented it as a 'model habitation', it had some of the worst conditions of the concentration camps, particularly in its overcrowded sleeping quarters. But Tereziń, was associated with remarkable artistic creation: Jewish stage producers and actors put on plays, composers wrote music, writers books, and artists produced the greatest body of paintings and drawings to come from the concentration camps. After some works were smuggled to Switzerland as early evidence of what the camps were like, most of the artists were interrogated, tortured and killed. Nevertheless, in the heroic manner of art, their work survives and speaks to the generations.

On the face of it, the resistance museums should be able to tell stories of a bravery that goes beyond the will to live or to die boldly, and moves to significant martyrdom. In every resistance museum there is praise for the basic revolutionary and liberal concept of the binding and transforming power of the printed word, with exhibits of illegal newspapers and pamphlets. Some museums have models of buildings in which clandestine printing was carried out. In Belgrade, one of these buildings has itself been preserved and turned into a museum. In the Georgi Dimitrov Museum, Sofia, another of the great liberal symbols is celebrated, in the court trial successfully used as a theatrical device to expose tyranny. It commemorates Dimitrov's successful defence of himself when, after being falsely accused of responsibility for burning down the Reichstag in Berlin in 1933, he was brought to a court presided over by Göring. It displays the navy blue pinstripe suit Dimitrov was wearing when he was arrested, a reconstruction of his cell and the notes he made during the trial.

Above all, the resistance museums celebrate Europe's tradition of hope through rebellion: the revolutionary belief that through action and purity of will, wrong can be righted and freedom can prevail. The museums display some symbols of obvious modernity: the secret wireless sets ingeniously concealed in telephones, the parachutes and containers and maps of dropping places, the microfilms and the microdots, the techniques of *plastique*. However, there is nothing new about the concept behind home-made bombs and rifles: they are from the same impulse as the improvised weapons in museums celebrating peasants' uprisings. The forage caps, the photographic records of acts of sabotage and the models of armed resisters' camps in the hills speak the same insurrectionary language as earlier museums of national liberation. And the symbols of the 'underground' – the false papers, the maps of escape routes, the typewriters and clandestine pamphlets – are in the same language as the symbols of revolution.

Though resistance museums celebrate the heroism of revolution, the revolution did not occur. Dimitrov's trial was one of the few public defeats the Nazis were to suffer; Tito's Partisans were one of the few resistance movements of any significance. The Soviet Union and the United States would have defeated Nazi Germany even if there had been no resistance movement.

In monuments to the victims of fascism, what is novel are reminders of the concentration camps. Museums display distinctive uniforms and photographs of incinerators, of patient queues obligingly waiting to be hanged, shot, or gassed, and of the piles of dead. In memorials to the persecuted, there is a new sculptural symbol, the 'living corpse' of the emaciated concentration camp victim. And there are visits to the concentration camps themselves.

A characteristic pilgrimage is to Auschwitz. The signs lead to a rather friendly-looking red wall behind which are the brick buildings of what might be a large, prosperous factory established at the turn of the century – perhaps a family firm. The road curves in towards the entrance. A slender silver birch rises high beside a gate that's crowned with the message that work brings freedom. Beyond the gate are two long, tree-lined avenues. Solid, two-storey redbrick villas of almost uniform design stand on either side of each avenue, producing a reassuring ambience of old-style German bourgeois solidity and comfort. Enter one of them and you find it is a storehouse. In a large hall the length of one wall, a huge storage area contains human hair. The building next door is also a storehouse; in one room it has hundreds of used brushes – boot brushes, men's shaving brushes, men's and women's hair brushes. Another room contains a stock of Jewish vestments; another, a large heap of spectacle frames and lenses; a whole room is taken up with basins, jugs, saucepans and other hardware; there is a big collection of artificial limbs, braces, trusses and crutches. In another hall are thousands of boots and shoes that stretch like walls of cracked mud; another has a huge array of old suitcases and baskets, lettered with owners' names; a smaller room displays babies' booties, dolls, children's clothes. These are just a few of the belongings of the millions of Jews, Slavs and others who died in the Auschswitz camps. When Auschswitz was captured there were 30 huts filled with such leftovers, awaiting recycling.

Another redbrick building displays the cans that contained the Zyclon B gas used to kill. It also houses the striped jackets of degradation, photographs of piled, naked corpses that look like dim, human shapes emerging from stone, examples of starvation rations, photographs of results of 'medical' experiments on humans, the execution wall, the whipping-blocks, the punishment cells and postcards on which prisoners wrote home saying they were well.

These people did not die so that Europe might be saved. They were merely innocents who were massacred. With a clear eye one can see the concentration camp museums not as monuments to the heroic, but to the sufferings of passivity: a record of the triumph in power of one of the possible forms of a modern industrial state. To the tourists on a horror pilgrimage, however, all this can seem exceptional – something that ended with the Nazis.

Industrialism and slavery

In the museum at Auschwitz, a note records the financial value of the prisoners hired out for slave labour. The average daily rental paid for a worker–slave was estimated at RM6; after subtracting deductions for food and clothing, each prisoner could be reckoned for a daily profit of RM5.30. Since a prisoner's life expectancy was nine months, the average profit per prisoner could be estimated at RM1,431. And after death there was a capital gain: a prisoner's corpse cost, on average, RM2 to incinerate, but tooth-gold, clothes, valuables and money were reckoned, on average, at more than ten times this. Therefore, after nine months the total profit from a prisoner was calculated at RM1,631, 'plus proceeds from the utilisation of bones and ashes'.

Behind the horror of the concentration camps as places of confinement, torture and death was the even wider horror that they were above all camps for industrial slaves. Even Auschwitz was not merely a corpse factory: its function was also to act as an encampment for a huge slave-labour army which worked in mines, steelworks, manufacturing plants, farms, and railway-maintenance depots. Plants were built near the camp – one was built within it – and 40 Auschwitz sub-camps operated beside other industrial enterprises. The inferior races were to be used, in the imperial manner, as forced labour and, in the industrial manner, as factory fodder.

The system of concentration camps was a system of labour supply, much of it to business firms. The continent that drew its history from the slave societies of Greece and Rome and, in the eighteenth and nineteenth centuries, much of its surplus wealth from incorporating the African slave trade into the world trading system, was now to see a modern nation attempt to build its dominance and prosperity on the transformation of its inferior races into a slave society. The uncommemorated labour camps of the Soviet Union played a similar industrial role: a dependable supply of cheap labour was essential to Soviet economic growth and, in particular, to the colonisation of the north and the north-east. As in Nazi Germany, the secret police were the nation's largest employment agency.

The smell of death so pervades memory at Auschwitz that it can almost seem to mock the dead to raise this other issue. Perhaps a concentration camp more aptly symbolising this form of industrial rationality is Dachau, the first concentration camp the Nazis built, and now listed under 'Museums and Galleries' in the monthly Munich tourist guide. The museum now set up in the former kitchen and 'shower bath' areas demonstrates how Dachau became the prototype of the *Konzentrationslager*. It was at Dachau that the cultural forms of the concentration camp were devised: the watchtowers, the barbed wire, the barracks, the roll-call square, which now seem so obvious as symbols of modern systems of surveillance. Other camps merely imitated what Dachau established. Exhibits in the museum convey the meticulousness of it all. To match the rational building-plan there was the rationality of camp documentation, adding reason to depravity: forms in triplicate, questionnaires, rubber stamps, signatures and counter-signatures, filing systems, card indexes, identity cards, directives, reports. A wall chart displays the precision that went into labelling prisoners accurately: on trousers, each prisoner wore a number and, alongside it, in rectangles, squares and circles of different colours and designs to mark different classes of prisoners, there was a neat cross-reference system. To know which type of inferior person they were dealing with, guards needed only to glance at trouser-markings. The museum has details of administrative codes, of training programmes for SS officers, work programmes for prisoners and directives on flogging, on the need for spotless cleanliness in each barracks, on specified layouts for prisoners' kits, on the way prisoners' beds should be made, on the drill to be followed by prisoners in assembling and marching to the square for roll call, on the songs prisoners were to sing as they marched.

Dachau presents the prototype, but it is to Auschwitz II (the Birkenau camp housing up to 100,000 prisoners) that one must go for one of the enduring images of this wasteland of the European imagination. In the first half of 1943, crematoria 2, 3, 4 and 5 were constructed at Auschwitz II. Each had a gas chamber built beneath it and was connected by an electric goods elevator which raised the bodies from the gas chamber so that they could be placed on trolleys and inside the ovens. Flower gardens were built around these complexes which, at their busiest, could eliminate 24,000 people a day. Trains were shunted into the camp siding and drove right through the camp, up to the flower gardens in front of the gas chambers. When the captives were unloaded, the doctors chose those fit to work. The others were killed at once. When the fit – housed in four camps, two on each side of the railway line – had become debilitated by forced labour, they, too, were killed.

In their last days the guards blew up gas chambers and crematoria, as well as other parts of the camp. Nevertheless, enough remains to be a most effective monument to the wastelands of the spirit and the demands of a merciless industrialism. After the pilgrim–tourists park cars or alight from coaches, they must walk the length of the three railway lines from the camp's impressive brick gate with its arch and its tower, past hundreds of huts, many still intact, others with only brick stove and chimney remaining. In front of the tourists, behind them, and on both sides are the squares and rectangles, in cement foundations, of a world forced to order.

When we stand piously in the presence of these ruins, we comfort ourselves by imagining that this is the *past* – never the present, never the future.

Epilogue: The tourist predicament

If this book were simply about power and imagination in Europe, I could leave it at that. Even from the perspective of the book's central theme – monuments as 'rhetoric', re-presenting history – Auschwitz would seem a suitable place to end. But the book also raises, sometimes directly, sometimes by inference, the whole intellectual and moral predicament of being a sightseeing tourist.

What intellectual worth can there be in sightseeing? The closer sightseeing comes to the mere ticking-off of objects on a ceremonial agenda, the closer the answer comes to being: 'None'.

For many tourists, the freest form of sightseeing – just 'wandering around' or 'meeting the people' or 'seeing another way of life' – can, by its very modesty of ambition, be the most intellectually satisfying. Not, of course, if this happens only within the tourist bubble. In that air-conditioned dreamland the only 'people' the tourists meets are waiters, door attendants, maids, guides, shop assistants; the only observation of lifestyles is of staged folk dances and musicians in national entertainment dress; and the only wandering around may be in a hotel's shopping complexes, buying 'souvenirs' which are reminders not even of what has been seen, but of the idea of the souvenir itself. For those who lack the money to buy a boastful imprisonment in the tourist bubble, or for those who have the knack of finding their own paths even from a luxury hotel, wandering around can allow a creative playfulness. Perhaps the wanderer may, in this state, imagine what it might be like to be someone else, or how things might seem to other people – or, possibly, come across some more formal tourist monument that arouses enough curiosity to provoke future reading. There are opportunities, as wide as human imagination, for those 'discoveries' which break through the grid of stereotypes that reduces tourism merely to scoring oneself, as in an elementary school examination, for skill in recognising, and therefore accepting, predetermined categories. Instead, sightseeing can provide some of the delights of the artistic or creatively intellectual experience: it is possible to believe that one has overcome conventional reality and can make up a hypothetical reality for oneself, to see how it goes.

But the tourism of the ceremonial agenda and the tourism of the ceremonial visit to the museum are tourisms of acquisition. Except for accidents of personal disposition, this can be a tourism drained of cultural meanings, apart from the meanings of acquisition itself. It is no accident that shopping can be one of the delights of tourism. A tourist 'buys a tour'. A tourist photographs tourist objects and appropriates them. A tourist buys souvenirs as another proof of appropriation. The very carrying out of a tourist itinerary – of 'doing Rome' – is a form of appropriation. The museums themselves are institutions of acquisition. As Roland Barthes says in his essay 'The Plates of the *Encyclopédie*': 'Inventory is never a neutral idea; to catalogue is not merely to ascertain . . . but also to appropriate.' Like an encyclopedia, a museum can be 'a huge ledger of ownership', fragmenting the world into finite objects that are controlled, because of their very discontinuity, by humans. A Soviet or a United States Space Museum is a declaration of human ownership of existence.

What can be most intellectually debilitating in a museum is the senseless reverence given to objects merely because of their authenticity. This reaches its worst excesses in the 'national museums', ethnographic museums, military museums, technology museums and other museums that are history museums but with such a worship of the object-in-itself that they do not tell its history; we are confronted by objects without social processes. It is as if relics of human society were dropped on us like meteors from outer space. Here, the very didacticism of the Communist museums makes them superior, in principle, because they do not assume that the objects tell their own story. In the same way, the Imperial War Museum in London shows intellectual responsibility in not merely displaying objects from the trenches, but in telling the story of the trenches. An overriding concern with authentic objects can be equally debilitating in a conventional history museum: it is as if historians stopped writing history and produced instead only volumes of documents, randomly collected and unannotated. What can these museums do that books cannot do better? Or that could not be better done in a more general exposition in which, if objects were needed to tell the story and no authentic objects were available, then there would be no shame in using facsimiles or even photographs? Within the museum world there is now considerable revulsion against the old ways and greater concern for the humanity of tourists. But some of the gimmicky remedies merely compound the problem. Tourists who are these days allowed to push the buttons that make the exhibits 'work' are being invited to become accomplices in their own mystification.

It is with art objects that the greatest problem arises, because actually to see them can provide an experience not obtainable in books. However, as Malraux says in *Le Musée Imaginaire*, the reverse is also true: a whole dimension of intellectuality can be given by collections of photographs in art books that is not available in the originals – because one cannot see the originals together, and because photographic presentation can give art objects greater meaning in reproduction than in the original. Cheap leaflets, cassettes and guided tours are not enough: we need more museums to emulate the boldness of the Groeningemuseum, Brugge, which has put up on its walls expository material, including reproductions.

How splendid it would be if all the great collections – the Louvre, the Hermitage, the Vatican, the Prado, the Zwinger, the Kunsthistorisches Museum, the Alte Pinakothek, and the others – might simply be broken up, and reduced to a series of smaller, intellectually comprehensible collections, placed in a number of small museums, preferably in different cities. Or, even better, if the great works of art could simply again be scattered, and put on display in public buildings, so that they became part of ordinary life, like advertisements and political slogans.

In speaking of the intellectual worth of tourism I am assuming, as Antonio Gramsci did, that all humans are intellectuals. We can't live without theories of reality that, by giving some shape to existence, enable us to think and act. Sightseeing can be one of the ways in which we can speculate on these 'reality-making' processes. Given this, most of the perils of sightseeing are simply special cases of our more general predicament. For instance, the difficulties of imagining the past as it really was are general limitations on human knowledge and speculation, not just limitations imposed by tourism. We have to learn to be as sceptical about the 'reconstructions' of tourism as we can learn to be sceptical about the 'reconstructions' of history. And it really should not be new to anyone with a critical interest in modern industrial societies that monuments have a 'rhetorical' function – more likely than not to serve certain prevailing interests – and that these 'rhetorical' functions shift, as society shifts. This is true of the whole public culture of such societies. Of course, if we want to use tourism to escape this kind of reality, we can do so: but we should recognise that we are simply using the past as therapeutic fantasy.

As with life, so with tourism: it is intellectually possible to train ourselves to swim against the tide. To be able to contemplate a monument not just according to the present stereotype, but to give it one's own meanings – and to know something about the other meanings it has had – is one of the ways of sharpening intellectual acuteness.

This is something that needs its own training. I realise that most people don't get that training or, more exactly, that they are trained *not* to act in such a way. Pierre Bourdieu is half right when he says in 'The Aristocracy of Culture' that while educated people are at home with scholarly culture, the 'least sophisticated' are reduced to a position similar to that of an 'ethnologist who finds himself in a foreign society and is present at a ritual to which he does not hold the key'. Where he is right is in suggesting that working-class people, in fact the whole realm of the 'uneducated', can be reduced to impotence, and sometimes insulted, when placed in the presence of most of the operations of high culture. (It is true that in all the industrial societies individuals from 'uneducated' families may acquire the language of high culture and it is also true that in some societies – the German Democratic Republic is one example – considerable educational resources are now deployed to overcome alienation from high culture. Nonetheless, these are merely qualifications to Bourdieu's statement.) Where he is plain wrong is in believing that all educated people are necessarily at home with high culture. It is precisely a characteristic of education that the opposite is often true.

Bourdieu misses the ambiguities in the position of high culture in a modern society. Unlike the period when the culture of a ruling class dominated visible culture, what is now thought of as high culture is not necessarily the culture of the rulers, and certainly does not dominate the public culture. Some of the most ignorant tourists can be found among the most powerful in a society. Public culture in a modern society is most concerned with prevailing social habits such as punctuality, timetabling, specialisation, obedience, diligence in performing set tasks, marginal adaptability – social habits which hold things together (and characterise the typical group tour). Its other great field of operation is the rhetoric that purports to explain and justify existing power and privilege (tourism again!). High culture plays a part in putting ordinary people in their place, but the specialisations of 'expertness' have become so great they can dry out belief in a general intellectual culture. Even the 'educated', when 'out of their field', can also find themselves in the presence of a ritual to which they do not hold the key.

But there is another side to it: in the popularisations of parts of the huge storehouse of cultural artifacts that are such an extraordinary feature of our age, there is also a subversive potential – for challenge both to expertness and to the ruling order. With the enormous experience this challenge can give us of what it might mean to be human, we may find the only real potential for giving substance to human liberation.

If we all became 'good' tourists, would tourism survive?

The answer may be that, under those circumstances, there would be no need for us to become tourists.

Further reading

This is not a book about other books, or a book built on other books. It is based primarily on seeing, rather than reading. And its combination of theme and style is sufficiently unusual for it to be difficult to recommend 'other books in the field'. (Which field, exactly, is that?)

Tourism now attracts some attention from sociologists and anthropologists. Valene L. Smith (ed.) *Hosts and Guests: The Anthropology of Tourism* (University of Pennsylvania Press, 1977) records the first national anthropologists' symposium on tourism, with two general chapters, on tourism as a sacred journey and on tourism as a form of imperialism, and a number of case studies. There is a study of the socially corrosive effects of tourism in Louis Turner and John Ash, *The Golden Hordes: International Tourism and the Pleasure Periphery* (New York, St Martin's Press, 1976) and an excellent example of how a 'social science' approach can be useful is provided by 'The Disney Universe: Morality Play' a chapter analysing the social functions of Disneyland in Michael R. Real, *Mass-Mediated Culture* (New Jersey, Prentice-Hall, 1977).

Museums can also attract some sociological interest, as in Alma S. Wittlin, *The Museum, Its History and Its Tasks* (London, Routledge & Kegan Paul, 1949) and Kenneth Hudson, *A Social History of Museums* (New Jersey, Humanities Press, 1975). There are studies of the museum predicament in Ian Finlay, *Priceless Heritage: The Future of Museums* (London, Faber & Faber, 1977) and Karl E. Meyer, *The Art Museum: Power, Money, Ethics* (New York, William Morrow, 1979), and T.R. Adams in *The Museum and Popular Culture* (New York, American Association for Adult Education, 1939) is remarkable for seeing some of the problems almost ahead of everyone. The best single study I could find of both the morality and the technology of the museum problem was Kenneth Hudson, *Museums for the 1980s: A Survey of World Trends* (London, Macmillan for UNESCO, 1977). If you try this, begin with the amusing and illuminating glossary.

What might seem more appropriate to this book are some of the essays of Roland Barthes – 'The Plates of the *Encyclopédie*' and 'The Eiffel Tower', for example, both in Susan Sontag (ed.) *Barthes* (London, Fontana, 1983) or 'The Blue Guide' in his own *Mythologies* (London, Granada, 1973). Also valuable are parts of Susan Sontag, *On Photography* (London, Penguin, 1979); all of John Berger, *Ways of Seeing* (London, Penguin, 1972); and, most of all, André Malraux, *Museum Without Walls* (London, Secker & Warburg, 1967), with its theory of the metamorphosis of objects into 'art' and their continuing changes in meaning, a view also expounded in some splendid passages in Malraux's *Antimemoirs* (London, Hamish Hamilton, 1968).

There was no attempt to provide footnotes. In the historical segments there had to be no footnotes, or too many. If there had been footnotes they would have been either too peripheral, if unexplained, or too long-winded if explained. But it is possible to get some of the feeling, passing beyond words, of being in the presence of both theories about history and objects given meaning by history, by reading intelligently illustrated, simply themed histories such as the Thames and Hudson series, *Library of European Civilisation*.

Before visiting a city, I had to devise and timetable my own itinerary, and do it in alarming detail. For this I found that, overall, the *Blue Guides* were best. In his essay Barthes attacked the *Blue Guides* (correctly) for their extreme emphasis on monuments. But if you want to see monuments, the *Blue Guides* provide, overall, the most reliable compendiums. I paid no attention to their ridiculously overburdened itineraries. The two best individual guides, however, were *Prague* (Prague, Olympia, 1973) and *Budapest* (Budapest, Corvina, 1970), both of them masterpieces of sympathy and intelligence, giving direction to those who like itineraries but also presented so that they were valuable for individual planning. Of the kinds of books or booklets you can take away from museums so that you can remember some of what you saw, the best I found (in terms of page size, text, quality of reproduction) were the series *The Greek Museums* (there are ten of them), published by Ekdotike Athenon.

Some of the most useful things I read are so inaccessible that I shall just give a few examples, to show how ridiculous it would be to go on: Dora Panayotora, *Bulgarian Mural Paintings of the Fourteenth Century* (Sofia, Foreign Language Press, 1966), Brigitte Geiser, *Musical Instruments in the Swiss Folk Tradition* (Zurich, Pro Helvetia, 1975), the summary in English at the back of Allan Ellenius, *Den offentliga konsten och ideologierna* (Stockholm, Almqvist & Wiksell, 1971), *Romania Revolutionara, 1848* (Bucharest, Editura Meridiane, 1978), *Le Temps des Gares* (Paris, Centre George Pompidou, 1978), *The Discovery of Scotland: The Appreciation of Scottish Scenery through Two Centuries of Painting* (Edinburgh, National Gallery of Scotland, 1978), Maurice Painzola, *Paysages Romantiques Genevois* (Geneva, Musée d'art et d'histoire, 1977) and Sigurd Aa Aarnes, 'Myths and Heroes in Nineteenth-century Nation Building in Norway', in J.C. Eade (ed.) *Romantic Nationalism in Europe* (Canberra, Australian National University, 1983). One of the pleasures of travel can be to make 'discoveries' like these.

As examples of books that in their own way deal with the 'rhetoric' of display and its relation to struggles for power, there are Lauro Martines, *Power and Imagination: City-States in Renaissance Italy* (New York, Vintage Books, 1980), which I found overstated, and Mark Girouard, *The Return to Camelot: Chivalry and the English Gentleman* (New Haven, Yale University Press, 1981) or Richard Jenkyns, *The Victorians and Ancient Greece* (Cambridge, Mass., Harvard University Press, 1980) both of which seemed to me understated. As being concerned, in passing, with the struggle for a useful monument-symbol, Marina Warner, *Joan of Arc: The Image of Female Heroism* (London, Weidenfeld & Nicolson, 1981) is an example of how this might have become a central theme.

The Great Museum lives on the edge of the 'mass culture' or the 'culture and society' debate, for which, of course, there is now a recognised section of the book industry and around which have developed academic career structures. For a relatively concise account of this debate, I would recommend Part One of Michael Gurevich and others, *Culture, Society and the Media* (London,

Methuen, 1982), particularly the chapter by Stuart Hall, 'The Rediscovery of "Ideology": Return of the Repressed in Media Studies'.

One of the reasons for recommending this is the simple introduction Stuart Hall gives to an idea central to my book – that 'reality' is a social construction. This is an idea that may be approached through Marx (but with the enormous difficulties involved in the concept of 'false consciousness') or through certain kinds of structuralist writings (with their own enormous difficulties). It can be approached somewhat more simply from the idea of 'definition of the situation', put forward in passing by the American sociologist W.I. Thomas, whose huge study, *The Polish Peasant in Europe and America*, is now remembered for a few illuminations in its footnotes. In his *The Child in America*, Thomas said: 'If men define situations as real, they are real in their consequences.' So far as thought and action are concerned, 'reality' is what it is defined to be. The argument is developed most fully in a non-structuralist way in Peter L. Berger and Thomas Luckman, *The Social Construction of Reality* (New York, Doubleday, 1966).

However, some social groups have greater resources to define 'reality' than others and of 'definitions of the situation', as of everything, one can always ask the great political question: Who wins? Who loses? It should be obvious to anyone who has read the Italian marxist Antonio Gramsci that the idea I put up of 'public culture' is related to his concept of 'hegemony'.

Index